THE EVOLUTION OF ANTITRUST IN THE DIGITAL ERA:
Essays on Competition Policy

Volume Two

Editors
David S. Evans
Allan Fels AO
Catherine Tucker

Competition Policy International, 2021

Copyright © 2020 by Competition Policy International
111 Devonshire Street · Boston, MA 02108, USA
www.competitionpolicyinternational.com
contact@competitionpolicyinternational.com

Printed in the United States of America

First Printing, 2021

ISBN 978-1-950769-68-1 (Paperback)
ISBN 978-1-950769-66-7 (Hardcover)
ISBN 978-1-950769-69-8 (Ebook)

Publisher's Cataloging-in-Publication Data
provided by Five Rainbows Cataloging Services

Names: Evans, David S. (David Sparks), 1954- author. | Tucker, Catherine, editor. | Fels AO, Allan, editor.
Title: The evolution of antitrust in the digital era : essays on competition policy, volume II / statement of responsibility.
Description: 1st edition. | Boston : Competition Policy International, 2021.
Identifiers: LCCN 2020951723 (print) | ISBN 978-1-950769-68-1 (paperback) | ISBN 978-1-950769-66-7 (hardcover) | ISBN 978-1-950769-69-8 (ebook)
Subjects: LCSH: Antitrust law. | Antitrust law--United States--History. | Competition, Unfair. | Electronic commerce--Law and legislation. | Big data. | Commercial law. | BISAC: LAW / Antitrust. | LAW / Commercial / General. | LAW / Essays.
Classification: LCC KF1649 .E93 2021 (print) | LCC KF1649 (ebook) | DDC 343.07/21--dc23.

Cover and book design by Inesfera. www.inesfera.com

Editors' Note

Antitrust and technology go hand in hand. Much like those in the first volume of this publication, the essays in this volume elucidate this relationship.

The relationship is longstanding. It dates back to the birth of antitrust in the late 19th century, when the important technology of the day was railroad. This tracks through the growth of the oil industry in the early 20th century, to the telecommunications boom of the mid-century and then the growth of the so-called "tech" industry from the 1970s on. At each step along the way, antitrust thinking has been defined and modified by the technologies that gave rise to its greatest challenges. Latterly, the focus has turned to the so-called "digital economy." Today's challenges bear comparison with the formative debates that faced policymakers throughout the first century of antitrust.

The pieces in this volume draw on the lessons of this evolving relationship to set out how competition rules might deal with today's concerns, throughout the world. Each contribution draws on aspects of this historical relationship to address specific aspects of the contemporary debate, many of which have dominated headlines for several years.

Pieces by **Jonathan B. Baker** and **David S. Evans** address one of the most pressing questions facing policymakers today: that of how to regulate so-called "platform" businesses. It is common ground that antitrust law has a role in protecting and fostering competition between online platforms. But how is "exclusionary conduct" in platform businesses properly to be defined? And how is it different from previous dilemmas antitrust has faced before? Courts and enforcers, not to mention policymakers, face important and -- some would say -- intractable problems in this regard. The questions relate not only to the need to deter bad behavior by platforms themselves, but also, crucially, by participants on such platforms.

In the latter regard, there is a key disconnect between public and private incentives. Private incentives may not provide sufficient motivation to limit harmful behavior. As such, governments and policymakers may need to enhance public regulation of the perpetrators of such bad behavior, and better align platforms' private incentives to engage in regulation with public incentives to do so. Consideration of the economic theory on the regulation of negative externalities is key to examining these issues and can provide valuable guidance for devising specific rules in this regard. Regulation of these negative externalities, in turn, raises important issues for antitrust policy.

Another key issue relates to how competition rules relate to data protection policies. So-called "big data" raises myriad antitrust-related concerns, both in regard to how companies compete between each other, and in terms of their potential to exploit consumers. **Lesley Chiou & Catherine Tucker** specifically address the latter concern. Do larger quantities of historical data affect a firm's ability to maintain market share in Internet search? They study whether the length of time that search engines retain server logs affect the accuracy of their results. Is there empirical evidence that reducing the length of storage of past search engine searches affects the accuracy of search results? Do limits on data retention impose fewer costs in instances where overly long data retention leads to privacy concerns such as an individual's "right to be forgotten"? These are also key questions that policymakers must address in months and years to come. The authors' analysis casts light on these questions, which will be key to the decisionmaking processes that will face enforcers for many years to come.

Similarly, **Alexander Elbittar & Elisa V. Mariscal** illustrate how digitization has not only changed the physical means by which firms capture valuable information on consumers, but also its scale, scope and detail. Companies can have direct contact with their consumers, thus opening the possibility for them to mine data directly, catered to their immediate and changing needs. Algorithms are built specifically to reap and unravel information, producing market equilibria that may not before have been possible.

As such, the central question for antitrust analysis is how such data can specifically be exploited and analyzed. Key to this question is whether there are endogenous and exogenous conditions in place that affect competition in a given market, that make it relatively easy or hard for economic agents to behave in anticompetitive ways, or for markets to tip, or to become increasingly less efficient.

Indeed, as **Pierre Régibeau** notes, data-based digital antitrust cases are in some senses distinct from non data-based cases. That said, so far, even in the (few) explicitly data-based cases thus far, the theories of harm are traditional: bundling, exclusive dealing, and foreclosure. While the remedies obtained in some such cases have been criticized, they seem to follow the traditional forward-looking goal of preventing continuing damage to competition. Nevertheless, there may be a need to focus more on the reparative function of remedies in future cases. Doing so, however, will require better definition of the rules concerning the intellectual property rights at issue, and their interaction with other regulatory rules.

Merger control is another area where the digital economy continues to raise distinct concerns. As **Stephen P. King** notes, mergers involving large digital platform companies often create unique challenges for reviewing authorities. Are the existing rules and standards adequate to deal with such platform companies, or do they need reform? Recent experience from the U.S., EU, UK, and Australia suggests that such laws may need some refinement, but it is as yet unclear that specific rules are required to deal with "digital platforms."

Moreover, as **Andy C. M. Chen** underlines, the arrival of the digital economy has spurred a new wave of enforcement interest in so-called "data-driven non-horizontal mergers" by competition agencies. New theories concerning potential competitive harms from such mergers are reshaping what used to be a relatively clear and predictable area of enforcement. Enforcement experience from the U.S., the EU, and Asia demonstrate how these theories can be applied in relevant cases. Though the issues appear novel, most of the competitive concerns raised by such theories are still amenable to well-established analytical frameworks for vertical and conglomerate mergers, with appropriate modifications.

Any discussion of the digital economy would, of course, be incomplete without consideration of the specific role of algorithms. One key question is whether algorithms increase the risk of tacit collusion between firms. At present, the answer to this question seems uncertain, as a mere empirical matter. That said, as **John Moore, Etienne Pfister & Henri Piffaut** discuss, any antitrust approach to potential algorithmic collusion must ensure that any risk of such conduct is reduced while simultaneously preserving firms' incentives to adopt the most efficient algorithms available. Any approach must be based on the best available scientific and economic evidence, and balance regulatory tools with traditional competition enforcement.

Another innovative technology that raises profound implications for various policy areas, including antitrust, is blockchain -- or "distributed ledger" -- technology. As **Antonio Capobianco & Gabriele Carovano** set out, the policy debate around digitalization and competition, and in particular blockchain, raises numerous questions around whether new laws, powers, standards, or regulatory interventions are needed. On the other hand, one particularly innovative use of blockchain mechanisms may be to employ them as part of remedies against allegedly dominant technology companies.

Finally, it is important to note that certain industries in the "physical" world, notably retail and media, have been arguably disproportionately disrupted by the rise of the digital economy. The debate concerning the latter has reached fever pitch in certain countries, including certain European countries, and most recently in Australia. As **Allan Fels AO** discusses, the Australian authorities have proposed a mandatory news media and digital platforms bargaining code, under which platform companies would be required to pay media companies for content reproduced on their platforms. The code has certain unique features, including a final offer arbitration process to determine the payments, and statutory powers to enforce its operation. Other countries will closely monitor developments in Australia, as media companies continue to assert more control over their content worldwide.

In sum, the digital economy represents an evolution in the relationship between technology and the competition rules. Like any solid relationship, it ebbs and flows, and the terrain can be tough. But as the pieces in this volume demonstrate, it is a robust relationship, and one that will surely endure. But its future contours remain to be seen.

Table of Contents

The Role of Antitrust Law in Protecting and Fostering Online Platform Competition

By Jonathan B. Baker[1]

Abstract

This essay provides a perspective on the role of antitrust law in protecting and fostering competition in the digital economy, with particular attention to online platforms. It highlights the danger of anticompetitive exclusionary conduct by dominant online platforms and describes ways that antitrust law can challenge and deter such conduct. The essay also identifies a number of difficulties that U.S. courts and enforcers face in challenging harmful exclusionary conduct by dominant platforms, and discusses some ways regulation can supplement antitrust law in fostering competition.

Many of these themes are pursued in more detail in my book, The Antitrust Paradigm,[2] though in some places this discussion goes beyond the book. Although some of the problems discussed here are distinctive to the U.S., others can impede enforcement in all jurisdictions.

I. ECONOMICS

Online platforms serve an important economic function: they facilitate economic interactions among end users and competition among sellers who connect to the platform. There are many varieties and many familiar examples. Amazon's Marketplace connects shoppers and manufacturers, and facilitates competition among manufacturers. Apple and Google (Android) have app stores that connect applications developers and smartphone or tablet users, and facilitate competition among developers. Social media platforms (e.g. Facebook, LinkedIn) connect members to one another, permit advertisers and advocates to reach members, and facilitate competition among advertisers and advocates. Search engines (e.g. Google and Microsoft (Bing)), allow advertisers to interact with consumers and to compete with other advertisers. Other online platforms include payment systems (e.g. Visa and MasterCard), broadband providers, and restaurant reservation services (e.g. OpenTable).

---

1   Research Professor of Law, American University Washington College of Law. The author is grateful to Andy Gavil and Steve Salop.

2   Jonathan B. Baker, The Antitrust Paradigm (2019).

Online platform markets often tend toward having a dominant platform. One reason involves network effects: as platforms gain more users, they often become more valuable to users, which may allow them to attract even more users. Network effects may be direct, as with social media and communications platforms. Or they may be indirect, as with shopping platforms. More shopping platform consumers make the platform more attractive to sellers, and vice versa.

Scale economies in supply also may lead to a dominant platform. The fixed costs of platform operation may be large while the costs of adding additional users may be small. Or important costs (e.g. for product delivery) may decrease as the number of users grows.

The emergence of a dominant platform is not inevitable. In some markets, network effects and user switching costs may be naturally low, or largely exhausted at a scale that allows multiple platforms to be viable. User control over data, as with portability, can reduce switching costs. Switching costs can be low in markets where users value multi-homing (use of multiple platforms), and it is not prevented by the platform's architecture or terms of use. Interoperability may permit multiple platforms to share network effect benefits. When users vary in their preferences for platform features, multiple differentiated platforms may successfully co-exist.

In markets with a dominant online platform, the most important competition may come from potential rivals and fringe competitors. If platform users are willing and able to switch to a rival with a superior product, dominance can erode. The market could even tip to the rival: as the rival benefits from increased network effects, it may attract even more users and it may become dominant. In some cases, even the mere possibility that a fringe rival or entrant could expand and replace the incumbent could constrain a dominant platform's exercise of market power to some extent.

Exclusionary conduct by a dominant platform can suppress this key competitive force. Think, hypothetically, for example, of Google excluding Bing, Amazon excluding Walmart, or Facebook excluding Snap (Snapchat). Here, "exclusion" means disadvantaging and possibly marginalizing rivals, in addition to possibly forcing them to exit or preventing their entry. The dominant platform also may find ways to exclude nascent or potential platform rivals, not just current rivals, by impeding entry and expansion.

At the same time, exclusion of competitors does not necessarily add up to harm to competition. If one pizza parlor sets fire to a neighboring store, and there are a number of other pizza stores in the neighborhood, the local pizza market would likely remain competitive so the exclusionary conduct is most likely just a business tort, not also an antitrust violation. But when a market has a dominant firm, the loss of any rival – even a small rival or a potential one – can often reasonably be expected to reduce the odds that competition will emerge. Under such circumstances, harm to a competitor can be expected to create a material risk of harm to competition.

Dominant online platforms can adopt a number of strategies to exclude actual or potential platform rivals.[3] One possible exclusionary strategy involves exclusive dealing: a dominant platform could simply forbid its sell-side users (e.g. manufacturers or advertisers) from patronizing a rival platform. Platform most favored nations (price parity) provisions may have a similar exclusionary effect when the rival platform's strategy is predicated on offering low seller prices. Or the platform may make it more difficult for rivals to attract users by increasing customer switching costs, for example, by introducing membership fees (perhaps combined with lower usage prices) or by preventing interoperability or multi-homing.

The anticompetitive conduct in several prominent pre-digital examples of exclusionary platform conduct can be thought of as locking-in users by preventing multi-homing or, alternatively, as exclusive dealing: the Lorain Journal newspaper excluded a local radio station entrant by declining to accept advertisements from merchants that advertised on the radio station;[4] the FTD (telephone) flower delivery network impeded the development of rival networks by preventing its florists from signing up with other networks;[5] and Mastercard and Visa prevented member banks from issuing credit cards offered by other payment systems including American Express and Discover.[6]

In the digital world, dominant online platforms may adopt similar strategies to exclude platform rivals. They may also exclude platform rivals by foreclosing their access to data generated by users. With less data, or less data of certain types, an entrant or rival may have less ability to exploit network effects or obtain scale economies. In addition, dominant online platforms can exclude by acquiring potential rivals, whether nascent platform competitors or sellers of complementary (or vertically-related) services that could become rivals. For example, some have suggested that Facebook harmed social media competition by acquiring Instagram, or Google maintained its advertising dominance or achieved dominance in advertising technology by acquiring DoubleClick.

---

3 These and other exclusionary strategies that dominant platforms could employ are discussed in more detail in chapter 7 of *The Antitrust Paradigm*.

4 *Lorain Journal Co. v. United States*, 342 U.S. 143 (1951).

5 See *American Floral Services, Inc. v. Florists' Transworld Delivery Ass'n*, 633 F. Supp. 201, 204 n.5 (N.D. Ill. 1986) (citing *United States v. Florist's Telegraph Delivery Ass'n, 1956 Trade Cas.* (CCH) ¶ 68,367 (E.D.Mich.1956)); *United States v. Florist's Telegraph Delivery Ass'n 1996 Trade Cas.* (CCH) ¶ 71,394 (E.D.Mich.1990); U.S. Justice Department Antitrust Division, "Justice Department Settles Charges Against FTD, The Leading Flowers-by-Wire Company, for Violating 1990 Consent Decree," press release, August 2, 1995.

6 *United States v. Visa*, 344 F.3d 229 (2d Cir. 2003).

When online platform owners also use the platform, moreover, they can employ exclusionary strategies against rival end users. It is not uncommon for platform owners to be users as well. Amazon runs a marketplace on which it sells private label products. Google has a search engine and also provides shopping services like flight information. Apple runs an app store and offers services similar to those provided by some apps. For example, it offers Spotify's music application as well as its own music application.

A platform that is also a user can impede entry or expansion by rival users through input or customer foreclosure–and it may have the incentive as well as the ability to do so by virtue of the fact that it is both user and provider. It could, for example, bias search results to favor its own products or to disfavor rivals' products, or refuse to link to rival users. It could also target rival users for product design or price competition, perhaps using its privileged access to customer data when rival users have less access to data so they cannot easily fight back. These possibilities do not exhaust the ways a dominant platform can exclude rival platforms or rival users, but they do illustrate economic incentives and mechanisms that could lead to such reductions in competition.

II. ANTITRUST LAW AND POLICY

Antitrust law and policy seek to deter and remedy conduct that harms competition, including exclusionary conduct by dominant platforms. Such conduct can be reached by U.S. antitrust law if undertaken by agreement,[7] if undertaken by a dominant firm (one with what the law terms "monopoly" power) or by a large firm with a dangerous probability of achieving monopoly power,[8] if undertaken through exclusive dealing or tying in the sale of goods,[9] or if undertaken through acquisition or merger.[10]

The evidentiary burdens of establishing competitive harm from exclusionary conduct can be demanding, however. Exclusionary unilateral conduct cannot be challenged under Section 1 of the Sherman Act, which requires proof of an agreement. If that conduct is undertaken by a firm with a share too low to prove monopoly power

---

7 15 U.S.C. § 1. Invitations to collude cannot be reached under Section 1 of the Sherman Act, but the F.T.C. challenges them under Section 5 of the FTC Act. 15 U.S.C. § 45.

8 15 U.S.C. § 2. Section 2 of the Sherman Act also prohibits conspiracies to monopolize.

9 15 U.S.C. § 14.

10 15 U.S.C. § 18.

or dangerous probability of successful monopolization,[11] the conduct cannot be challenged under Section 2 of the Sherman Act.[12]

Beyond satisfying the agreement prerequisite for Section 1 liability, or the monopoly power (or dangerous probability of success) prerequisite for Section 2 liability, the plaintiff must demonstrate that the exclusionary conduct harms competition. Yet a variety of judicially-created hurdles may impede doing so in meritorious cases. Courts have treated exclusionary vertical conduct as presumptively procompetitive, even in settings such as oligopoly markets and markets with dominant firms where it is well-established that vertical restraints can harm competition.[13] In some cases, courts have declined to condemn exclusionary conduct that harms competition on balance if the conduct benefits competition in any way, or plausibly could do so, regardless of the magnitude of the competitive benefit.[14] Importantly for dominant platforms, the Supreme Court has suggested that the prohibition on monopolization would not reach unilateral refusals to deal with a rival by a vertically integrated platform, that is, one that is also a supplier (or seller of a complementary product), unless the platform had previously supplied the rival.[15]

The Supreme Court's *American Express* decision may create additional hurdles for plaintiffs bringing meritorious exclusion cases against dominant platforms.[16] It suggests that market definition is required, and direct evidence is insufficient for proving market power, in exclusionary vertical restraints cases (conduct involving an agree-

---

11 Courts often require a 70 percent share for finding monopoly power in a monopolization case, and a 50 percent share with a prospect of achieving a monopoly share for finding dangerous probability of success in an attempted monopolization case. ANDREW I GAVIL, WILLIAM E. KOVACIC, JONATHAN B. BAKER & JOSHUA D. WRIGHT, ANTITRUST LAW IN PERSPECTIVE: CASES, CONCEPTS AND PROBLEMS IN COMPETITION POLICY 640 (3d ed. 2017). While monopoly power and dangerous probability of success are almost always demonstrated with proof of market share, it is also possible to make these showings with direct evidence. *Re/Max Int'l, Inc. v. Realty One, Inc.*, 173 F.3d 995 (6th Cir 1999).

12 See *Spectrum Sports, Inc. v. McQuillan*, 506 U.S. 447, 456, 459 (1993); cf. *Copperweld Corp. v. Independence Tube Corp.*, 476 U.S. 752, 767-68 (1984). See also *Verizon Communications Inc. v. Law Offices of Curtis V. Trinko, LLP*, 540 U.S. 398, 415 n.4 (2004).

13 See ANDREW I GAVIL, WILLIAM E. KOVACIC, JONATHAN B. BAKER & JOSHUA D. WRIGHT, ANTITRUST LAW IN PERSPECTIVE: CASES, CONCEPTS AND PROBLEMS IN COMPETITION POLICY 913-15 (3d ed. 2017).

14 E.g. *Novell, Inc. v. Microsoft Corp.*, 731 F.3d 1064, 1072, 1075 (10th Cir. 2013) (Gorsuch, J.).

15 *Verizon Communications Inc. v. Law Offices of Curtis V. Trinko, LLP*, 540 U.S. 398, 409 (2004); *Aspen Skiing Co. v. Aspen Highlands Skiing Corp.*, 472 U.S. 585 (1983). *Aspen* may also support a challenge to unilateral refusals to deal with a rival by a vertically integrated platform that excludes rivals while voluntarily dealing with non-rivals. The defendant in that case declined to sell to its rival, even at a retail price, while continuing to sell to consumers (skiers and tour operators).

16 *Ohio v. American Express Co.*, 138 S. Ct. 2274 (2018).

ment between a firm and its suppliers or distributors).[17] This may require courts to analyze, for example, the extent to which different social media compete for attention, online advertisers compete with cable and print ads, or general-purpose online retailers compete with brick and mortar retailers or specialized online retailers–even when direct evidence would make it possible to demonstrate competitive harm or market power reliably without making an inference from market shares, and thus without reaching potentially difficult market definition questions. *American Express* may also require courts to analyze the competitive effects of conduct by transaction platforms within cluster markets encompassing end users on both sides[18] – which can create confusion when evaluating competitive harms.

Beyond these legal issues, there are a number of practical impediments to bringing meritorious exclusion cases against dominant platforms. The most important problems impede challenges to the exclusion of nascent rivals and potential entrants. The antitrust laws reach such conduct,[19] but it can be difficult for governmental or private plaintiffs to prove that nascent or potential rivals are a competitive threat, even when that is in fact the case, simply because those firms, by definition, lack a track record showing what they can do. When exclusionary conduct deters potential rivals from even attempting entry, an antitrust case may be difficult to prove because it may be hard to tell whether the excluded firm is truly a potential entrant that would become a viable and effective competitor. These problems, particularly when exacerbated by judicial delays, mean that a range of damaging exclusionary conduct may not be deterred and that courts may be unable to restore competition (as by preserving the excluded firms).

In addition, foreclosed rivals, whether actual or potential competitors, may have little incentive themselves to challenge the exclusionary conduct of well-heeled platforms. Even where its case is strong, moreover, a rival may do better accepting a large financial settlement that leaves the platform's monopoly power intact, rather than litigating to create competition.[20]

When a potential entrant is acquired, it can also be difficult to show competition is harmed. Courts now require that the plaintiff, which is usually a government agency, show that the potential entrant would have otherwise entered the market rap-

---

17 138 S.Ct. at 2285 n.7. *American Express* was brought under Section 1 of the Sherman Act, which is concerned with unreasonable agreements.

18 The Court defined a cluster market encompassing both sides of a two-sided platform in a narrow setting: when users on different sides are matched in a single, simultaneous transaction, 138 S. Ct. at 2286, and when network effects are so strong as to make it impossible for firms other than transaction platforms to compete on either side. 138 S. Ct. at 2287.

19 *United States v. Microsoft Corp.*, 253 F.3d 34, 79 (D.C. Cir. 2001).

20 Cf. *FTC v. Actavis, Inc.*, 133 S.Ct. 2223 (2013).

idly and been viable, and that there are few other likely potential entrants.[21] Evidence of competitive harm may be hard to come by because a potential entrant that has been acquired for a high price would have little incentive to support the government's challenge.

Meritorious exclusion cases against dominant platforms are also impeded by the erroneous assumptions that some courts accept, at times encouraged by defendants and non-interventionist commentators.[22] Some erroneous assumptions are about markets. It is wrong to suppose, as a general rule, that monopolies lead to more innovation than competitive markets, that forcing a monopoly platform to admit rival users will reduce innovation by both the monopolist and its rivals, that the exercise of market power rapidly self-corrects through entry, or that business practices prevalent in competitive markets, such as vertical restraints, are unlikely to harm competition when employed in oligopoly markets or markets with a dominant firm.

Other erroneous assumptions are about courts. It is also wrong to suppose, in general, that courts cannot tell whether exclusionary conduct harms competition or promotes it, that erroneous judicial precedents are more durable than the exercise of market power, or that the litigation process is manipulated by complaining competitors.

III. REGULATION

Most discussions of competition policy, including my book, *The Antitrust Paradigm,* are concerned primarily with ways the courts can and should apply the antitrust laws to address and deter competitive problems – including anticompetitive exclusionary conduct by dominant online platforms. Yet other public policy responses are also available. Congress could amend the antitrust laws to address impediments to the success of meritorious challenges to exclusionary conduct. In addition, regulation may usefully supplement antitrust in fostering platform competition.

Regulation has a number of general advantages and disadvantages. On the one hand, it can be a cost-effective way of addressing a market failure – such as externalities, providing public goods (which may include competition), or overcoming problems associated with moral hazard or adverse selection – particularly when Coasian bargaining among private actors would be a costly or inadequate substitute. On the other hand, regulation has at times suffered from ineffectiveness, delay, or misuse

---

21   *FTC v. Steris Corp.*, 133 F. Supp. 3d 962 (N.D. Ohio 2015). The potential competition jurisprudence addresses the loss through merger of anticipated rivalry in current products, not a loss of rivalry in innovation or future products.

22   These erroneous assumptions are discussed in Chapter 5 of *The Antitrust Paradigm*, with the exception of the assumption about the consequences of forcing a monopoly platform to admit a rival user, which is addressed in Steven C. *Salop* and R. Craig *Romaine, Preserving Monopoly: Economic Analysis, Legal Standards and Microsoft*, 7 GEORGE MASON L.R. 617 (1999).

(as when regulators are captured by regulated industries). In addition, over-regulation can create social costs by impeding efficiency-enhancing firm conduct, including innovative effort and productivity-enhancing activities, and by entrenching existing market structures and business models.

Regulation can supplement antitrust law by fostering competition among dominant online platforms. When used for this purpose, regulation has a number of advantages. Regulators typically have expertise that generalist courts enforcing the antitrust laws do not. For example, agencies like FERC and the FCC have developed and enforced interoperability and non-discrimination requirements, which some have suggested for encouraging competition among or on online platforms. Regulation may also reduce delays. If remedies for competition problems like platform interoperability, data portability, or open standards are desirable,[23] regulators may be able to impose and enforce them more quickly than courts. Regulators relying on rulemaking may be able to alter practices across an industry more easily than can courts relying on case-by-case adjudication.[24] Regulation may also reach conduct that antitrust cannot reach easily or at all, such as dominant platform conduct that chills potential competition and innovation by firms that are not yet a success or have not yet been imagined, or government-imposed restrictions on entry that impede competition.

Finally, regulatory solutions may usefully supplement antitrust remedies for exclusionary conduct by dominant platforms when the conduct creates important non-competition problems that fostering platform competition would not fully solve, such as protecting privacy or preventing discrimination or other harms to vulnerable consumers. Similarly, a regulator attuned to consumer protection issues may do better

---

23 See Unlocking Digital Competition, Report of the Digital Competition Expert Panel (March 13, 2019), available at https://www.gov.uk/government/publications/unlocking-digital-competition-report-of-the-digital-competition-expert-panel; Economy and Market Structure, Report of the Market Structure and Antitrust Subcommittee, Committee for the Study of Digital Platforms, George J. Stigler Center for the Study of the Economy and the State, The University of Chicago Booth School of Business (July 1, 2019), available at https://research.chicagobooth.edu/stigler/events/single-events/antitrust-competition-conference/digital-platforms-committee; Jacques Crémer, Yves-Alexandre de Montjoye, and Heike Schweitzer, Competition Policy for the Digital Era (European Commission 2019), available at https://ec.europa.eu/competition/publications/reports_en.html; Harold Feld, The Case for the Digital Platform Act (2019), available at https://www.publicknowledge.org/documents/the-case-for-the-digital-platform-act/.

24 On the Federal Trade Commission's competition rulemaking authority, see Jonathan B. Baker, *Two Sherman Act Section 1 Dilemmas: Parallel Pricing, the Oligopoly Problem, and Contemporary Economic Theory*, 38 Antitrust Bull. 143, 207-19 (1993); Rohit Chopra & Lina M. Khan, *The Case for "Unfair Methods of Competition" Rulemaking*, 87 U. Chi. L. Rev. 357 (2020); C. Scott Hemphill, *An Aggregate Approach to Antitrust: Using New Data and Rulemaking to Preserve Drug Competition*, 109 Colum. L. Rev. 629, 673–82 (2009).

than a court in developing means of promoting competition through data portability that does not undermine user privacy.

IV. CONCLUSION

Deterring and remedying anticompetitive exclusionary conduct by dominant online platforms creates an important challenge for competition policy today. Competition authorities in Europe have taken the lead in evaluating the behavior of large online platforms, and the U.S. antitrust agencies have recently announced plans to do the same. Antitrust law, by itself or supplemented by regulation, is a critical tool for fostering platform competition.

Search Engines and Data Retention: Implications for Privacy and Antitrust

By Lesley Chiou & Catherine Tucker[1]

Abstract

This paper investigates whether larger quantities of historical data affect a firm's ability to maintain market share in Internet search. We study whether the length of time that search engines retained their server logs affected the apparent accuracy of subsequent searches. Our analysis exploits changes in these policies prompted by the actions of policymakers. We find little empirical evidence that reducing the length of storage of past search engine searches affected the accuracy of search. Our results suggest that the possession of historical data confers less of an advantage in market share than is sometimes supposed. Our results also suggest that limits on data retention may impose fewer costs in instances where overly long data retention leads to privacy concerns such as an individual's "right to be forgotten."

I.   INTRODUCTION

Currently, Internet search attracts legal scrutiny on both sides of the Atlantic.[2] In this heavily concentrated market, one firm, Google, accounts for 70 percent of the search market in the U.S. and over 90 percent of the search market in the European Union.[3] Public and legal controversy surround why and how such dominance in the market may arise.

One argument presented in the policy debate is that the ability of search engines to store historical data on its users' searches may confer long-term advantages. These advantages subsequently allow a dominant search engine to maintain its market share in the long-term. This practice of "data retention" has been quite controver-

---

1   Lesley Chiou is Professor of Economics at Occidental College. Catherine Tucker is the Sloan Distinguished Professor of Management Science and Professor of Marketing at MIT Sloan.

2   Goldfarb, A. & C. Tucker (2011), "Substitution between offline and online advertising markets," Journal of Competition Law & Economics 7(1), 37–44.

3   Pouros (2010) reports Google's market share for the five most populous countries in the European Union: United Kingdom (93 percent), France (96 percent), Germany (97 percent), Spain (97 percent), and Italy (97 percent). Population measures were obtained from nationsonline.org, and the list of countries within the European Union was obtained from the official European Union website.

sial. Proponents indicate that the storage of data is necessary to provide high quality searches to users in the future. Critics allege that any benefits from such "network effects" in search are minimal and are outweighed by a loss in privacy and data security and accompanied by an increase in antitrust concerns.

This antitrust debate reflects how data retention is deeply intertwined with legal developments in privacy and data security. At the moment, much privacy regulation focuses on obtaining informed consent, and less emphasis exists over how long data may be stored after a person's consent has been acquired. However, the length of time of data storage is key for both privacy protection and the security of an individual's data.[4]

Despite the policy debate and interest surrounding search engines and data retention, no empirical work exists to date on the effects of data retention on the accuracy or quality of search results. When establishing the legal framework for data retention, policymakers must weigh the benefits and costs of data retention to firms, private citizens, and society, so it is important to establish first whether and how much benefit exists from the practice of data retention.

We report the results of our empirical study that measures the benefits companies may receive from having large quantities of data. Specifically, we use variation in guidelines surrounding the length of time that search engines can store an individual's data as an exogenous shifter of the amount of data available to a search engine.[5] We then study how the accuracy of search results changes before and after the policy change. We measure the accuracy of search results by whether the customer navigates to a new website or whether the customer had to repeat the search either on that search engine or another search engine.

We find no empirical evidence of a negative effect from the reduction of data retention on the accuracy of search results. Our findings are apparent in the raw data as well as in a regression analysis of panel data with fixed effects to control for changes over time and across search engines. Our regression analysis suggests not only insignificance, but also that the likely economic effects of the imprecisely measured coefficients are small.

We believe that absence of a decline in the accuracy of searches suggests little long-term advantage in market share bestowed by longer periods of data retention. Some potential explanations exist for the lack of an advantage. First, historic data may be less useful for accurately predicting current news than is sometimes supposed. Given consumers' desire for current and more recent news, large of amounts of his-

---

4 Successful attempts at de-anonymizing clickstream or search engine log data have relied on providing a history or time series of people's searches or web browsing behavior that did not reveal an identifiable pattern.

5 The term "exogenous" shifter refers to how differences in the length of data retention policies are independent of the outcome of the policy.

toric data may not be useful for relevancy. Second, the precise algorithms that underly search engines algorithms are shrouded in secrecy. Third, a substantial fraction of searches are unique: 20 percent of searches that Google receives each day are searches that Google has not received in the last 90 days.[6] Of course, we also recognize the possibility that our measure of search accuracy may be too direct to pick up nuances in the precise quality of search results.

Our results have implications for the new debate in the legal literature on the right to be forgotten.[7] In the European Union in particular, this "right to be forgotten," is gaining traction as a potential foundation of privacy regulation.[8] As pointed out by Korenhof et al. (2014), the timing of data retention plays a part in this debate, as longer periods of data retention make it difficult for digitally recorded actions to be forgotten.[9] As U.S. policymakers, companies, and consumers keep an eye towards developments in the EU, concerns exist over whether legal actions abroad could "take over the American Internet, too."[10]

Part II provides the background for this debate, including context on the existing regulatory landscape, controversies over search data, and the changes in data retention policies that we study. Part III describes our study design and methodology and presents our empirical results. Part IV discusses our results and their implications. Finally, Part V concludes with recommendations for future study.

II.   BACKGROUND AND INSTITUTIONAL SETTING

A. Existing Regulatory Landscape

Firms' policies on data retention are deeply intertwined with legal and policy concerns over privacy, security, and antitrust. Privacy laws encompass any policy or legislation that governs the use and storage of personal information about individuals

---

6   AdWords, G. I. (2008), "Reach more customers with broad match," available at https://adwords.googleblog.com/2008/11/reach-more-customers-with-broad-match.html.

7   Rosen, J. (2012), "The right to be forgotten," Stanford Law Review online 64, 88.

8   Bennett, S. C. (2012), "The right to be forgotten: reconciling EU and US perspectives," Berkeley Journal of International Law 30, 161–195. See also "Europe's `Right to be Forgotten' Clashes with U.S. Right to Know," Forbes, May 16, 2014.

9   Korenhof, P., J. Ausloos, I. Szekely, M. Ambrose, G. Sartor, & R. Leenes (2014), Reforming European Data Protection Law: Law, Governance and Technology Series, Volume 20, Chapter Timing the Right to Be Forgotten: A Study into "Time" as a Factor in Deciding About Retention or Erasure of Data, pp. 171 – 201.

10   Dewey, C. (2015), "How the 'right to be forgotten' could take over the American internet, too,: The Washington Post, available at https://www.washingtonpost.com/news/the-intersect/wp/2015/08/04/how-the-right-to-be-forgotten-could-take-over-the-american-internet-too/.

whether by the government, public, or private entities. As Hetcher (2001) points out, the Internet can often lead to a "threat to personal privacy" due to the "ever-expanding flow of personal data online."[11] This notion of privacy and security of personal data has become one of the significant public policy concerns regarding the Internet, leading to legal and regulatory challenges.

One challenge faced by the U.S. legal system is that most privacy laws at the federal level predate technologies, such as the Internet, that "raise privacy issues."[12] In recent years, innovations such as behavioral advertising, location-based services, social media, mobile apps, and mobile payments have led to heated debates over an individual's privacy and security. The issue is pressing among lawmakers, as the U.S. Government Accounting Office ("GAO") prepared a report in conjunction with the inquiry by Senator Rockefeller over data collection for marketing purposes.[13] According-ing to Sableman (2013), the report suggests that the "U.S. privacy debate will increas-ingly look to international standards and privacy concepts."[14] For instance, the report cites the Fair Information Practice Principles as the *de facto* international standard.

Consequently, the need for understanding the effects of data retention on search quality is a crucial component for the debate. Given that most innovations and regulations occur in the EU, our study examines changes in those policies and their implications for the U.S. Internet.

Our study is related to a privacy concern that began abroad and quickly spread to U.S.: the right to be forgotten. The right to be forgotten "soared into public view" internationally when the European Court of Justice ordered Google to grant a Spanish man's request to delete search results that linked to 1998 news stories about his unpaid debts.[15] While no formal right currently exists in the U.S. for individuals to request the deletion of data from the Internet, proponents of privacy laws argue that such a right to be forgotten exists in the U.S. through privacy torts and credit reporting rules.

---

11   Hetcher, S. (2001), "Changing the Social Meaning of Privacy in Cyberspace," Harvard Journal of Law and Technology 15(1), 150–206.

12   *Ibid.*

13   United States Government Accountability Office, "Information Resellers: Consumer Privacy Framework Needs to Reflect Changes in Technology and the Marketplace," December 18, 2013.

14   Sableman, M. (2013), "The US data privacy debate, in a nutshell," Thompson Coburn LLP, available at https://www.thompsoncoburn.com/insights/blogs/internet-law-twists-turns/post/2013-12-19/the-u-s-data-privacy-debate-in-a-nutshell.

15   Roberts, J. (2015), "The right to be forgotten from Google? Fortune Magazine," available at https://fortune.com/2015/03/12/the-right-to-be-forgotten-from-google-forget-it-says-u-s-crowd/; See *Google Spain SL, Google Inc. v. Agencia Espanola de Proteccion de Datos.*

As a result, companies must often determine their own policies for the storage and use of data. Differences in policies across companies may reflect external pressure such as court rulings and public sentiment. In our empirical analysis below, we use variation in data-retention policies from the European Commission and driven by public pressure.

B. Changes in Data Retention Policies

Table 1 summarizes the variation in data-retention policies that we use in our study. The first two changes in retention of search data that we study were prompted by pressure from the European Commission's data protection advisory group, the Article 29 Working Party. In April 2008, the group recommended that search engines reduce the time they retained their data logs.

The first search engine to respond to this challenge was Yahoo!. Yahoo's Chief Trust Officer Ann Toth declared that the decision to anonymize its user personal information after 90 days "set a new industry standard for protecting consumer privacy. This policy represents Yahoo!'s assessment of the minimum amount of time we need to retain data in order to respond to the needs of our business while deepening our trusted relationship with users."[16]

In January 2010, the chief privacy strategist at Microsoft announced that Microsoft would delete the Internet protocol addresses associated with search queries at six months rather than 18 months.[17]

Table 1: Timeline of policy changes

Date	Search Engine	Change in Storage Policy
December 2008	Yahoo!	13 to 3 months
January 2010	Bing	18 to 6 months
April 2011	Yahoo!	3 to 18 months

In the last example, we study a change in Yahoo! policy where they increased the length of data retention. Yahoo! claimed that "going back" to 18 months was required in order to "keep up" in the competitive environment against other search engines. Yahoo!'s reasoning was that it offers highly personalized services, including shopping recommendations, customized news pages, and search tools, that must "anticipate what users are looking for." According to Anne Toth, Chief Trust Officer at Yahoo!, "[t]o pick out patterns for such personalization, Yahoo needs to analyze a larger set of data on user behavior." Since this change was prompted by internal com-

16 http://www.ft.com/cms/s/0/f6776768-cc6b-11dd-9c43-000077b07658.html#axzz1Jyh-QBZ2u.

17 http://blogs.technet.com/b/microsoft_on_the_issues/archive/2010/01/19/ microsoft-advances-search-privacy-with-bing.aspx.

petitive motivations rather than exogenous changes in the enfrocement of EU directive, we use this policy as a robustness check to our main analyses.[18]

In sum, our study focuses on three changes in data retention policies. We observe changes in the length of data retention for Yahoo! and Bing. Since Google did not change its data retention policy during this time, we do not observe changes in Google's policy.

It is also important to highlight that not all de-identification and anonymization procedures were the same. Figure 1 is a representation of search engine policies as of February 2009 by Microsoft. The figure makes a distinction between de-identification (which removes the ability to match search queries with personal identifying information) and anonymization (which involves the removal of IP addresses). In general, the policies we studied were targeted towards anonymization. The policies arrive in the wake of the release of AOL search engine log query data for 658,000 users within the U.S., which demonstrated how a series of search engines queries over time could reveal an individual's identity. For example, reporters were able to identify Thelma Arnold, a 62-year-old widow who lives in Lilburn, Georgia as AOL searcher "No. 4417749" from the content of her searches.[19]

---

18   For more details see http://www.ypolicyblog.com/policyblog/2011/04/15/ updating-our-log-file-data-retention-policy-to-put-data-to-work-for-consumers/.

19   http://www.nytimes.com/2006/08/09/technology/09aol.html?pagewanted=all&_r=0.

Figure 1: Microsoft comparison of Search Data Retention Policies of Major Search Engines in February 2009

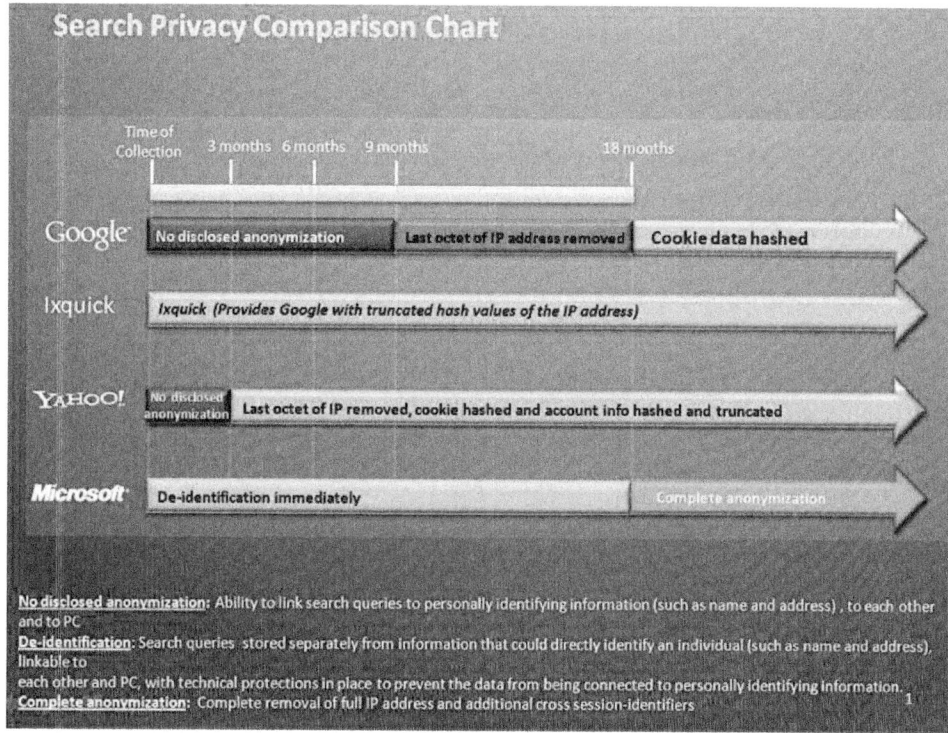

Source: *http://blogs.technet.com/b/microsoft_on_the_issues/archive/2009/02/10/comparing-search-data-retention-policies-of-major-search-engines-before-the-eu.aspx*

III. EMPIRICAL ANALYSIS

A. Study Design and Methodology

Our study design relies on natural experiments to exploit changes in the data-retention policies of major search engines. A natural experiment is a situation in which entities are randomly exposed to a treatment policy.[20] In our study, we compare companies with different policies on the length of data retention due to external pressure from policymakers. The treatment group is the search engine with the change in the length of its data retention policy, and the control group consists of search engines with no change in data-retention policies. The idea is that the control group will allow us to

---

20   See The New Palgrave Dictionary of Economics, "natural experiments and quasi-natural experiments."

control for other seasonal patterns in users' search behavior that are unrelated to the change in data retention. In this way, we will not attribute spurious factors to the change in data retention. In other words, the control group describes the counterfactual of how we would expect the treatment group to behave in the absence of the policy change.

Given recent changes in data-retention policies at major search engines, this methodology provides us with several experiments to study. We describe below the search data that we use, and then we report our analysis of the policy changes in the raw data as well as regressions. Our regressions model a measure of the quality of search as our as the outcome variable.

B. Search Data

Our analysis relies on data from Experian Hitwise. Hitwise assembles aggregate data using the website logs from Internet Service Providers. The information is combined with data from opt-in panels to create a geographically diverse sample of usage data from 25 million people worldwide.[21] Since we study policy changes that affect search engines in Europe, we use data from Hitwise on the search behavior of UK residents.

Table 2: Summary statistics

	Mean	Std Dev	Min	Max	Observations
% clicks	0.85	1.29	0	9.08	2882
Google	0.31	0.46	0	1	2882
Yahoo!	0.51	0.50	0	1	2882
Bing	0.18	0.39	0	1	2882
Observations	2882				

Notes: We observe the fraction of traffic to each "downstream" search website from a major search engine. Each observation in our final sample represents a search engine-website-week combination.

We are interested in whether a change in policies of data retention affected the accuracy of search results. As a measure of accuracy, we examine whether a consumer repeats a search or navigates to a new site. Hitwise reports the top 20 sites that users navigate to after visiting a particular site. We observe the fraction of outgoing traffic to each of these "downstream" sites from each of the major search engines in a given week.

We restrict our sample to outgoing traffic from the three major search engines: Yahoo!, Google, and Bing. We identify which of the downstream sites are search sites by examining whether the URL contains the domain of any major search engine.

---

21   For further details, Chiou & Tucker (2012) also use this data.

Our category of search sites excludes mail, book, or wiki sites, which serve a different purpose than general search. We collect data for the two months before and after each policy change in our sample.

Table 2 reports the summary statistics for the downstream search sites in our sample. Each observation in our final sample represents a search engine-website-week combination. For instance, we can observe the percent of outgoing traffic from Yahoo! Search that navigated to a particular search site during the first week of February 2009. The average search site received 0.85 percent of all outgoing clicks from a search engine.

C. Graphical and Regression Analysis

As a preliminary analysis, we explore the change in traffic to search sites before and after each major policy change. Figure 2 summarizes the fraction of traffic to search engines among the top 20 downstream sites from Bing and other search engines. The pre- and post-periods refer to the time before and after the Bing's policy change from 18 to 6 months of data retention. As seen in the figure, traffic to search sites remained relatively constant over this period of time.

In Figure 3, we summarize the fraction of traffic to all downstream search sites before and after Yahoo's policy change from 13 to 3 months of data retention. Total traffic to search sites from Yahoo! remained relatively unchanged over this period compared to traffic from other search engines.

Figure 2: Downstream search sites visited after Bing and other search engines before and after Bing reduced its length of data retention

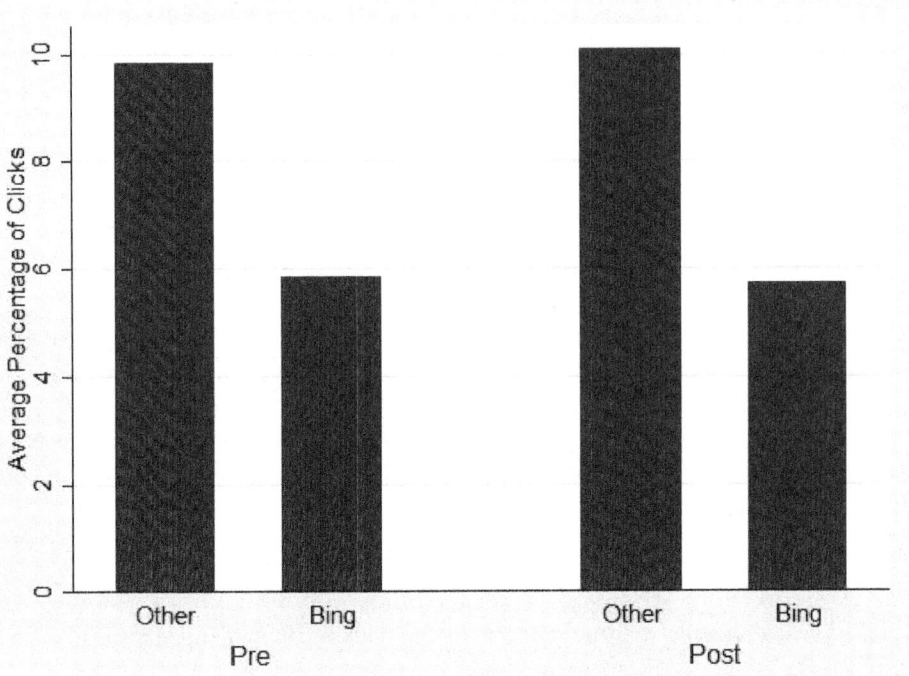

Note: This figure shows the average percentage of visits to "downstream" search websites after users visited Bing and other search engines (Yahoo! and Google) before and after Bing reduced its length of data retention from 18 to 6 months in January 19, 2010.

Figure 3: Downstream search sites visited after Yahoo! and other search engines before and after Yahoo! reduced its length of data retention

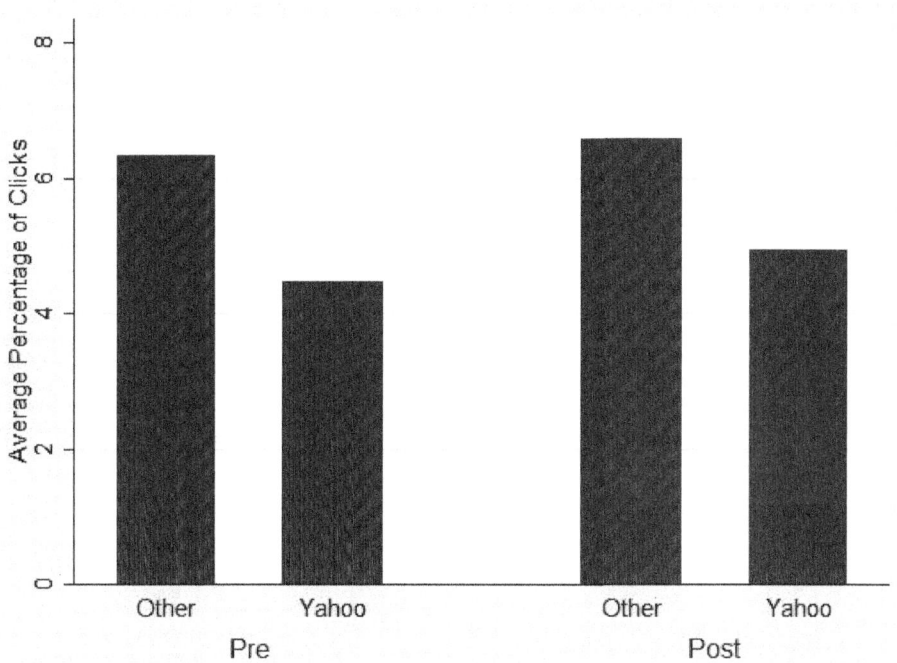

Note: This figure shows the average percentage of visits to "downstream" search websites after users visited Yahoo! and other search engines (Bing and Google) before and after Yahoo! reduced the length of its data retention from 13 to 3 months in December 17, 2008.

The figures suggest that changes in data retention policies did not shift downstream traffic from search engines. To formalize the analysis, we run difference-in-differences regressions at the website level for downstream traffic to the top 20 website for each of the policy changes in our sample. For instance, to analyze Bing's policy change, we estimate the percentage of visits to website i after visiting search engine j in week t:

$$\%visits_{ijt} = \beta_0 + \beta_1 Post_t \times Bing_j + \delta_j + \alpha_i + \rho_t + \epsilon_{ijt}$$

where δ is fixed effect for the originating search engine j, and *Post* is an indicator variable equal to 1 for the weeks after Bing's change in storage policy. The controls are downstream-website fixed effectsto allow each website to have a specific intercept in the regression line. The controls ρ_t are weekly fixed effects to allow each week to have a specific intercept, since variation in the volume and interest of searches may occur across weeks. The coefficient β_1 on the interaction term *Post x Bing* measures the effect of a change in Bing's storage policy on subsequent visits to search sites from Bing relative to traffic from Yahoo! or Google as a control. We estimate this specification using ordinary least squares and cluster our standard errors at the website level to avoid the downward bias reported by Bertrand et al. (2004).[22]

To summarize, the regression model describes the relationship between the dependent or outcome variable and a group of explanatory variables. Our coefficient of interest β_1 measures the extent to which storage policy may increase or decrease subsequent visits to search sites. If the coefficient is positive, this suggests that reducing the length of data retention increased the number of repeat searches on the search engine, i.e. the quality of search results decreased. If the coefficient is negative, this suggests that reducing the length of data retention decreased the number of repeat searches on the search engine, i.e. the quality of search results increased.

---

22 Bertrand, M., E. Duflo & S. Mullainathan (2004), "How much should we trust differences-in-differences estimates?" The Quarterly Journal of Economics 119(1), 249–275.

Table 3: Downstream traffic to search websites before and after Bing's reduction of the length of its data retention from 18 to 6 months in January 2010

	(1) 2 months	(2) 4 months	(3) 6 months
Post Bing	-0.0516 (0.0405)	-0.0373 (0.0978)	-0.0463 (0.140)
Website Fixed Effects	Yes	Yes	Yes
Search Engine Fixed Effects	Yes	Yes	Yes
Week Fixed Effects	Yes	Yes	Yes
Observations	464	928	1392
R-Squared	0.952	0.833	0.790

Notes: Robust standard errors clustered at website level. $*p < 0.1$, $**p < 0.05$, $***p < 0.01$. The dependent variable is the percentage of visits to search websites.

We test for whether a positive or negative coefficient is statistically significant. As de-scribed in Schwartz and Seaman (2013), "statistical significance is the probability that an observed relationship is not due to chance."[23] If a coefficient is not statistically significant, this means that we cannot reject the hypothesis that the coefficient is equal to zero, i.e. the policy had no effect on the outcome variable.

We report our results in Table 3 for the specification above that analyzes Bing's policy change. We run a similar regression that analyzes the effect of Yahoo!'s policy change, and we report those results in Table 4. Both tables indicate that the change in storage policy did not have an effect on downstream visits to search sites. The estimated effect is small and statistically insignificant. To rule out possible delays in implementation, we run our regressions using varying windows of 2, 4, and 6 months.

23   Schwartz, D. & C. Seaman (2013), "Standards of Proof in Civil Litigation: An Experiment from Patent Law," Harvard Journal of Law & Technology 26(2), 430–480. See also Getting Started with Statistics Concepts. "A p-value of less than 0.05 is usually considered statistically significant … ("When a result has less than a 5 percent change of having been observed but is observed anyways, it is said to be statistically significant.") A 5% probability is equal to a p-value of 0.05 or less. Results with a p-value of less than 0.01 are considered highly statistically significant … (a 1% chance "represents a 'higher' level of significance because it indicates a less probable outcome and hence a more rigorous statistical test."

Table 4: Downstream traffic to search websites before and after Yahoo!'s reduction of the length of its data retention from 13 to 3 months in December 2008

	(1) 2 months	(2) 4 months	(3) 6 months
Post Yahoo	-0.0148 (0.122)	-0.123 (0.195)	-0.173 (0.229)
Website Fixed Effects	Yes	Yes	Yes
Search Engine Fixed Effects	Yes	Yes	Yes
Week Fixed Effects	Yes	Yes	Yes
Observations	210	322	434
R-Squared	0.948	0.904	0.885

Notes: Robust standard errors clustered at website level. *p < 0:1, **p < 0:05, ***p < 0:01. The dependent variable is the percentage of visits to search websites.

Table 5: Downstream traffic to search websites before and after Yahoo!'s increase in the length of its data retention from 3 to 18 months in April 2011

	(1) 2 months	(2) 4 months	(3) 6 months
Post Yahoo	0.0133 (0.121)	0.0648 (0.110)	0.0687 (0.104)
Website Fixed Effects	Yes	Yes	Yes
Search Engine Fixed Effects	Yes	Yes	Yes
Week Fixed Effects	Yes	Yes	Yes
Observations	352	704	1056
R-Squared	0.910	0.928	0.933

Notes: Robust standard errors clustered at website level. *p < 0:1, **p < 0:05, ***p < 0:01. The dependent variable is the percentage of visits to search websites.

D. Robustness Check

As a robustness check, we examine a third policy change where Yahoo! lengthened its data retention period from 3 to 18 months. This policy change contrasts with the two policy changes analyzed in the prior section, where search engines decreased the length of data retention. Reassuringly, we find that our results are also statistically insignificant.

IV.   DISCUSSION AND POLICY IMPLICATIONS

Our findings suggest that long periods of data storage do not confer advantages in search quality, which seems contrary to an often-cited benefit of data retention by companies. Of course, a few caveats exist. First, our study focuses on blanket policies by firms towards data retention policies and finds little observable effects on search accuracy as measured by the need to repeat searches. However, we do want to highlight that the kind of policies studied in this paper are very different from the recent cases concerning the right to be forgotten in the European Union, which have focused on the individual rather than blanket data retention policies.[24]

Furthermore, our finding of little effect of longer periods of data retention contrasts with other work that has found significant costs from different types of privacy regulation on commercial outcomes.[25] We recognize that the difference may reflect the importance of the recency of data and current results to the business models of search engines.

Our findings also suggest important policy implications. Unlike the EU, the U.S. does not have a "single overarching privacy law."[26] If long periods of data retention do not generate higher quality of searches, this suggests that the costs of privacy laws for users and companies may be lower than otherwise presumed. The debate thus far has centered on whether more privacy is worth the cost. Our results suggest that the costs of privacy may be lower than currently perceived.

Privacy concepts differ between the U.S. and other legal regimes in the EU.[27] In the EU, the user owns a "set of legal rights entitling him to control data that are describing him, regardless of who had access to the data." In the U.S., whoever has rightful access to the data "owns" the data. While our results do not necessarily suggest that privacy concepts in the U.S. need to change, our results suggest that other policy innovations such as consent use may be useful. In the EU, a consent requirement allows a user to prevent any use of the data that he or she does not agree to. This notion

---

24   For instance, in an ECJ case, a Spanish man requested to have details of his foreclosure deleted from Google. *Google Spain SL, Google Inc. v. Agencia Espanola de Proteccion de Datos.* Accessed at http://curia.europa.eu/jcms/upload/docs/application/pdf/2014-05/cp140070en.pdf.

25   Miller, A. R. & C. Tucker (2009, July), "Privacy protection and technology adoption: The case of electronic medical records," Management Science 55(7), 1077–1093. Goldfarb, A. & C. E. Tucker (2011), "Privacy regulation and online advertising," Management Science 57(1), 57–71.

26   "Differences between the privacy laws in the EU and the US," Management, Compliance, & Auditing, January 10, 2013.

27   Laux, C. (2007), "Privacy Concepts: US v. EU," The Center for Internet and Society at Stanford Law School, available at http://cyberlaw.stanford.edu/blog/2007/09/privacy-concepts-us-v-eu.

is similar to intellectual property rights, e.g. copyright, patent, and trademark rights. Alternatively, policymakers may choose to adopt blanket policies that directly govern the length of data retention.

In addition, our empirical results contribute to the antitrust debate over search engine dominance. We do not find evidence of an advantage in search quality for search engines that adopt longer periods of data retention. This suggests that a dominant search engine with a large fraction of market share does not necessarily maintain its dominance in the long-term due to its access of historical data on users. Of course, we do not rule out that other antitrust concerns may exist as to why market concentration remains so high in Internet search markets.

V.   CONCLUSION AND RECOMMENDATIONS FOR FUTURE STUDY

This paper investigates whether retention of large sets of data by firms provide measurable changes to search performance from the perspective of consumers. Specifically, we study how the length of time that search engines retained their server logs affected the apparent accuracy of subsequent searches. Our analysis exploits changes in these policies prompted by the actions of the European Commission. We find little empirical evidence that reducing the length of storage of past search engine searches affected the accuracy of search. Our results suggest that the possession of historical data confers less of an advantage to firms that own the data than is sometimes supposed.

Our results also suggest that restrictions to data retention provoked by privacy concerns may impose fewer costs if directed at limiting the recency of data (e.g. "right to be forgotten" policies). More generally, the length of data retention has become an issue in this debate over privacy.[28] The question is whether the benefits of privacy (less data retention) for consumers outweigh any potential costs to consumers (lower quality search results). Our study suggests that retaining data for shorter periods of time does not lead to lower quality searches; in other words, we do not find a cost to privacy in our setting.

Several avenues beyond the scope of this study exist for future research. The first is that it is not clear that search engine responsiveness to a search query is the only area where consumer might benefit from a search engine retaining data. Other benefits may include testing new algorithms or fraud prevention. The second is that the policy changes we study occurred in Bing and Yahoo!. Unsurprisingly, these two

---

28   Korenhof, P., J. Ausloos, I. Szekely, M. Ambrose, G. Sartor, & R. Leenes (2014), Reforming European Data Protection Law: Law, Governance and Technology Series, Volume 20, Chapter Timing the Right to Be Forgotten: A Study into "Time" as a Factor in Deciding About Retention or Erasure of Data, pp. 171 – 201.

search engines lacked the market share of Google and were experimenting with differentiating themselves via user privacy in order to attempt to gain market share. Consequently, we study the effects of a reduction in data retention for firms that were not the market leader. If in the future, Google changes its data retention policy, this would a useful exercise for study. The third avenue for future research is that we do not know whether longer-term effects exist due to the change in retention policies. Our data is truncated partly because Yahoo! reversed its previous data retention policy.

Given several interesting directions for future study, we believe that our study is a useful first step in measuring the effect of data retention policies on consumer behavior.

Deterring Bad Behavior on Digital Platforms

By David S. Evans[1]

Abstract

This paper is about the regulation of bad behavior by participants on digital platforms. It shows that these platforms have private incentives to limit this bad behavior and, in fact, have rules, monitoring, and enforcement systems to do so. However, these private incentives may not provide motivation to limit harmful behavior enough. That may require the government to enhance public regulation of the perpetrators and better align the platform's private incentives to engage in regulation with public incentives to do so. The paper uses the economic theory of the regulation of negative externalities to examine these issues and provide general guidance for devising interventions. It identifies issues that policymakers should consider in determining the optimal regulation of bad behavior on digital and applies these to current discussions over the regulation of speech, privacy, and copyright. Finally, it shows that these negative externalities, and governance systems to address them, also raise important issues for antitrust policy.

I.   INTRODUCTION

Long before terrorists used social media platforms to broadcast live attacks there was the case of thirteen-year old Megan Meier, who lived outside of St. Louis, Missouri. She struck up an online romance on Myspace, with a boy, Josh, who, after encouraging her, became vicious. His final message said that the "world would be a better place without you." Shortly after, on October 17, 2006, this already troubled girl committed suicide. It turns out that "Josh" was a fake account created by Lori Drew who used it to get back at Megan over a disagreement her daughter had with the girl.[2] Myspace was

---

1   Evans is Chairman, Global Economics Group, Boston, Mass and Executive Director, Jevons Institute for Competition Law and Economics, and Visiting Professor, University College London, London, UK and. The author has benefitted greatly from comments by Henri Piffaut of the French Competition Authority and thanks Nicholas Giancarlo for excellent research support. None of the views expressed in this paper should of course be attributed to them or any organization with which the author is affiliated.

2   The Economist, "Megan's law" July 9, 2009, available at https://www.economist.com/united-states/2009/07/09/megans-law.

the leading social network, linking more than 100 million people in 2006, and one of the most trafficked digital platforms in the United States.[3] In the aftermath there was a flurry of activity to pass "Megan's Laws" to make cyberbullying a crime.[4] Really, though, not much happened. There was little discussion of whether this digital platform behaved badly by, for example failing to deter fake accounts, and if so what laws and regulations could make digital platforms like it, or its participants, behave better.[5]

More than a decade later there are increasing complaints that bad things are happening on, or because, of digital platforms, some of which are harming society at large. There is now intense consideration of laws and regulations to deal with worrisome activity. The European Union has imposed stringent privacy regulations and the U.S. Congress is holding hearings on various aspects of digital platforms in preparation for possible legislation.[6] It would be hard to find a jurisdiction where reigning in bad behavior on, or by, platforms is not a serious topic of discussion. This chapter develops economic principles for laws and regulations to limit harmful behavior and then highlights

---

3   Mashable, "MySpace Hits 100 Million Accounts," August 9, 2006, available at https://mashable.com/2006/08/09/myspace-hits-100-million-accounts/; Mashable, "MySpace, America's Number One," July 11, 2006, available at https://mashable.com/2006/07/11/myspace-americas-number-one/.

4   The Economist, "Megan's law" July 9, 2009, available at https://www.economist.com/united-states/2009/07/09/megans-law; ZDNet, "Megan's Law: Mo. prosecutors using new cyberbullying laws," December 21, 2008; Megan Meier Cyberbullying Prevention Act, H.R. 1966, 111th Cong. (2009), available at https://www.congress.gov/bill/111th-congress/house-bill/1966/text.

5   A digital platform is a multisided platform that relies on the Internet to connect its participants. Non-digital platforms range from payment card networks to physical shopping malls. For an introduction to multisided platforms see Evans, David & Richard Schmalensee (2016) Matchmakers: The New Economics of Multisided Platforms, Harvard Business Review Press.

6   See European Commission, "EU data protection rules," available at https://ec.europa.eu/commission/priorities/justice-and-fundamental-rights/data-protection/2018-reform-eu-data-protection-rules_en; There have been multiple U.S. congressional hearings related to digital platforms. For example, see House Committee on Energy and Commerce, "Hearing on 'Protecting Consumer Privacy in the Era of Big Data," February 26, 2019, available at https://energycommerce.house.gov/committee-activity/hearings/hearing-on-protecting-consumer-privacy-in-the-era-of-big-data; United States Senate, "Hearing on foreign influence operations' use of social media platforms," September 5, 2018, available at https://www.intelligence.senate.gov/hearings/open-hearing-foreign-influence-operations%E2%80%99-use-social-media-platforms-company-witnesses; United States Senate, "Facebook, Social Media Privacy, and the Use and Abuse of Data," April 10, 2018, available at https://www.judiciary.senate.gov/meetings/facebook-social-media-privacy-and-the-use-and-abuse-of-data. Legislation to govern digital platforms has been proposed by multiple members of the U.S. Congress. For example, see United States Congress, "S.2728 - Social Media Privacy Protection and Consumer Rights Act of 2018" (available at States Congress, "Social Media Privacy Protection and Consumer Rights Act of 2018," available at https://www.congress.gov/bill/115th-congress/senate-bill/2728; United States Congress, "American Data Dissemination Act of 2019," available at https://www.congress.gov/bill/116th-congress/senate-bill/142.

some of things that policymakers should consider in devising sound interventions.[7] The paper focuses on digital platforms, but the analysis applies to platforms more generally.

Economists have developed guidance on when and how to intervene in the economy to improve social welfare and have applied this in considering laws and regulations. Much of this work has concerned negative externalities in which one economic actor can impose a cost on another without having to pay for the other actor for doing so. This chapter applies this approach to platforms in which participants impose negative externalities on other platform participants, with possible spillovers outside the platform, and where the platform may engage in behavior that promotes, or does not restrict, these negative externalities. The analysis concentrates on problems that stem from the behavior of participants on the platform, possibly with the tacit encouragement of the platform, which is a unique aspect of platform regulation.[8] That naturally leads to the question of the extent to which public policy interventions should focus on the participants rather than the platform. The framework has implications, however, for addressing negative externalities that platforms themselves impose on their participants or society at large, such as failure to guard private data.

Digital platforms have incentives for dealing with bad behavior on their platforms insofar as it reduces their profits. If people post gross stuff on a social media platform, for example, it may make it harder to attract advertisers which account for the preponderance of revenues. Digital platforms typically have rules, and penalties for violating those rules, that prohibit bad behavior. In fact, the existence of these governance systems differentiates platform businesses from traditional ones. The private incentives of platforms, however, may be weaker than society would like and thereby result in too much harmful behavior happening on the platform. And the platform participants, or the platform itself, may impose harm on the larger communities in which the platform is embedded.

There may be reasons to pass laws and regulations to limit negative externalities when private deterrence is insufficient. Interestingly, some of the contemporary concerns over bad behavior stem from decisions in the late 1990s to limit the scope of long-standing laws for the physical world for platforms in the incipient online world. For example, Section 230 of the Communications Decency Act of 1996 exempted digital

---

7   Unlike some recent scholarship this chapter analyzes the governance of bad behavior for platforms generally rather than social networks and relies on the economic literature on multisided platforms and optimal regulation of externalities. See Klonick, Kate (2017), "The New Governors: The People, Rules, and Processes Governing Online Speech (March 20, 2017). 131 Harv. L. Rev. 1598, pp. 1598-1670. Also, see Gillespie, Tarleton (2018), *Custodians of the Internet: Platforms, Content Moderation, and the Hidden Decisions that Shape Social Media* (New Haven, Yale University Press).

8   The analysis is therefore not intended to address platforms directly causing harm as a result, for example, of engaging in anticompetitive conduct. However, as discussed below, the enforcement of other laws and regulations concerning platforms could consider their indirect effects on negative externalities created by platforms.

platforms from liability for content, including cyberbullying, posted by their participants.[9] This history highlights the point that laws and regulations for the online world, just as with the physical world, require careful thought and analysis that accounts for costs, benefits, and unintended consequences. To be clear, that means taking the right action, not inaction, when it comes to negative externalities caused by digital platforms.

The chapter has five sections in addition to this introduction and a brief conclusion. Section II situates digital platforms in the larger social context in which polities develop laws and regulations to deal with a myriad of negative externalities created by people and businesses that comprise communities. Section III describes multisided platforms and the role that positive externalities play in creating value for members of these platforms. Section IV then shows that platforms have private incentives to limit negative externalities caused by their members but possibly not enough from society's standpoint. Section V develops principles for devising socially optimal interventions to limit bad behavior on and by platforms, based on the economic theory of first and second-best interventions. Section VI considers past laws and new proposals involving interventions in digital platforms, including the role of competition authorities in addressing negative externalities for digital platforms.

II. EXTERNALITIES, COMMUNITIES, AND POLITIES

Traditional businesses hire workers, buy inputs, and sell products and services directly to customers. The analysis of negative externalities, such as pollution, for these traditional, single-sided, businesses is well-trod territory. Multisided businesses bring different types of participants together on a single platform and give one type of participants access to the other type. Multisided businesses essentially organize communities of people and businesses who benefit from getting together. The harmful behavior by these participants on the platforms is similar in nature to harmful behavior in society at large. The platform then develops rules, similar to polities, for dealing with some of this behavior. These platform communities are subsets of broader communities and polities. We therefore begin then by considering externalities, communities, and polities more generally.

A. Externalities

An externality is an action by one person, that changes the well-being of another person, for better or worse, for which there is no compensation.[10] The person who creates the benefit, or positive externality, doesn't get anything for doing so. The person who creates the harm, or negative externality, does not incur any cost for doing so. Planting

---

9   47 U.S. Code § 230.

10   Green, Jerry, Andreu Mas-Colell, Michael Whinston (1995), *Microeconomic Theory*, Oxford University Press, at p. 351-352. For simplicity, this discussion focuses on people but businesses and other organizations cause externalities too.

beautiful roses and painting the house an ugly color, that neighbors can see, are typical examples of positive and negative externalities. People have too little incentive to create good ones and too much incentive to cause bad ones given the lack of compensation.[11]

The Coase Theorem says that the price system could eliminate negative externalities if there were no transactions costs.[12] In this frictionless world, a homeowner could charge her neighbors for planting roses and neighbors could pay a homeowner to repaint his house in a more appealing color. Too few positive externalities and too many negative externalities arise because there are transactions costs. Those costs are especially large for multilateral externalities such as many neighbors and passersby benefitting from a homeowner's roses.

Economists use the phrase "internalize the externalities" to refer to mechanisms that give actors the incentives to take the external effects of their actions into account. These mechanisms are the focus of this paper.[13]

B. Communities

Humans form communities because doing so enables them to benefit from interacting with each other.[14] By living near one other they can more easily engage in trade, find mates, and realize economies from specialization. They can also share common resources. By forming and joining communities, and engaging in collective action to create shared resources, people create positive externalities.[15]

When humans come together some of them also engage in harmful activities. They steal, trespass, inflict bodily harm, lie, cheat, and a myriad of other lesser and greater sins. They also overuse shared resources. Undeterred, they impose negative externalities because they benefit from doing bad things and they don't have to pay for the harm they inflict.

---

11   The economic definition of externality excludes any action that is intermediated through the price system which does provide incentives for efficient behavior.

12   Coase, Ronald (1960) "The Problem of Social Cost," *The Journal of Law and Economics*, Vol. 3, pp. 1-44; Posner, Richard (1992) *Economic Analysis of Law* 4th Edition, Little, Brown and Company, at pp. 8, 49-52.

13   Harrington Jr., Joseph, John Vernon & W. Kip Viscusi (2005) *Economics of Regulation and Antitrust* 4th Edition, The MIT Press, at p. 878.

14   McMillan, David & David Chavis (1986) "Sense of Community: A Definition and Theory" *Journal of Community Psychology* 14(1), pp. 6-23.

15   Glaeser, Edward & Joshua Gottlieb (2009) "The Wealth of Cities: Agglomeration Economies and Spatial Equilibrium in the United States," *Journal of Economic Literature*, 47(4), pp. 983-1028.

Communities do not just involve people agglomerating in one place. People also form communities to pursue some shared purpose such as a profession, a hobby, or some civic activity. Even in these cases members of the community could harm one another.

Whether it pays to be a hermit, or join a community, depends on the degree of positive and negative externalities. Communities manage to secure positive externalities and limit negative ones by becoming polities in which they have processes for governing themselves. With these governance systems in place they can promote positive externalities and limit negative ones.

C. Polities

Polities can enact a variety of policies to create positive externalities. Economists have found that one of the most important of these is the rule of law including the creation and enforcement of property rights.[16] Another is money which among other things provides a standard method for exchange.

Polities are particularly important for deterring negative externalities.[17] To do so requires shared resources such laws, monitoring, and enforcement and the right to impose penalties that society would not want private actors to use. The polity has the ability to levy punishments, from jail time to fines, to deter personally harmful behavior such as violence and theft as well as other harmful behavior such as depleting shared resources by overusing the commons or polluting the environment for example.

Of course, polities take many forms, and maximize the well-being of their participants to varying degrees.

III. EXTERNALITIES, EXCHANGE, AND PLATFORMS

A multisided platform is a physical or virtual place, at which participants can enter into beneficial exchanges, which the platform facilitates by helping participants

---

16 La Porta, Rafael, Florencio Lopez-de-Silanes, Andrei Shleifer & Robert Vishny (1998) "Law and Finance" *Journal of Political Economy* 106(6), pp. 1113-1155; La Porta, Rafael, Florencio Lopez-de-Silanes, Andrei Shleifer & Robert Vishny (1999) "The Quality of Government" *The Journal of Law, Economics and Organization* 15(1), pp. 222-279.

17 For further discussion of the interpretation of criminal and civil laws as responses to negative externalities, and citations to relevant economic literature, see Evans, David (2012) "Governing Bad Behavior by Users of Multi-Sided Platforms," *Berkley Technology Law Journal* 27(2), pp. 1201-1250.

find good matches and consummating an interaction.[18] The participants form a community that has come together in the same place, the physical or virtual platform, for a common purpose, the subject of the beneficial interaction. To understand the basic economics of these businesses, consider platforms with two types of participants.

A. Basic Economics of Multisided Platforms

Two-sided platforms enable members of the two distinct types of participants to enter into beneficial interactions with each other often involving exchange.[19] Of course, two members of distinct groups could just meet and agree to interact. The platform, however, reduces the transaction costs, or frictions, between the two parties thereby making it easier for parties to find each other and consummate a beneficial interaction.

When OpenTable, the pioneering restaurant-reservation platform, started out in 1998, for example, restaurants often had someone to answer the phone to take reservations, which were then written down in a book; diners sometimes had to call several restaurants to find a table on a particularly busy night. Many tables went empty, and people went without reservations, because it was inefficient for diners and restaurants to make suitable matches. OpenTable reduced the transactions costs in making reservations for diners and restaurants. The diners saved time and had more choices while the restaurants earned more profit from filling unused capacity.

Two-sided platforms have indirect network effects for at least one type of participant. An "indirect network effect" refers to a situation in which participants on one side of the platform (e.g. drivers on a ride-sharing platform) value having more participants on the other side of the platform (e.g. passengers on a ride-sharing platform) with whom they can have a mutually beneficial interaction (e.g. transport).

---

18   Evans, David & Richard Schmalensee (2016) Matchmakers: The New Economics of Multisided Platforms, Harvard Business Review Press.

19   Evans, David & Richard Schmalensee (2016) *Matchmakers: The New Economics of Multisided Platforms,* Harvard Business Review Press at Chapter 1. The distinct types of participants refer to how the participants use the platform as opposed to the identity of those participants. For example, on a communication network, one person sends a message (e.g. makes a mobile call, makes social media post) and another receives it (e.g. takes the call, reads the social media post). The demand for engaging in these activities can vary across people although most people do both to some degree. For example, small portion of participants on social media platform contribute most of the posts. See Erlandsson, Frederik, Pitor Brodka, Anton Borg & Henric Johnson et al. (2016) "Finding Influential Users in Social Media Using Association Rule Learning," *Entropy* 18(164); Goulet, Lauren, Keith Hampton, Cameron Marlow & Lee Rainie (2012) "Why most Facebook users get more than they give," *Pew Research Center and Facebook Joint Research Report.* As a result, many of the online attention platforms discussed later have at least three sides. YouTube, for example, consists of people who upload videos (content creators), people who view videos (content viewers), and advertisers.

Indirect network effects arise because, with more potential partners on the other side, there is a higher probability of finding a partner for a better value-increasing exchange. A passenger is more likely to find a driver, and get picked up more quickly, if there are more drivers around. Indirect network effects refer to increasing the pool of *relevant* partners for each type of user (e.g. drivers near your home) and not the sheer number of participants in the platform (drivers in the entire country).[20]

Indirect network effects result in a positive feedback loop between the two sides. When more relevant members of one group join the platform, such as restaurants, the platform becomes more valuable to the other group, such as diners, which leads more members of that group to join. Then the platform becomes even more valuable to the first group, the restaurants, leading even more of them to join. These positive feedback loops, which are sometimes referred to as the virtuous circle, drive the dynamics of platform businesses.

Studies of two-sided platforms typically find that managing these indirect network effects, and the resulting positive feedback loop, is a central part of starting and running their business.[21] When a platform starts out, for example, it cannot provide a valuable service to members of either group unless it has members of both groups on board. This results in the "chicken-and-egg problem" for platform startups. A platform needs to figure out how to get enough of both types of participants to join. As they mature, platforms must balance the interests of both groups because business decisions that affect the value of one group in using the platform affects the value of the other group.

The prices that different types of users pay for platform services are interrelated because of these feedback loops. Platforms have to select prices that balance the participation of each group against the profits from that group. A higher price for one group reduces the demand by that group which makes the platform less valuable to the other group. The platform therefore has to juggle prices to find ones that maximize its profits taking price and demand on both sides of the platform into account. The economic theory of two-sided platforms shows that the price charged to either group does not necessarily track the costs of serving that group, and this feature sets them apart from single-sided businesses.[22] Ad-supported media platforms often provide their content at less than marginal cost and some, including most digital platforms, do so for free.

---

20 Veiga, André, E. Glen Weyl & Alexander White (2017) "Multidimensional Platform Design" *American Economic Review: Papers & Proceedings* 107(5), pp. 191-195 at p. 191.

21 C. Cusumano, Michael, Annabelle Gawer & David Yoffie (2019) *The Business of Platforms: Strategy in the Age of Digital Competition, Innovation, and Power*, HarperCollins, at Chapter 3 Section 2.

22 Rochet, Jean-Charles & Jean Tirole (2003) "Platform Competition in Two-Sided Markets," *Journal of the European Economic Association* 1(4), pp. 990-1029 at p. 990.

B. Platforms, Positive Externalities, and Value Creation

Modern platforms, including digital ones, start by identifying frictions that prevent mutually beneficial interactions. They reduce those frictions by figuring out ways to agglomerate participants onto a platform. To do so, they try to persuade one type of participant that they will have more beneficial interactions with other participants if they join the platform. They use prices, including subsidies, to get more of each type of participants on board. They also employ methods such as search, matching, and payments to increase the expected value of the interactions for participant. Each participant who joins the platform as a result of these price and non-price strategies generates a positive externality for other members which is the source of the indirect network effects. In effect, the two-sided business partly internalizes positive externalities by devising mechanisms to give people incentives generate these externalities; the platform then makes money by taking a share of the increased value they create.

Ride-sharing platforms, for example, recruit drivers to join their platforms in local areas and then sign up people who want rides. They use mobile phones, apps, GPS, mapping, and matching algorithms to make it easier for drivers to find passengers and passengers to find drivers. That helps them recruit more drivers and riders. The value of the platform increases to both sets of participants as more join. The increased density of passengers and drivers in particular areas, for example, reduces the wait times for drivers and riders.[23] That enables drivers to handle more rides, and thereby make more money, and save riders valuable time and inconvenience. These innovations clearly generate value for drivers and riders because both chose to use these platforms instead of options they had been using. One study found that the UberX platform generated $2.9 billion consumer surplus for passengers in four cities in the United States.[24]

C. Attention Platforms

Ad-supported media businesses, such as newspapers, are platforms that use content to attract viewers and sell ads to businesses that want to market to those viewers.[25] The way these businesses internalize externalities, and the feedback loops between the two sides, are different than transaction platforms, such as restaurant-reservation businesses, that facilitate a direct exchange between a buyer and seller. Since

---

23   Cramer, Judd & Alan Krueger (2016) "Disruptive Change in the Taxi Business: The Case of Uber" *The American Economic Review* 106(5), pp. 177-182.

24   Cohen, Peter, Robert Hahn, Johnathan Hall, Steven Levitt, Robert Metcalfe (2016) "Using Big Data to Estimate Consumer Surplus: The Case of Uber" *NBER Working Paper* 22627.

25   Evans, David (2019) "Attention Platforms, the Value of Content, and Public Policy" *Review of Industrial Organization* 54(4) pp. 775-792; Evans, David (2017) "The Economics of Attention Markets" *Working Paper*, available at https://papers.ssrn.com/sol3/papers.cfm?abstract_id=3044858.

ad-supported platforms, such as Facebook, are the focus of much of the current discussion over policy interventions, it is helpful to describe these platforms in a bit more detail. Economists refer to them as "attention platforms" because, as discussed below, they effectively buy attention from consumers and sell that attention to advertisers.

Advertisers would like to present messages to consumers in the hope of persuading them to buy their product. If consumers could be confident that the message was valuable to them, perhaps because it provided information on a sale price for a product they want to buy, they should be happy to receive that message. But, even if it was possible to target messages so precisely, advertisers want the opportunity to persuade people who are not initially receptive to buy their products and therefore wouldn't willingly hear the message. Advertising can also be annoying since marketers seek ways, including hyperbole, to get people's attention. Thus, while consumers might like to receive some advertising, they may not want to receive as many messages as advertisers would like to deliver.

Nevertheless, so long as advertisers value delivering a message more than a consumer values avoiding the message, there's an opportunity for an exchange that makes them both better off. Business sellers, for example, sometimes take buyers to expensive dinners, or lavish resorts, in order to pitch them. That mutually beneficial bilateral exchange is not a realistic option when there are many buyers and their interests aren't well known. Frictions make it difficult for advertisers and consumers to enter into mutually beneficial exchanges to deliver and receive messages.

Ad-supported media emerged in the 17th century to solve this problem. Newspapers produced content that got people to spend time looking through the paper. They then sold advertisements that appeared in their pages. The advertisers hoped that people would see their ads, some of those people would be interested, and they would make a sale as a result. The content, like the expensive dinner, compensated the newspaper reader, and the advertising revenue compensated the newspaper for producing and distributing the content.

Although the media and technologies have evolved since the 17th century the basic economics has remained the same. Content is key. It provides the payment to consumers for spending time on the platform; the medium into which ads are inserted to attract some of their attention; and an efficient mechanism for securing attention since same material can attract many viewers. Content can also be tailored to attract particular types of consumers (moms with young children) that are of interest to particular types of advertisers (products for young children). The provision of content is the mechanism by which these platforms internalize the externalities for viewers and advertisers.

At given prices, and holding the amount of content they are getting, consumers often prefer to be exposed to fewer ads. Although viewers could ignore them, these messages can provide a distraction and increase the amount of time they have to devote to consuming content. It may be easier, for example, to just listen to an ad on the radio than finding something else to. The ads on attention platforms do not impose, however, negative externalities on the viewers insofar as those viewers are being compensated with content for being exposed to them.[26]

Online attention platforms differ from traditional ad-supported media platforms. They usually provide people with content for free unlike traditional newspapers, magazines, and cable television. Some of them, and the largest ones, rely on user-generated content. They can realize substantial global scale economies in ways that traditional media cannot. Online attention platforms also use algorithms and data to target ads to people unlike traditional media that broadcasts the same ad to many. They often charge advertisers based on whether a person clicked on an ad unlike traditional media that charge on the basis of the number of views who might have seen an ad.

IV.   PLATFORM REGULATION OF NEGATIVE EXTERNALITIES

Managing positive externalities is a key feature of two-sided platforms. So are negative ones.

To distribute its app to iPhone users in the App Store a business has to follow the Apple Store Review Guidelines.[27] They are intended to "provide a safe experience for users." They prohibit, for example, "content that is offensive, insensitive, upsetting, intended to disgust, in exceptionally poor taste, or just plain creepy." Apple has a team that reviews apps to make sure they are suitable for their users. Apple's rules also extend to the behavior of developers who are in the App Store. Its guidelines tell developers that, "If you attempt to cheat the system (for example, by trying to trick the review process, steal user data, copy another developer's work, or manipulate ratings) your apps will be removed from the store and you will be expelled from the Developer Program."[28]   It turns out that many platforms have rules that prohibit their users from imposing these sorts of negative externalities on other

---

26   The economic literature assumes that ad-supported businesses have to determine the ad-load (the ratio of ads to content) as part of the balance they strike between attracting viewers to the platforms and selling ads. The literature often refers to this relationship as a negative indirect network effect for viewers. Of course, while viewers may not like ads, they do like content, which result to the platform being able to sell and display ads. See Evans, David (2019) "Attention Platforms, the Value of Content, and Public Policy" *Review of Industrial Organization* 54(4) pp. 775-792.

27   Apple, "App Store Review Guidelines," available at https://developer.apple.com/app-store/review/guidelines/.

28   Apple, "App Store Review Guidelines" available at https://developer.apple.com/app-store/review/guidelines/.

users.[29] They enforce these rules mainly by using their "bouncer's right" to exclude those who violate them.[30]

A. Participants Behaving Badly on Platforms

Not surprisingly, since platforms are communities, many of the bad things that people, and businesses, do to each other happen on platforms as well.

People can inflict bodily harm on those they interact with on platforms. Sexual predators have used Craigslist, for example, to meet, and in some cased kill or rape victims.[31] People can also cause bodily harm by using verbal interactions to drive people, or encourage them, to commit suicide as we saw with Megan Meier. They can engage in a variety of other behavior that could harm other participants such as hate speech, bullying, and pornography. The unwanted exposure to this content imposes costs on participants.

Platform users can engage in various types of fraud, libel misrepresentation, and deception. Sellers can purvey counterfeit goods or fail to ship goods for which they have taken payment. Buyers can also try to manipulate auctions or make fraudulent payments that harm sellers. Participants can engage in a variety of deceptive practices through providing misleading or false information. Examples include posting pictures on a dating site that make the person look more attractive than they are, manipulating reviews to inflate their scores as sellers, or not disclosing shipping or other charges. Platform users could also post reviews to make their rivals appear less attractive and drive them off the platform. Finally, platform users could violate intellectual property laws by posting copyrighted content on the site.

Congestion is a common result of negative externalities generally. It can occur on platforms as well. The obvious cases involve physical platforms such as nightclubs and shopping malls. Beyond some point additional people reduce the value of the platform. Online platforms can have congestion as well because more participants may increase the search costs for finding partners. That is particularly the case when people who are likely to be poor matches join the platform.

This recitation is hardly an exhaustive list of how platform participants can harm each other. Basically, almost anything that could happen in communities in the physical world can happen in communities in the online world.

---

29   Evans, David (2012) "Governing Bad Behavior by Users of Multi-Sided Platforms" *Berkley Technology Law Journal* 27(2), pp. 1201-1250; Evans, David (2014) "The Antitrust Analysis of Rules and Standards for Software Platforms" *Competition Policy International* 10(2), pp.71-85.

30   For discussion of the "bouncer's right" see Lior Jacob Strahilevitz, *Information Asymmetries and the Rights to Exclude*, 104 MICH. L. REV. 1835, 1837 (2006).

31   The New York Times, "Medical Student Is Indicted in Craigslist Killing," June 21, 2009, available at https://www.nytimes.com/2009/06/22/us/22indict.html.

B. *Platform Governance of Bad Behavior*

Much of this litany of bad behavior is subject to criminal and civil laws or could be. Platforms could simply leave it to the government to address these problems. In fact, many platforms, unlike most traditional businesses, have prominent rules for governing conduct on their platforms, and these rules are particularly common for digital platforms.[32] Often these rules, which prohibit certain forms of conduct, are incorporated into a contract, in the form of terms and conditions, that that users must enter into to join and use a platform.

The Apple App Store Guidelines, with roughly 12,000 words, outline various prohibitions and requirements organized into safety, performance, business methods, design, and legal. Much of the document concerns prohibiting various aspects of developer behavior that could harm app users. It prohibits "inflammatory religious commentary" and "medical apps that could provide inaccurate information" and thereby cause physical harm. It requires accurate data because "[c]ustomers should know what they're getting"; "ongoing value to the customer" for auto-renewing subscriptions; and compliance with a set of privacy rules.

eHarmony has a lengthy terms and conditions for users of its dating site.[33] The posting and communication section lists 17 prohibited activities. These include anything "intended to or tends to harass, annoy, threaten or intimidate any other users"; "intended to defraud, swindle or deceive other users"; and even anything "off-topic, meaningless, or otherwise intended to annoy or interfere with others' enjoyment" of the platform. Users are also prohibited from providing false or misleading information about themselves.

Amazon has a "Selling Policies and Seller Code of Conduct" that prohibits various kinds of behavior. Sellers are prohibited from sending unsolicited or inappropriate communications; from attempting to "damage or abuse another "Seller, their listings or ratings"; and from attempting to "influence customers' ratings, feedback, and review." Sellers are also prohibited from providing misleading information and doing things such as attempting to increase the price after an order has been confirmed. Amazon customers are also prohibited from engaging in certain kinds of behavior such as posting offense content in comments on the site.

Platforms devote resources to monitoring the behavior on the platforms. The most extensive information on the scope of these activities concerns Facebook. As of

---

32 Evans, David (2012) "Governing Bad Behavior by Users of Multi-Sided Platforms" *Berkley Technology Law Journal* 27(2), pp. 1201-1250; Evans, David (2014) "The Antitrust Analysis of Rules and Standards for Software Platforms" *Competition Policy International* 10(2), pp.71-85. As discussed below, Section 230(c)(2) of the 1996 Communications Decency Act limited the liability of digital platforms for enforcing these rules.

33 eHarmony, "Terms & Conditions," available at http://static.eharmony.com/files/us/images/terms-conditions/terms-and-conditions-us.pdf.

2009, Facebook had about 150 employees, nearly 20 percent of its total workforce, engaged in monitoring and enforcement efforts to ensure there was no nudity, porn, or fake people.[34] The company invested in software to detect prohibited nudity on the platform and has been successful. As the social network has gotten larger, and there are more opportunities for harmful behavior, the company has encountered difficulty in using software-based solutions. It has expanded its use of "content moderators" who spend their time identifying bad, and often horrible, behavior on the platform, and tagging it for removal. It employed 7,500 content moderators as of 2018.[35]

To enforce their rules platforms can punish violators, and prevent further bad behavior, by excluding them from the platform or by preventing them from getting on the platform in the first place. The Apple Store Review, eHarmony, and the Amazon rules all list exclusions as the sole remedy for violations. The enforcement of Google's "quality guidelines," which prohibit, websites from using deceptive and manipulative practices to artificially inflate their rankings offers a well-documented example of the use of disciplinary measures based on exclusion.

Google punishes websites that have done so by pushing them down the search rankings for some period of term. This is known as going to Google Jail. Websites that aren't listed in on the first search engine results page get few clicks so pushing websites beyond that essentially excludes them from the relevant search results. J. C. Penney, an American retailer, for example, engaged in several practices designed to fool Google's algorithms into determining that it was a more relevant website for certain consumer product queries than it was. Google punished the company by manually forcing them down the search rankings for 90 days. For example, for one query involving luggage the retailer was pushed down from the first to the 72nd position, so 10 pages in. This downgrading resulted in temporary exclusion from Google's search results for all practical purposes. In one highly publicized case Google delisted BMW.de—that is banned the site entirely from Google—for using doorway pages to boost its rankings. Delisting is the death penalty for a website. BMW ultimately got a reprieve.

C. The Limitations of Platform Enforcement

The tools available to platforms to govern bad behavior are limited. Platforms enter into contracts with participants. In principle they could use those contracts to impose penalties for violating rules or seek compensatory damages. Doing so could impose significant transactions costs for platforms with many participants. The risks of entering into contracts with potential financial costs could also deter participants

---

34 Newsweek, "Facebook's 'Porn Cops' Are Key to Its Growth" April 30, 2009, available at https://www.newsweek.com/facebooks-porn-cops-are-key-its-growth-77055.

35 See The Atlantic, "Inside Facebook's Fast-Growing Content-Moderation Effort," February 7, 2018, available at https://www.theatlantic.com/technology/archive/2018/02/what-facebook-told-insiders-about-how-it-moderates-posts/552632/.

and thereby slow the growth of the platform. There does not appear to be any evidence that digital platforms use financial penalties much to enforce rules.

The "bouncer's right," given by property law, to exclude participants from their platforms or prevent them from joining in the first place, is the main tool used by platforms to enforce rules.[36] Digital platforms can exclude participants easily by simply disabling their account, and short of that they can delete or edit their content. Platforms do not need to go to court to do that although they may be subject to lawsuits for having done so.[37] To borrow a phrase, dispossession is nine-tenths, and much more, of the law.

Denying or limiting users' access to the platform is, however, a blunt instrument for dealing with negative externalities. OpenTable, for example, automatically deactivates the accounts of diners who miss four reservations in a 12-month period. According to its terms and conditions, "No-shows are quite disruptive to a restaurant's business, so if any user accumulates four no-show reservations within the same twelve-month period their OpenTable account will automatically be deactivated." So there is no penalty for missing three or less, even though it is harmful to restaurants, but a permanent ban for the fourth.[38] Facebook, to take another example, reserves the right to disable an account for violating its terms and conditions.[39] Someone who uses a fake name faces the same penalty as someone who engages in cyberbullying or posts a live murder.

Platforms using the bouncer's right do have some advantages over governments. They can act very quickly and even algorithmically. They can also do this in principle across jurisdictions thereby creating effectively global rules for their platforms and a uniform experience for their users.

V.   SOCIALLY OPTIMAL REGULATION OF NEGATIVE EXTERNALITIES ON PLATFORMS

Negative externalities on platforms raise new issues for government intervention because there is another polity, the platform, ruling a community, standing between the government and actors that cause the negative externalities. Unlike a fac-

---

36   That is true for the many sets of terms and conditions discussed in my earlier papers on this topic. See Evans, David (2012) "Governing Bad Behavior by Users of Multi-Sided Platforms" *Berkley Technology Law Journal* 27(2), pp. 1201-1250; Evans, David (2014) "The Antitrust Analysis of Rules and Standards for Software Platforms" *Competition Policy International* 10(2), pp.71-85.

37   For example, see The Wall Street Journal, "Writer Sues Twitter Over Ban for Criticizing Transgender People," February 11, 2019, available at https://www.wsj.com/articles/writer-sues-twitter-over-ban-for-mocking-transgender-people-11549946725. The lawsuit was dismissed by the court which determined that Section 230 of the Communications Decency Act shielded Twitter from liability for suspending and banning a user's account for violating the platform's policies. See *Murphy v. Twitter, Inc.*, No. CGC-19-573712 (Cal. Superior Ct. June 12, 2019).

38   OpenTable, "What is your no-show policy?" available at https://help.opentable.com/s/article/What-is-your-no-show-policy-1505261059461?language=en_U.S.

39   Facebook, "Disabled Accounts," available at https://www.facebook.com/help/185747581553788.

tory that causes pollution, a platform has private profit incentives to restrict harmful activities by their users and, also unlike a factory, often has a sophisticated governance system to do so. Government intervention needs to consider the extent to which the platform is already dealing with the negative externalities, when social regulation is needed to supplement or displace private regulation, and the interaction between government and private interventions when both are used.

These are not small issues. Private restrictions on speech on platforms, for example, may conflict with public benefits from free speech. Should government delegate the regulation of hate speech to platforms because they are more efficient at detecting and stopping it? Should government take this regulation on entirely rather than having private businesses making decisions on what speech to allow? Or should government adopt a mixture of public and private enforcement? These particular choices have substantial ramifications for societies that value free speech.

This section provides a framework for considering the interplay between public and private methods for regulation negative externalities that can help policymakers work their way to sound policies.

A. Economics of Regulating Negative Externalities

The basic solution to a negative externality is to make the perpetrator bear the cost it imposes thereby aligning private and social incentives. Consider a factory that emits pollution in the course of manufacturing a product.[40] The social cost of making the product exceeds the private cost. To maximize its profits, the factory increases output until the marginal private cost equals the marginal revenue it receives. Marginal revenue measures how consumers value an additional unit and is normally equal to marginal social benefits.[41] To maximize social welfare, society would like the factory to produce out to the point where the marginal social cost, including the pollution, equals marginal revenue.

Government intervention could reach that socially desirable result in two simple ways. It could impose a tax on the factory equal to the marginal social cost of the pollution, which would thereby make the marginal private and marginal social cost coincide. Alternatively, it could simply mandate that the factory produce the right amount of output corresponded to were marginal social costs equal marginal social benefits.

---

40   Harrington Jr., Joseph, John Vernon & W. Kip Viscusi (2005) *Economics of Regulation and Antitrust* 4th Edition, The MIT Press, at Chapter 21.

41   This assumes that the product itself does not cause any negative externalities on society so that private marginal revenue and social marginal revenue are the same.

These are known as "first-best" interventions because they achieve the social optimum, assuming there are no other costs related to them.[42]

Getting the first-best solution, however, requires a great deal of information. Even if they could be measured accurately, marginal social cost could vary across forms of pollution, different industries, and different location. Price and output restrictions may impose other costs on society such as increases in prices from less competition if the regulation forces some companies to close down. Regulation may also be costly for the government to administer and for the company to comply with.

In practice, government intervention means finding a "second-best solution" that tries to get as close to the social optimal as possible while minimizing other costs that society would bear. These include administrative costs incurred by private businesses as well as the government, error costs incurred as a result of designing interventions in the face of imperfect information and the frailties in human judgment, indirect costs from other distortions caused by the intervention, and risks of unintended consequences that could flow from the intervention. To take the example above, imposing an overall cap on pollution could require less information and be prone to less error than coming up with a tax schedule.

Different types of negative externalities raise special design issues for optimal interventions. Consider an egregious social harm such as first-degree murder.[43] There is no doubt that the optimal amount of first-degree murder is zero. A first-best intervention would arguably impose an infinite cost on those committing murder. But this first best solution is not feasible in practice. Government must consider the costs of enforcement mechanisms including police to investigate, courts to prosecute, and prisons to hold relative to the benefit of those mechanisms in terms of reducing the likelihood of murder and the value of justice. Government also has to consider error costs in determining that someone has convicted murder. Given the number of people saved by DNA testing from life in prison or death row the likelihood and cost of error is material in the U.S.[44]

To take another example, some negative externalities may involve tradeoffs between activities that are mixtures of costs and benefits. Free speech provides individual and social benefits but can be used to impose individual and social harms. Even

---

42 Governments use carbon taxes or tradeable emission rights to limit carbon emissions which among other things have harmful effects on global climate.

43 Posner, Richard (1985) "An Economic Theory of the Criminal Law," *Columbia Law Review* 85(6), pp. 1193-1231.

44 Lachman, Pamela, John Roman, Kelly Walsh & Jennifer Yahner (2014) "Post-Conviction DNA Testing and Wrongful Conviction," *Urban Institute Research Report*; Connors, Edward, Thomas Lundregan, Neal Miller, Tom McEwen (1996) "Convicted by Juries, Exonerated by Science: Case Studies in the Use of DNA Evidence to Establish Innocence After Trial," *U.S. Department of Justice Research Report*.

in countries where free speech is a fundamental right, laws and regulations implicitly trade off these costs and benefits. People can face civil liabilities for engaging in libel under some circumstances and businesses are subject to consumer protection laws that prohibit advertising that goes too far in misleading consumers.[45]

Of course, there are sound economic and social reasons why more serious violations should face stiffer penalties and there is wide variation in penalties even for homicides.

B. Why Private Platform Governance May Not Be Enough

While it is possible that platforms could devise a second-best intervention that makes public regulation unnecessary, they could may not do enough to limit harmful behavior in many circumstances. It is useful to begin, however, with the conditions under which further government involvement is not needed, and then explore the reasons for departure.

1. Conditions Under Which Platforms Have Socially Optimal Incentives to Regulate Negative Externalities

The platform would have the incentive to devise the best intervention from society's perspective in the absence of spillovers; when it bears the marginal social cost of the negative externalities; and when its second-best solution, including the particular penalties, is better than what the government could do.

Absence of spillovers. The social cost of the negative externality would have to impact only participants on the platform for the platform to have enough incentives to stop them. The consequences of the negative externalities must not spill beyond the platform walls. Some harmful behaviors meet this condition. It is hard to see how people on dating sites posting inaccurate flattering pictures or developers on app stores selling apps that don't really work would harm anyone outside of the people they interact with on those platforms. In both cases the behavior reduces the value of the platform which should have strong incentives to curtail it.

Platform bears full marginal cost of network externalities. Even if negative externalities were only borne by its participants, for the platform to have the right incentives, the marginal cost of the negative externalities would have to be the same for the platform owner as for the platform participants. In general, platforms internalize both the negative externalities imposed on the marginal user, and the value that these marginal users bring to other users that can be extracted from

---

45   Posner, Richard (1992) *Economic Analysis of Law* 4th Edition, Little, Brown & Company, at pp. 211-213, 669-670; U.S. Federal Trade Commission, "Truth in Advertising," available at https://www.ftc.gov/news-events/media-resources/truth-advertising.

infra-marginal users. This equals the marginal social value of combating negative externalities if the marginal and average users are the same in these respects.[46] The platform would then have an incentive to reduce the negative externality to the point where the marginal benefit of reducing the externality is equal to the marginal cost. The marginal cost to the platform equals the marginal loss of profits from the negative externalities.

Platforms may lose profits in several ways from negative externalities that could result in their bearing much of the marginal costs of the negative externalities. Potential users may factor in the platform's reputation for regulating negative externalities in the decision to join. If they don't join, the platform loses not just a customer, but the positive indirect network effects created by that participant. Actual users may factor in the likelihood of negative externalities in their decisions to interact on the platforms, which leads to reduced revenue for the platform, and the fees they are willing to pay the platform for these interactions. Platforms may also face the standard lemons problem: if participants cannot sort out good interactions from bad ones, they may decide not to interact at all.

Platform Has Better Second-Best Intervention than the Government. Even under these two conditions, however, the platform is unlikely to find a first-best intervention for the same reason governments have. It is possible, however, that the platform could devise a better second-best intervention than the government because it has more immediate information and can act more quickly. It may be able, for example, use an algorithm to detect harmful behavior and disable an account in essentially real time. With the bouncer's right the platform does not have to provide due process. Given the administrative costs and uncertainty there may be cases where the platform governance system is good enough that it isn't worth the government getting involved. Even if the first two conditions do not hold, it may be that the platform can still achieve a better second-best solution that the government.

2. Conditions Under Which Platforms Do Not Deter Negative Externalities Enough

The conditions under which private regulation yields the socially optimal outcome provide the baseline for assessing whether there is scope for public laws and regulations. There is room for government intervention when there are spillovers, platforms lack the right marginal deterrence incentives, and government has a better solution including the use of superior enforcement and punishment mechanisms.

---

46 This is a generalization of the famous monopoly quality distortion of Spence, Michael A. (1975) "Monopoly, Quality, and Regulation," *Bell Journal of Economics* 6(2), pp. 417-429. For details of the generalization to multi-sided platforms with heterogeneous users, see Weyl, E. Glen (2010) "A Price Theory of Multi-Sided Platforms" *American Economic Review* 100(4), pp. 1.642-1.672; Veiga, André, E. Glen Weyl & Alexander White (2017) "Multidimensional Platform Design," *American Economic Review: Papers & Proceedings* 107(5), pp. 191-195.

Spillovers. The costs of negative externalities could spill over into the broader community. Negative externalities that harm participants, such as sexual violence, could also harm the family and friends of participants. Bad information supplied to participants could spread outside the platform into the markets for goods, information, and ideas as they pass that bad information around to people who aren't participants in the platform. The negative externalities could also harm social norms that benefit society broadly.

Insufficient Platform Incentives. Even without spillovers, platforms may not have the marginal incentives to limit negative externalities to the degree society would prefer. The economic literature shows that, even putting market power considerations aside, platforms would not maximize social welfare because they may have private incentives to favor one side or the other.[47] Market power could provide further incentives to deviate from the socially optimal prices on each side. While this literature does not address negative externalities, it shows that there is no presumption that platforms will regulate negative externalities, which have different effects on the relative values for the two sides, to the optimal degree.[48] Platforms could decide to spend less resources on regulating negative externalities than society would prefer because the losses they incur at the margin are less than society would incur.[49] For example, an attention platform that uses content to attract viewers and viewers to get advertising revenue could produce more attention-getting, but socially harmful content, than society would choose after balancing private and social benefits of the content and advertising.

Government May Have Better Second-Best Intervention. Even where the platform's and society's interest are aligned it may be that best platform intervention is substantially worse than the best government intervention. The government may be able to devise a better second-best intervention because it has more tools at its disposal including police, courts, and jails. As noted above, the primary method of enforcement available to and typically used by platforms — using the bouncer's right to deny platform access — is a blunt instrument. The fact that platforms do not have tailored penalties for violations, as civil and criminal law systems, strongly suggests that they lack the ability to do so.

---

47 Rochet, Jean-Charles & Jean Tirole (2003) "Platform Competition in Two-Sided Markets" *Journal of the European Economic Association* 1(4), pp. 990-1029; Rochet, Jean-Charles & Jean Tirole (2006) "Two-sided markets: a progress report" *RAND Journal of Economics* 37(3) pp. 645–667; Weyl, Glen (2010) "A Price Theory of Multi-Sided Platforms" *The American Economic Review* 100(4) pp. 1642-1672; Veiga, André, E. Glen Weyl & Alexander White (2017) "Multidimensional Platform Design" *American Economic Review: Papers & Proceedings* 107(5), pp. 191-195.

48 In practice, this departure from the social optimum could be immaterial or a second-best intervention to improve the situation may not be available.

49 At least in theory the platforms could spend more resources reducing the negative externality than society would because its private losses at the margin are greater than society's losses.

3. Either, Or, or Both?

There may be cases where public or private regulation dominates the other and only one polity should be involved in dealing with negative externalities. These different forms of regulation, however, could also be complements. The government could specialize in solutions that rely on the power of the state while the platform could specialize in solutions that rely on informational advantages and ability to act quickly and decisively. The combination gets closer to the social optimum than either could do on its own. In some cases of mixed regulation, the government mainly fills in the gaps resulting from underdeterrence by the platform. It either nudges the platform to do more on its own or supplements what the platform does with its own regulations.

In fact, the current regulation of negative externalities on platforms typically involves a mixture of private and public regulation. Platforms can be used, for example, to facilitate crimes which are subject to governmental laws. The platform may disable the account of a retailer that commits fraud, but that retailer may also be subject to criminal prosecution. Platform participants may be banned because they engage in prohibited practices that inflict emotional distress, but the victim may be able to sue the perpetrator for civil damages in some cases.

C. Designing Interventions for Deterring Negative Externalities

The consideration of interventions to address bad behavior by participants on platforms can arise because of concern that existing private and public enforcement don't do enough, or by a desire to deter previously allowed behaviors. The concern could arise because of a change in circumstances. Perhaps there is an increase in the type or seriousness of the bad behavior and a realization that the behavior causes spillovers that were not previously recognizes. New types of bad behavior occur on platforms for which there is no, or insufficient, deterrence. Finally, there may be a concern that certain platforms, through their own actions rather than the actions of participants, may impose negative externalities on society.

1. The Need for Intervention

Whether there is a need for an intervention depends on whether there really is a problem for which an intervention is a solution. That begins with a determination that the conduct to be regulated actually gives rise to a negative externality. But an action by one party isn't a negative externality if the other party has been compensated for it perhaps because the platform has fully internalized the negative externalities. Advertising, for example, could be a negative externality when the recipient doesn't have any choice about receiving it such as when someone shoves a flier in our face when we are walking in a city. Attention platforms, however, provide content to viewers in return for their being exposed to advertising messages. The viewer doesn't incur a negative externality because he is receiving compensation for the harm and can easily avoid the harm by not using the platform.

The analysis should also determine whether the negative externality is likely to cause material harm given that interventions are always costly and can have unintended consequences. Consider online dating sites. Participants may be sufficiently experienced to account for a certain amount of misinformation, including flattering pictures, about people they encounter online. Once we move past fake pictures, or clearly inaccurate ones, it may be costly to decide what information is sufficiently truthful or not. And perhaps rigorous rules would have unintended consequences by, for example, discouraging online romance.

Current private and public rules, monitoring, and enforcement adequately may already deal with the negative externality in question. The fact that some bad behavior persists is not by itself a reason to consider additional intervention. Society tolerates some level of some of the most egregious negative externalities, such as murder, because the marginal costs of further efforts exceed the marginal benefits of further efforts. To assess the need for further intervention it is helpful to have information on the extent of current public and private deterrence efforts and the likely scope for further cost-effective reductions.

Of course, there are many types of bad behavior by platform participants that would benefit from greater intervention. They involve serious negative externalities that cause material harm and existing methods aren't sufficient.

2. Participant and Platform Liability

Governments can choose the extent to which they want to regulate platform participants directly or make platforms liable for doing so.

Existing public laws and regulations could be modified to deal with bad behavior that is particular to digital platforms. For example, consumer protection laws could to extended to deal with problems that are specific to digital platforms. Fines and other penalties could be strengthened for digital platforms if there is a basis for concluding that there is under-deterrence for these businesses. Perhaps there is evidence that a particular type of negative externality, such libel is more virulent when done online. That would argue for having heightened enforcement efforts and fines for online activity.

New laws or regulations could be enacted to deal with negative externalities. Platforms could give rise to other new methods for individuals by themselves, or through organizing individuals, to cause social harms. Existing laws may not provide avenues to deal with these, and the platform may have neither the incentive nor ability to address. "Megan's Laws" against cyberbullying were enacted because social media platforms were viewed as providing a new mechanism for causing harm for which specific laws were needed to impose liability on perpetrators.

It would be possible to impose liability, through laws and regulations, on the platform. That would give the platform the incentives to use its governance system to address the problem. In effect, shifting liability to the platform attempts to align its private incentives to address negative externalities with society's incentives. The platform, for example, could be held liable for harms inflicted on platform users, or society, that it could have limited by taking reasonable precautions through its governance system. Or there may be cases where strict liability is the better option.

These approaches are not mutually exclusive. In a world of second-best it is likely that a mixture of solutions is the best way to deal with negative externalities on platforms. Governments could impose sanctions on participants for bad behavior while also making the platform itself liable for harmful actions its participants make on the platform.

3. Benefits and Costs of Solutions

A proposed "intervention" in the following discussion involves the set of proposed public and private solutions.

Deciding on the optimal solution for negative externalities on platforms is likely to be more complex than usual because of the role of the platform itself as a regulator. The starting point is determining whether the benefits of a particular intervention being considered outweigh its costs. The following provides an overview of relevant factors in considering benefits and costs. This isn't just an accounting framework though. By carefully thinking through benefits and costs policymakers can refine their approaches by trying to devise solutions that increase the benefits, while limiting the direct costs, and reducing the risk of unintended consequences.

The analysis must begin by determining the benefits of the proposed intervention. The benefits of the intervention consist of the social value of the negative externalities reduced as a result of the intervention. To put this another way, the benefits equal the social value of the negative externalities under existing private and public rules less the social value of the negative externalities that would result from the intervention. In practice the benefits of reducing negative externalities on platforms are likely to be difficult to quantify because they involve goods that are not traded in markets. They may also involve concepts that are difficult for respondents to put a value on in contingent-valuation types surveys. Nevertheless, the only way to proceed with a cost-benefit analysis is to have at least some idea of the magnitude of the benefits that could be secured through reduced negative externalities.

Interventions involve costs. They include the usual ones for public interventions. Solutions that impose liability on the platform or that require it to modify its business practices could impose financial costs that are passed through to the participants. They could also induce the platform to reduce the value of services provided to participants. The risk of liability for harmful interactions, for example, could induce the platform to limit beneficial interactions thereby reducing the value of the platform. Regulations on selling counterfeit goods, for example, induce the platform to adopt certification policies that could reduce the sale of valid goods on the platform. Interventions could reduce the incentives on online attention platforms to provide content and services which, although free, are valuable.

Finally, interventions could have unintended consequences. By definition these are hard to anticipate. Prohibiting some behavior on platforms could drive it to other platforms where it is harder to detect. Intervention could reduce incentives for innovation. They could increase barriers to entry if there are scale economies in complying the regulations. The government is also not immune to agency problems. The legislative process or regulators could both captured by special interests that are motivated by raising rival's costs or excluding rivals altogether. Indeed, the jostling for advantages among digital platforms, and their rivals, may be one of the greatest risks to efforts to devise sound government interventions for excessive bad behavior on, and by, platforms.

4. Evaluating Alternative Solutions

The theory of second-best teaches us that none of the interventions will be perfect. The task is finding the best imperfect intervention. By definition, that's the one that generates the largest net benefits — the difference between the value of reduce negative externalities and the direct and indirect costs from intervention. Even if the considerations above aren't reduced to numbers they can be used in conjunction with various forms to evidence to perfect and choose solutions.

5. Platforms Behaving Badly Themselves

Platforms themselves may engage in activities that cause negative externalities. One situation in which this occurs relates to the previous discussion. If a platform's incentives to regulate negative externalities are too weak it may design the platform in ways that result in too much harmful behavior by its participants. A platform may design the platform so that it is too easy for people who engage in bad behavior to join the platform and then cause harm. An extreme version of this situation, discussed below, is when the platform makes money from negative externalities that arise from spillovers, which gives it a strong financial incentive to promote the bad behavior.

Another situation occurs when the platform itself engages in activities, rather than its participants, that cause negative externalities for its participants or society at large. A platform may have deceptive practices regarding the use of data that harm its participants directly with possible spillover effects. The basic principles for intervention outlined above apply in these cases as well.

VI.   APPLICATION OF THE NEGATIVE EXTERNALITY FRAMEWORK TO PAST, NEW, AND PROPOSED INTERVENTIONS

Governments have grappled with how to regulate bad behavior in the digital world since its beginnings in the early 1990s. This section uses the negative externality framework to highlight some of the key issues in the evolution of public and private regulation and some recent proposals. Its modest goal is help policymakers and others think about whether, and how, to modify public and private regulation of bad behavior on platforms, and not to devise solutions, which is a far more difficult, and evidence-demanding, undertaking. Its main message is that many of problems of today result from legislative decisions in the past that, with the benefit of hindsight, were not well though through—and that evidence-based analysis with careful consideration of long-term consequences is necessary to make the right decisions.

A. Section 230 and the Division of Public and Private Responsibility

Backpage.com displays classified ads for adult entertainment, including escorts, along with other things. Three young women, as young as 15 at the relevant times, claimed that the website "with an eye to maximizing its profits, engaged in a course of conduct designed to facilitate sex trafficker's efforts to advertise their victims on the website."[50] Among other claims they alleged that Backpage had rules and processes, such as not requiring phone or email verification, that were designed to encourage sex trafficking. The district court, and an appeals court, both very reluctantly, dismissed their case. Under Section 230(c)(1) to the Communications Decency Act of 1996 (CDA) an internet service provider is not liable for content posted by users.[51]

1. The Origin and Scope of Section 230

Section 230 was enacted to deal with an odd feature of freedom of speech laws in the U.S.U.S. Publishing certain kinds of content such as obscene or defamatory material is unlawful. Distributing that content is lawful unless the distributor knew or should have known that the content was unlawful and didn't take any action to prevent its distribution.[52] In 1995, a New York State court held that Prodigy, an

---

50   *Jane Doe No. 1 v. Backpage.com, LLC,* 817 F.3d 12, 16 (2016).

51   All of the substantive issues raised in this section also concern the 1998 Digital Millennial Copyright Act (DCMA) which immunized digital businesses from users posting copyrighted content so long as they took measures to take down the content when notified. The DCMA is covered briefly in the discussion concerning the impact of digital platforms on the supply of news.

52   For background on the legislation and its consequences see Kosseff, Jeff (2019) *The Twenty-Six Words That Created the Internet,* Cornell University Press.

online service that operated over a pre-Internet private network, was liable for posting a defamatory statement made by a user on a message board, because the company moderated the message board. Prodigy settled the case, before an appeal, with a public apology. An earlier decision, involving CompuServe, another pre-Internet online service, had determined the business was not liable because it did not moderate content.

These court decision, and the state of the law, raised the concern that users would post objectionable content on the new online businesses and that those businesses would have incentives not to police that content because doing so would expose them to liability. U.S. Congress believed this perverse standard would limit the growth of digital businesses and stifle innovation in addition to encouraging the proliferation of harmful material.[53] A year after the Prodigy decision it passed the Communication Decency Act.

Section 230 distinguishes between internet service providers ("ISPs") who connect multiple users to a service from internet content providers ("ICPs") that create information. Section 230(c)(1) says that ISPs, and users of ISPs, are not publishers for the purpose of the law. As a result, at least as the courts have interpreted the law, only the publisher of the content in question could be held liable for it. The ISP, and any ISP users that distribute the original content, have immunity. That immunity doesn't extend to violations of federal criminal law and intellectual property law but does extend to state criminal law. Section 230(c)(2) provides ISPs protection for "blocking and screening offensive material … whether or not such material is constitutionally protected."[54] The ISP therefore has a largely unfettered right to block and delete content and users. Over the years most courts have interpreted these provisions strictly in favor of the ISP.[55]

Section 230 was a very consequential decision on the allocation of public and private enforcement of harmful behavior on digital platforms. Digital platforms were no longer subject to long-standing public laws for a wide class of harmful behavior, including state criminal laws, that took place on their platforms. Congress further decided to empower digital platforms to limit harmful behavior on their platforms thereby essentially shifting responsibility from public to private enforcement. It did this by lim-

---

53 Brannon, Valerie (2019) "Liability for Content Hosts: An Overview of the Communication Decency Act's Section 230" *Congressional Research Service Report;* 141 Cong. Rec. H8470 (Aug. 4, 1996); Kosseff, Jeff (2019) *The Twenty-Six Words That Created the Internet,* Cornell University Press, at pp. 59-60.

54 47 U.S.C. §230.

55 In 2018 Congress amended to the CDA to expressly provide that Section 230's immunity provisions will not apply to certain sex trafficking offenses. See Allow States and Victims to Fight Online Sex Trafficking Act (FOSTA) of 2017. Pub. L. 115-164. 132 Stat 1253-1256. Apr. 11, 2018.

iting the ability of users to complain about having their content taken down, or being excluded from the platform, thereby enhancing bouncer's right for digital platforms.

2. Striking the Right Balance

Section 230 gave the U.S. a mixed regulatory regime in which digital platform users who directly caused harmful behavior by posting offensive content remained liable under prevailing public laws and in which the digital platform was given enhanced tools for operating whatever governance system it chose to employ. This regime could get close to socially optimal deterrence of harmful behavior on platforms if digital platforms had the incentives to do so, if the ability to exclude content and users was sufficient for them to accomplish that goal, and if the residual liability for participants who directly cause harm could fill in the gaps. Even if this mixed regime could not achieve the socially optimal deterrence, government may have decided that a more stringent regulatory regime would impose social costs by discouraging the development of the Internet. In fact, the legislative record suggests that Congress believed that making digital platforms liable would retard the growth of the Internet and that private governance could deal with harmful behavior.[56]

Without second-guessing Congress's decision to pass Section 230, it is useful to identify some issues that should have been considered based on the framework presented above and that provide insights into evaluating interventions in the future. The decision to immunize digital platforms for distributing harmful content likely increased the relative returns for digital platforms that focused on user-generated content and on content and behaviors could cause harm. That may have led entrepreneurs and investors to focus more on starting these platforms than they would have done in the absence of Section 230(c)(1). In addition to fostering the development of the Internet, the law may have had the unintended consequences of biasing the development of the Internet towards particular business models such as ad-supported ones and those relying on third-party content.

The decision to immunize digital platforms was also made with little information about the degree and type of harmful behavior that could occur on these platforms. There were only 20 million Internet-users in the U.S. in 1996.[57] Most online sites were new, with few users. It was another five years before social media platforms became popular and long before the rapid global growth in the use of these platforms. Congress could anticipate the harm from existing laws discouraging digital platforms

---

56 Kosseff, Jeff (2019) *The Twenty-Six Words That Created the Internet,* Cornell University Press, at pp. 59-60.

57 Nearly 20 million American adults reported that they used the World Wide Web regularly during 1996. See Specter, Michael, "World, Wide, Web: 3 English Words," *The New York Times,* April 14, 1996, available at https://www.nytimes.com/1996/04/14/weekinreview/computer-speak-world-wide-web-3-english-words.html.

that relied on third-party content from forming but not the harm from those platforms operating subject mainly to private regulation. According to Professor Kosseff, who interviewed the sponsors of Section 230, they had no idea what would become of the Internet or the impact of Section 230 on it.[58]

Congress also appears to have placed great stock in self-regulation. As we saw above, platforms have incentives to deter harmful behavior that lowers the value of the platform and their profits. There is no economic presumption, however, that they have strong enough incentives to curtail negative externalities to the degree society would like. Backpage is an example. It made money from classified ads placed by pimps and sex traffickers, in addition to sex workers, and from having users who wanted to view those ads to procure sex. It apparently didn't have any financial interest in caring about the people being trafficked or broader impacts on society.

Discussions of Section 230 typically suggest that the Internet could not have gotten off the ground in the absence of this law.[59] The argument is that companies such as Google and Facebook could not have existed in an environment in which they face legal liability for third-party content. That could be true, but the claim is not based on any reasoned analysis of a counterfactual world in which Section 230 was not enacted. The decisions that raised concerns were by state trial courts and not appealed. It is not clear how the courts would have sorted out of novel issues arising with the new platforms. There wasn't any evidence that platforms faced ruinous financial liability from moderating content. Prodigy was undone by the Internet, not by defamation lawsuits. And, as noted above, we don't know how digital platform business models would have evolved in the face of liability. Lastly, we don't know how the Internet would have evolved under alternatives to Section 230 that made digital platforms more liable for failing to take measure to limit harmful contents on their site.

3. Proposals to Modify Section 230

To limit the amount and nature of harmful content on digital platforms the government would need to give these platforms stronger incentives to limit that content, by making them more liable for the harm generated by this content; increase enforcement efforts and penalties for platform users who publish the content or who knowingly redistribute harmful content; or a combination of these measures. Imposing more stringent public and private regulation now, however, would result in different costs than had this been done in the infancy of the Internet. Back then the costs

---

58 Kosseff, Jeff (2019) *The Twenty-Six Words That Created the Internet,* Cornell University Press, at Location 74-89 of the Kindle Edition.

59 Kosseff, Jeff (2019) *The Twenty-Six Words That Created the Internet,* Cornell University Press, at Location 99-123 of the Kindle Edition; "Note: Section 230 as First Amendment Rule" *Harvard Law Review* 131(7), pp. 2027-2048; Klonick (2018) op. cit., p. 1604.

involved deterring the creation of new businesses and particular types of businesses and limiting innovation.

Now the costs include the disruption of long-standing business models and ways in which users behave in the online world. And unlike 1996, billions of people and businesses covering almost all countries use digital platforms a few of which account for bulk of activity. Interventions that can reduce negative externalities, including particularly serious ones, can also reduce, possibly substantially, the value that these platforms create for society, including positive externalities. As a result, policymakers need to exercise considerable care in designing interventions involving digital platforms. Therefore, any modified or new laws would need to account for the potential costs.

There have been recent concerns over digital platforms distributing fake news, facilitating terrorism, creating social unrest, interfering in elections, and aiding sex-trafficking and other crimes.[60] This has resulted in proposed legislation to modify Section 230 some of which are under active consideration by Congress as of the end of July 2020.[61] The U.S. Department of Justice, in a June 2020 report, has proposed eliminating immunity for platforms that are purposely facilitating third-party content or activity that would violate federal criminal law; for claims related to child abuse, terrorism, and cyber-stalking, The Justice Department would also limit immunity to private actions and thereby allow federal enforcement.[62] The bipartisan *Platform Accountability and Consumer Transparency Act*, like the DOJ, eliminates immunity from federal enforcement, and also allows states attorney generals to bring claims, when their state has a law that is analogous to a federal statute. It remains to be seen what, if any legislation, will emerge, but efforts to eliminate the most egregious consequences of Section 230 are sensible. That doesn't mean they couldn't have unintended consequences, though, and that risk will depend on the final language.

President Trump issued an Executive Order targeted at platforms censoring content. Under the FCC is tasked with considering regulations that would limit immunity for content removal that is "deceptive, pretextual, or inconsistent with the provider's terms or service" or "taken after failing to provide adequate notice, reasoned explanation, or meaningful opportunity to be heard." Republican members of Con-

---

60   Chen, Angela, "What is Section 230 and why does Donald Trump want to change it?" *MIT Technology Review*, August 13, 2019, available at https://www.technologyreview.com/s/614141/section-230-law-moderation-social-media-content-bias/.

61   Bedell, Zoe and John Major, "What's Next for Section 230? A Roundup of Proposals," *Lawfare*, July 29, 2020, available at https://www.lawfareblog.com/whats-next-section-230-roundup-proposals. The following discussion is based on this survey.

62   U.S. Department of Justice, "Department of Justice's Review of Section 230 of the Communications Decency Act of 1996," June 30, 2020, available at https://www.justice.gov/ag/department-justice-s-review-section-230-communications-decency-act-1996?utm_medium=email&utm_source=govdelivery.

gress have proposed legislation that would limit the ability of platforms to moderate content deemed to be political speech.[63] Several of the proposed bills only apply to very large platforms and seem to be targeted to Facebook, Google, and Twitter.

B. Attention Platforms, Content, and Privacy Regulation

Privacy policies highlight the potential role costs from laws and regulation. These policies mainly target attention platforms which collect data from users, and other sources, to increase the accuracy of targeting ads and the accuracy of presenting content to viewers.

1. The Value of Free Content

With the exception of a some relatively small subscription-based businesses, digital platforms provide content to users for free. This content is very valuable to consumers. People spend a great deal of their scarce time consuming digital content. Based on Nielsen data, American adults spent 5 hours a day on average during 2019 Q1[64], and over 1.2 billion hours per day in total[65], during which they were viewing or listening to content online, including on their mobile devices. They must have valued the content by at least the opportunity cost of their time.[66]

Several recent economic studies have used large-scale surveys to estimate the value of digital content based on the willingness to accept ("WTA") payment to not

---

63 See Bedell and Major, op. cit., for an overview of the proposals.

64 Nielsen (2019) "The Nielsen Total Audience Report Q1 2019" at p. 3.

65 Based on multiplying the average daily time spent online per adult by the U.S. adult population. U.S. adult population is sourced from U.S. Census Bureau, Current Population Survey, Annual Social and Economic Supplement, 2018, available at https://www.census.gov/cps/data/cpstablecreator.html.

66 Evans, David (2019) "Attention Platforms, the Value of Content, and Public Policy," *Review of Industrial Organization* 54(4), pp.775-792.

consume it.[67]   One study ensured that it was receiving accurate answers by actually preventing respondents from getting access to Facebook in return for payment in excess of their WTA for a month.[68]   Other studies have used the value of time to estimate the consumer surplus from online activities.[69]

2. Data, Privacy and Negative Externalities

Digital platforms invest in providing content to people, which involves developing and running the platform, because they are seeking to earn revenue from advertisers.[70] The returns to investing in content is greater when platforms expect more advertising revenue. With better data digital platforms can present more relevant ads to people. That increases the revenue it can earn since consumers are more likely to click

---

67   For estimates of the WTA not using online services, see Hunt Allcott, Luca Braghieri, Sarah Eichmeyer & Matthew Gentzkow (2019), "The Welfare Effects of Social Media," Working Paper, https://siepr.stanford.edu/sites/default/files/publications/19-002.pdf (median willingness to accept Facebook deactivation for four weeks of $100 for the first four weeks); Erik Brynjolfsson, Avinash Collis & Felix Eggers (2019), "Using Massive Online Choice Experiments to Measure Changes in Well-Being," PNAS, 116(15): 7250-7255 (median willingness to accept one year of no use in 2017 of $17,530 for all search engines, $8,414 for all email, $3,648 for all online maps, $1,173 for all online video, $842 for all e-commerce, $322 for all social media, $155 for all messaging, and $168 for all online music); Jay R. Corrigan, Saleem Alhabrash, Matthew Rousu & Sean B. Cash (2018), "How Much Is Social Media Worth? Estimating the Value of Facebook by Paying Users to Stop Using It," PLoS ONE, 13(12): e0207101 (median willingness to accept one week of Facebook deactivation of $15); Roberto Mosquera, Mofioluwasademi Odunowo & Trent McNamara (2019), "The Economic Effects of Facebook," Working Paper, https://papers.ssrn.com/sol3/papers.cfm?abstract_id=3312462 (willingness to accept Facebook deactivation for one week of $67). But note that looking at willingness to pay for online services instead of willingness to accept leads to substantially lower estimates of the value of these services. Cass Sunstein (forthcoming), "Valuing Facebook," Behavioral Public Policy (median willingness to pay for one month of Facebook of $1, but median willingness to accept for one month without Facebook of $59).

68   Erik Brynjolfsson, Avinash Collis & Felix Eggers (2019), "Using Massive Online Choice Experiments to Measure Changes in Well-Being," *PNAS* 116(15), pp. 7250-7255.

69   For estimates of the consumer surplus from online services, see Ergin Bayrak (2012), "Valuing Time-Intensive Goods: An Application to Wireless and Wired Internet," in Serge Allgrezza & Anne Dubrocard (eds.), Internet Econometrics, London: Palgrave Macmillan, 130-141 (annual consumer surplus from the internet of around $7,000, with wireless internet users receiving at least $824 more surplus than wired internet users); Brynjolfsson, Erik & Joo Hee Oh (2012) "The Attention Economy: Measuring the Value of Free Digital Services on the Internet" 33rd International Conference on Information Systems, at pp. 7-9 (consumer surplus from the internet of $1,196 billion in the United States in 2011); Austan Goolsbee & Peter J. Klenow (2006), "Valuing Consumer Products by the Time Spent Using Them: An Application to the Internet," American Economic Review Papers & Proceedings, 96(2): 108-113 (annual consumer surplus (equivalent variation) from the internet of $3000).

70   See Evans, David (2019) "Attention Platforms, the Value of Content, and Public Policy" *Review of Industrial Organization* 54(4), pp.775-792.

on a relevant ad, which generates a fee under the standard pay-per-click model, and because they can charge advertisers more because there is a higher likelihood the ad will generate a sale. With better data digital platforms can also present more relevant organic content to people. That makes users more likely to come to the platform and spend time there which in turn enables the platform to earn more from advertising.

The collection and use of this data come at a cost to the extent that people value privacy of data about themselves. Getting data from people and using it therefore does not necessarily impose a negative externality. The platform and user may have entered into an exchange in which the user has obtained the ability to consumer content and services on the platform as compensation for providing the platform with data, and the right to use their data. If the user didn't believe they were being adequately compensated they would not use the platform or, if there is a continuing risk of having data taken, use the platform less.

Users could encounter negative externalities, however, if they don't know what data they are disclosing or how the platform is going to use their data. Perhaps the platform hasn't disclosed its data policies sufficiently. Or it has raised the transactions costs to make it hard for the consumer to learn about the data policies. It is also possible individual users make decisions concerning their data which impose social costs. Perhaps by combining data from many users, platforms could impose some other cost on society such as foreign adversaries using the data to target cause harm. Government could consider interventions to limit these perceived negative externalities.

3. Value Creation and Optimal Regulation

Consider a proposed regulation that limits the amount of data online platforms can acquire from and about their users. The regulation might raise the cost to platforms of acquiring the data by requiring various disclosures and explicit grants of permission from users. It could also restrict the use of data collected for the purpose of matching advertisers with consumers. Platforms would provide poorer targeting and measurement to advertisers as a result of collecting less data or being able to use data less effectively for matching.

All else equal, the returns to advertisers from delivering messages would decline, the demand for advertising would and the equilibrium price of advertising would decline. The platforms would have lower incentives to invest in providing content given that the returns from advertisers, and therefore the returns on their investments in content, would be lower. The returns to making fixed cost investments in content are lower when the value of the attention generated from that content is lower. As the supply of content is restricted consumer welfare would decline.

These costs of regulating negative externalities by attention platforms have two practical implications. First, they should be considered as part of the calculus to assess whether a proposed intervention increases social welfare. Government would need to weigh benefits of reduced negative externalities, from greater privacy protection, outweigh the costs of the reduced value of content. Second, they should be considered in the first instance in designing interventions. The preferred second-best alternative would consider interventions that mitigate the impact on the supply of content.

C. Coase Theorem, Externalities, and Property Rights

In the U.S., the 1998 Digital Millennium Copyright Act ("DCMA") was enacted two years after the Communications Decency Act. Section 512 limited the liability of ISPs for claims that could arise from their users sharing material the infringe copyrights.[71] In exchange for protection from most forms of liability, the DMCA requires service providers to cooperate with copyright owners to address infringing activities performed by providers' users.[72] The DCMA does not require service providers to actively monitor its service for infringing activity. However, it does require that the ISP, upon proper notification by the copyright owner of online material being displayed or transmitted without authorization, to "expeditiously" remove or disable access to the allegedly infringing material.[73] To enforce their copyrights users have to send in a "take-down notice" to the ISP which is then supposed to remove the content.[74]

The CDA and DCMA both sharply reduced long-standing property rights in the physical world for the digital world. The CDA enhanced the bouncer's right for ISPs and reduced the rights of people to be protected from speech-related harms. The DCMA reduced the rights of copyright holders. The Coase Theorem tells us that in the absence of transactions costs these changes in property rights would not have any real consequences for economic efficiency. Parties could just bargain to the right solution. It also tells us that in the presence of transactions costs it is efficient to allocate property rights in a way that minimizes transactions costs.

The DCMA made it difficult for rightsholders to negotiate with platforms or with users who shared unlawful content. There were many potential victims of harm each of which had a small probability of being harmed. The costs of organizing themselves were high and the benefits were low. Large holders of copyrights, such as media conglomerates and music publishers, could have negotiated with ISPs. Since copyrighted material is easy reproduced and transmitted, they would have to negotiate with many ISPs who could enter easily with the expectation of being compensated. The CDA eliminated the possibility of class action lawsuits, representing many potential victims,

---

71   17 U.S. Code § 512.

72   Yeh, Brian (2014) "Safe Harbor for Online Service Providers Under Section 512(c) of the Digital Millennium Copyright Act" *Congressional Research Service Report.*

73   17 U.S. Code § 512.

74   *Id.*

against platforms for having adopted general policies that promoted bad behavior such as that for Backpage. Of course, the ultimate victims could pursue the perpetrators.

The property rights that were in place before the passage of the CDA and DCMA were the result of longstanding state and federal laws and interpretations by courts. The legislative records of the CDA[75] and DCMA[76] suggest that they were passed based on a belief that the transactions costs of existing laws would be excessive for new digital business. But those records do not suggest that there any serious consideration the optimal allocation of property rights or the risks of such a radical separation of property rights in the online and physical worlds.

D. Antitrust and the Regulation of Negative Externalities

Digital platforms are receiving great attention from competition authorities which leads to a question of whether the sorts of negative externalities discuss above should be considered in investigations and decisions.

Long experience has shown that antitrust is most effective when focused on promoting competitive markets for the benefit of consumers and not getting sidetracked into pursuing other policy goals such as protecting small businesses or reducing unemployment. It would be a mistake to deploy competition policy to deal with negative externalities digital platforms beyond the harms that antitrust ordinarily addresses.[77] Laws and regulations that are targeted directly towards reducing negative externalities are likely to be more effective than the blunt instruments of antitrust. Some of the more serious issues involving regulating negative externalities on digital platforms concern difficult tradeoffs that legislators must make in the first instances.

That doesn't mean, however, that negative externalities, or positive ones, are irrelevant for antitrust enforcement involving digital platforms. The generation of positive and negative externalities are elements of the non-price dimensions of platforms. They should therefore be accounted for in analyzing the impact of business behavior on consumer welfare. In fact, these non-price dimensions can be substantial for platforms. That is clear from online attention platforms which provide valuable content for free. There is also reasonable concern that these platforms generate negative externalities only some of which are curtailed by their private governance systems or by public law.

---

75   Kosseff, Jeff (2019) *The Twenty-Six Words That Created the Internet,* Cornell University Press, at pp. 59-60.

76   Yeh, Brian (2014) "Safe Harbor for Online Service Providers Under Section 512(c) of the Digital Millennium Copyright Act" *Congressional Research Service Report.*

77   Some competition authorities have dual responsibility for consumer protection which, by contrast, does provide a framework and set of tools that are directly relevant for addressing many negative externalities caused by platforms and their participants.

1. Business Behavior Subject to Antitrust Laws That Could Increase Negative Externalities

Competition authorities could find that negative externalities on platforms are germane to their analysis of mergers, cartels, and monopolization/abuse cases.

A merger could increase the combined firm's incentives to generate negative externalities in a variety of ways. (a) Suppose two firms compete in part by providing users safer spaces to interact. It is possible that the merged firm would have incentives to soften this non-price competition just as it has to soften price competition. The merged firm could end up having weaker enforcement efforts regarding bad behavior by users. Myspace acquiring Facebook in the mid 2000s could have raised this issue. (b) Suppose the acquiring firm has a business model that involves weak governance of negative externalities. It could impose that governance system on the target thereby increasing the overall generation of network externalities. Backpage buying Craigslist could raise just this sort of issue.

A cartel could have incentives to limit competition along dimensions that involve negative externalities. Suppose firms compete by offering varying degrees of privacy protection. The firms could adopt a "code of conduct" that has the effect of getting firms to weaken those privacy protections. They could agree to a code of conduct that results in weaker protection than competition would eventually generate. A related situation involves cases in the U.S. in which online competitors have agreed not to bid on each other's trademarked keywords (e.g. the name of the company) and to require search engines not to display an ad in response to a search query that included a competitor's trademarked keyword.[78]

The question of whether an excluded rival is an "as efficient competitor" comes up in monopolization and abuse of dominance cases. The typical analysis focuses on the competitor's costs and prices. For digital platforms the effectiveness of the competitor in governing bad behavior on the platform could be an important dimension of competition as could its ability to compete without imposing negative externalities itself. The efficiency of the competitor involves the non-price terms it can offer consumers—the bundle of valuable content, relevant ads, and privacy.

2. Exclusionary Conduct and Negative Externalities

As we saw, exclusion, based on the bouncer's right, is the main tool for regulating negative externalities caused by users of digital platforms. It is the one that was strengthened and enshrined into law in the U.S. Digital platforms, however, can also use their governance systems to limit competition by actual or potential rivals by excluding them from the platforms or raising their costs. This poses a challenge

---

78 *Federal Trade Commission v. 1-800 Contacts; Tichy v. Hyatt Hotels Corporation et al.*

for competition enforcement. Competition authorities and courts have to distinguish between the use of the bouncer's right to limit negative externalities on the platform from anticompetitive conduct through platform governance. They also have to consider the effect on any injunction on the use of governance systems for exclusionary conduct on the ability of digital platforms to limit negative externalities.

These governance systems create two conflicting incentives which magnify the difficulty of distinguishing pro-competitive from anti-competitive applications of exclusion. Digital platforms have incentives to engage in exclusionary conduct relying on governance systems, which provide the cover of pro-competitive explanations. Meanwhile business users that are imposing negative externalities have incentives to claim that they are the victims of anticompetitive conduct.

The good and bad uses of governance systems, and the incentives of platforms and their users to exploit them, increase the likelihood of false positive and false negative determinations. In previous work this author has argued that conduct related to governance systems should be subject to a three-step test.[79] (1) The initial screen is whether the platform has established a governance system and the practice at issue results from the application of that system; if not the standard analysis applies. (2) If platform has, the plaintiff should bear the burden of demonstrating that the governance system is not reasonably related to the enforcement the lawful goals of the governance system; if the defendant fails in this showing the case moves to the standard analysis. (3) If the plaintiff succeeds in showing that the action is not reasonably related to enforcing lawful governance goals, then the standard antitrust analysis of exclusionary conduct applies. These three steps seek to balance the pro-competitive benefits of platform governance for negative externalities and the anti-competitive costs of platform governance in particular cases.

VII. CONCLUSIONS

Myspace didn't have any legal culpability for Megan Meir's death. Megan's parents couldn't sue it on the ground that it hadn't done enough to prevent fake accounts or to prevent people from using them to cause harm. Section 230(c)(1) was a complete shield. Not only that, Myspace could, if it chose, actively encourage people to use fake accounts and create an online culture in which cyberbullying was acceptable.

In fact, Myspace did countenance fake accounts. It gained traction because the leading social network, Friendster, had purged "Fakesters." Myspace embraced a laissez-faire policy towards participants and accepted the "Fakesters" with open

---

79 Evans, David (2012) "Governing Bad Behavior by Users of Multi-Sided Platforms," *Berkeley Technology Law Journal* 27(2), pp. 1201-1250.

arms. Friendster was then besieged by "Fraudsters" who, as part of an effort to punish Friendster, assumed the identities of real people rather than fake ones.

Myspace soon learned lax governance had a price.[80] Among other problems it attracted minors who lied about their ages and child sex predators. Myspace also did not discourage users from posting objectionable content. It gained a reputation as a "vortex of perversion." It lost advertisers, the source of most of its revenues, who didn't want their ads appearing next to objectionable content.

In 2004, Facebook entered with a business model that was based on a strict governance system. In its first two years it only accepted people with valid email accounts (.edu), prohibited fake accounts, and banned nudity, pornography, and other objectionable content. Famously, it ejected recent child star, Lindsay Lohan, from Facebook for having a fake account. By the latter 2000s Myspace was in serious decline. It was sold for a reported sum of around $35 million in 2011. A year later Facebook did its IPO and was valued at a bit more than $100 billion.

Market forces, and private regulation, can discipline negative externalities by platform participants to some degree as this history reveals. This paper has shown, however, that there are limits to the incentives and ability of platforms to deter negative externalities to the degree society requires. Finding public interventions that can supplement or supplant private platform regulation requires, however, careful consideration of costs, benefits, and unintended consequences.

---

80   For details on the evolution of Friendster, Myspace, and Facebook see Evans, David (2012) "Governing Bad Behavior by Users of Multi-Sided Platforms" *Berkley Technology Law Journal* 27(2), pp. 1201-1250.

THE EVOLUTION OF ANTITRUST IN THE DIGITAL ERA

Antitrust Regulation in the Digital Economy

By Pierre Régibeau[1]

Abstract

I distinguish between data-based digital antitrust cases and non data-based cases. So far, the emphasis has been on traditional cases where data did not play a direct role. Although new names are used, the theories of harm are also traditional: bundling, exclusive dealing, and foreclosure. While the remedies obtained in some cases have been criticized, I believe that they are appropriate "looking forward" (preventing continuing damage to competition). There might however be a need to focus more on the "damage repairing" function of remedies. There have been few data-based cases. One of the reasons is that property rights on data and basic regulatory rules have not yet been spelled out. In this sense the ongoing allocation of tasks between regulation and antitrust is important.

I. INTRODUCTION

While the digital revolution has brought many new products and improved on the delivery of goods and services, it has also raised concerns about increased concentration and potentially abusive conducts that might not be captured adequately by a traditional application of competition policy tools. Of particular note is the increasingly powerful position of so-called digital "gatekeepers," i.e. digital platforms with significant market power – or even a dominant position – in at least one of the markets in which they are active. While the GAFAMs are the posterchildren of digital gatekeepers, other strong digital players such as various booking platforms, matching platforms or marketplaces might also well fall within the category, now or in the near future.

The competitive issues raised by digitalization of course extends beyond the realm of "platforms" – in the domain of standard setting for example – and they have implications for the fool toolset of competition authorities, from merger review to

---

1 Chief Economist, DG Competition, European Commission. Before joining the Commission, the author worked for VISA and against Google in both the Russian and EU *Android* cases. The views presented in this paper are the personal views of the authors. They do not reflect the view of the European Commission, DG Competition or the Chief Economist's team.

state aid. However, in this short note, I will limit myself to the "antitrust" part of the EU's portfolio, with special emphasis on gatekeepers. In doing so I will discuss not only the application of traditional antitrust instruments within the framework of Articles 101 and 102, but I will also comment on the possible emergence of a new "market investigation" tool and the necessary balance between traditional approaches, the new tool and *ex ante* regulation.

I begin by discussing what I see as the main characteristics of the digital economy in general and digital platforms in particular, briefly sketching out why these features matter for competition policy. I then briefly review the main antitrust actions in the digital sector before coming back in more detail to some of the concerns raised in the first section. I conclude with my thoughts as to how "new instruments" might help us address the specific competition issues raised by the digital sector.

II.   FEATURES OF THE DIGITAL ECONOMY

While the digital economy shares many relevant competition characteristics with non-digital sectors, it is nonetheless with a number of features that make it sufficiently distinct to warrant a separate analysis. In order to set up the scene for the following discussion I briefly review these features. I start with aspects that seem fairly unique to the digital sector and then move to characteristics which, although common in other sectors, seem to assume a particular importance in a digital context.

A. *"Unique" Features*

"Digital" technologies deal with data, be it accumulated data sets, or the information exchanged in any interaction over electronic means of communication. So, data treatment is inescapably at the core of any digitalized sector. What makes the digital economy special though is the manner in which it deals with data: data can be stored and made accessible in huge quantities, they can be processed or analyzed at high speed and they can travel over large distances in the blink of an eye. These characteristics have consequences for competition analysis.

Firstly, they affect market definition both because physical distance becomes less relevant (geographic markets) and because the availability of consumer-specific data enables individually tailored offerings. Secondly, because data is central to the digital sector, the creation, accumulation, sale and use of data can have important implication for competition. As discussed further below, this raises important questions about the nature of the data, their ownership, and their transferability. Finally, both organized data storage and data processing at speed and scale rely on the use of ever more sophisticated algorithms. Unfortunately, algorithms are often complex, are constantly modified and, since they can be key competitive advantages, they are closely held. This makes both the detection of abusive conduct and the enforcement of effective remedies challenging.

B. Other Relevant Features

The digital economy is also characterized by a few factors, which are also found in other sectors, but take on a special importance in the digital context. The main such feature is the ubiquity of "platforms," i.e. of undertakings simultaneously involved in several interdependent markets. In the digital work, such interdependence has two major sources: the fact that there are direct or indirect network effects across markets linked to the platform and the fact that information collected in one market can be economically valuable in another market. So again, potential economies of scope and scale in data matter. Still, the greatest concern stemming from the prevalence of platforms, some of which with significant market power, is interoperability: interoperability between different sides of the platform so that undertakings with more limited scope are not at an undue disadvantage and compatibility of data. Ensuring that data exists in a well ordered (standardized?) format has two main advantages. Firstly, it facilitates the emergence of "data markets" and data intermediaries. This enables smaller players to (at least partially) bridge the data gap with larger players. Secondly, it also simplifies potential data-sharing remedies if, for example, some of the data controlled by an undertaking were judged to constitute an essential facility.

A second feature of interest is that, currently at least, most digital sectors are "fast moving." This has a number of countervailing implications for competition policy. On the one hand, one cannot assume that large market shares can be sustained for very long, as the risk that a current position is undermined by drastic innovation might be substantial. This, of course, has been the mantra by which many large digital platforms defend themselves against finding of dominance. On the other hand, precisely because new technologies usually offer quite significant improvements, consumers are keen to switch to new, innovative platform. In other words, entry, at least entry based on drastic innovation, might impose a more significant competitive constrained than in other sectors. What is the correct balance between these two opposing forces, and how might such a balance be achieved?

Finally, whenever some of the cross-platform externalities relate to the supply of complementary products ("indirect" network effects), platforms might become dominant in the corresponding aftermarkets. The best known of such digital aftermarkets are probably the "apps stores" run by both Apple and Google on their respective IOS and Android platforms. Of course, the extent of the market power enjoyed in these markets depends itself of the degree of interoperability existing between various platforms.

III. ANTITRUST

Over the last five to ten years, competition authorities have investigated a number of potentially anti-competitive conducts by digital platform. These can be organized into data-related cases and other, more traditional cases.

A. Non-Data Case

So far, the investigation of digital platforms has focused on three broad types of conduct[2] – and hence of theories of harm.

1. Theories of Harm

As discussed above, hotel booking platforms were investigated for their contractual MFN clauses. While not an explicit agreement between horizontal competitors, such clauses soften competition between rival platforms by modifying the hotels' optimal response to response to platforms offering reduced commissions. We are therefore in the traditional category of "clauses that reference rivals," such as "meet any price." While such clauses are generally considered anti-competitive[3] they might also be a defense against "show rooming," which is the practice of getting product-related information at a full-service site before completing the transaction, at a better price, at a bare-bone site. The only specifically "digital" aspect of these cases is that such "free riding" might be more prevalent in the online world than when brick and mortar outlets are concerned, as potential clients can "travel" more easily from one seller to the next.

Digital platforms have also been investigated for allegedly leveraging their dominance in one market into another related market. In the Google Android case, for example, both the Russian antimonopoly Bureau and DG Competition is also, at first sight at least, a traditional bundling/exclusive dealing case where dominance in one market (Google store) was used to improve or entrench Google's position in mobile search. Interestingly, the formal economic theory of harm had to make allowances for the fact that Google does not normally charge for users' access to either their browser or their store. While such zero, or even negative, prices on one side of the platform is not unique to the digital world, it is still more likely to arise in this context: if marginal costs are low, accounting for cross-platform externalities can easily lead to no charge or even bonuses (payment cards).

---

2 Outside of these three main categories of conduct, one must still mention the *VISA, Mastercard,* and *Amex* cases. Clearly though the main theory of harm relating to the interchange fee or to contractual clauses such as the no surcharge rule where not "digital" in nature.

3 See F. Scott-Morton, 2012-2013, "Contracts that Reference Rivals," 27 Antitrust 72, Heinonline.

The growing number of cases involving "self-preferencing" fall in the same broad category in the sense that dominance in one market is used in order to help the digital platform succeed in other market. However, this involves direct deterioration of rivals' access to a crucial input rather than contractual means such as bundling or exclusive dealing. I believe that it is important to underline that, in many respects, "self-preferencing" is *not* a new theory of harm. It is just the application of traditional input foreclosure/access degradation theories of harm to a context where access is managed through opaque algorithms that the dominant platform can readily manipulate to its advantage.

The fact that important aspects of the daily competitive conduct of some digital platforms are driven by non-transparent algorithms is problematic indeed, both for establishing competitive harm and for finding – and enforcing – effective remedies. The *Google Shopping* cases illustrates these difficulties. Without direct access to and, crucially, complete understanding of the search algorithm, determining whether or not price comparison sites were actually discriminated against is not an easy task. Moreover, even if one observes a change in the treatment of those sites overtime, one needs to determine that this was not the result of a legitimate change in the ranking algorithm. Moreover, if the algorithms are also modified for legitimate business reasons, one must also examine whether there was any other way of pursuing a legitimate business objective with less collateral competitive damage. Carrying out these tasks required enormous use of resources for DG Competition. As for remedies, the flexibility of algorithms makes it relatively easy to achieve a similar anticompetitive effect without infringing the formal commitments or, at least, without making such a breach obvious and hence easy to monitor.

Other theories of harm depend on the business model of the digital platform. There are two broad templates. In the first approach, most of the platform's activities are aimed at gathering data, which are then mostly monetized through online advertising. Because data is so central, issues relating to the advertising market will be (briefly) touched upon in the next section. The second dominant business model is that of the *digital marketplace*. This model has two important variants, one where the platform is mostly a marketplace (think Amazon) and another where the access to the marketplace involves the acquisition of hardware and/or operating system (Apple being the purest example). This second business strategy naturally leads to *aftermarkets*.

Overall then we see that, so far at least, non-data antitrust cases in the digital sector have not in fact focused particularly on the specific features of digital sectors discussed at the beginning of that note. In this sense, while we can already identify a significant number of antitrust cases in the digital sector, one might say that the era of digital antitrust enforcement has barely begun. This, however, does not mean that these "traditional," cases do not themselves have a strong "digital" flavor, as they at least consider specific aspects of pricing and platform organization in the digital sector.

2. Antitrust versus Regulation

Over the last several years, there has been a growing clamor to regulate some aspects of the behavior of large digital platforms. This is coming to a head with DG Competition's recent consultation about the introduction of a "new competition tool) and DG Connect's own regulatory plans. While the final form of any regulation and of its relationship with antitrust is yet to be determined, some clear principles are emerging.

Ex ante regulation offers three main advantages over competition policy: it saves resources, it is faster, and it generally provides greater legal certainty. Regulation is also best applied to conducts that have clear-cut implications for competition and consumer welfare and can be applied to a sufficiently large, and well-defined, population of undertakings. This creates some trade-offs. On the one hand, regulation can react quickly to the evolution of the industry, but a fast-moving sector is also likely to accelerate the obsolescence of current rules. This introduces a trade-off between responsiveness and legal certainty. The scope of application of digital regulation also requires some careful balancing. Limiting its application to a few undertakings might help find types of behaviors that are uniformly harmful or pro-competitive across all undertakings. The larger the set of sectors or undertakings to which the digital regulation would apply, the least ambitious this regulation can be as it can only apply to the "common denominator" of good and bad conducts. In this respect, it seems worth remembering that the GAFAMs themselves display such variety in terms of their conduct and business model that the number of rules, which could sensibly apply to all of them is already likely to be limited. There might then be little additional loss in extending the scope of application of the regulations to more digital platforms and/ or digital sectors.

I would welcome a division of tasks between antitrust and regulation. From my personal view, regulation would be especially helpful in dealing with what we usually refer to as "unfair business practices," over which DG Competition does not have jurisdiction and with matters of transparency. So, for example, transparency in the rules applied by marketplaces and robust appeals procedures would seem to be a low-hanging fruit. One might also set up basic about "display boxes" which are a feature of several platforms, at least requiring transparency in the criteria applied and a guarantee that these criteria are applied uniformly. More controversially, perhaps, one might even consider a broader type of "access regulation" to platforms, which might encompass technical conditions, contractual clauses of even the amount of the access fee.

Digital platforms are complex objects, relying on technologies that make their conduct less than transparent. Complexity and transparency complicate the task of developing appropriate theories of harm and of tying them to the facts. In this perspective then, "clearing the decks" by entrusting several dimensions of this environment to a regulator would, one would hope, lead to more targeted and rigorous antitrust enforcement. Clearly though, the relationship between regulation and antitrust must remain fluid. In particular, it would make sense to start with regulation of a moderate scope, adding to the rules as we learn more about other types of conducts. Some of this learning can come from traditional antitrust. Takes the example of "self-preferencing." In my view, jumping to a regulatory rule banning this type of conduct in general would be premature as self-preferencing can take many forms and entail different effects. However, antitrust investigations can improve our understanding of this family of conduct to the point where some more specific conduct can safely pass in the hands of regulators.

The development of a "new tool," making it possible to investigate the obstacles to competition in particular digital sectors or subsectors might also smooth the interface between antitrust and regulation in two respects. Firstly, such a tool could be used, even in the absence of dominance. Not only does this increase the number of investigations that could be opened, thereby increasing the speed of our learning, but it also means that potentially anticompetitive conduct, or potentially anti-competitive aspects of an industry's environment can be identified before they have led to excessive concentration or even to "market tipping."

B. Data Cases

1. The Problem with Data

As mentioned at the outset, the digital sector revolves around data. It is therefore somewhat odd that, while rumors of investigations abound, we have not yet much in terms significant data-related decision (the German Facebook case standing as a rather lonely exception). There are two main reasons for this state of affair. Firstly, property rights over various types of data have not yet been clearly established. Secondly, the use of some type of data and the competitive advantage that they might confer are still poorly understood.

Digital companies, and digital platforms in particular collect different types of data. Broadly, one can distinguish between information about how users behave on the platform and information about consumer behavior outside of the platform (e.g. through cookies). Furthermore, for digital marketplaces, one can add a third category: information about interactions between consumers and non-affiliated sellers in the marketplace. It should be clear that unambiguous property rights are a pre-condition for rigorous antitrust analysis. For example, a dominant platform demanding the right to use the first type of data (platform interaction), without providing a viable alternative for access, might conceivably be seen as an exploitative abuse if the consumer has property rights over this data. This line of argument would not be appropriate if the legal view were that this type of data is actually created by the platform. The allocation of property rights is also crucial to enable (if desired) the trading of data. In turn, such trading might enable smaller players to piece together datasets, which are not dwarfed by the data available to the larger players. Such trade would also be facilitated by the development of interoperability standards for online data sets.

In order to develop coherent theories of harm we also need to understand what the three different types of data mentioned above are, or can be, used for. We know that data about the interaction with the platform can help improve the user's experience. This, for example seems to be the situation in search. We also know that information about a users' purchasing behavior or about characteristics that are closely related to her purchasing behavior (and can come from outside the platform) improves the targeting of online advertising, allowing the platform to charge heftier fees to its advertising clients. But can the same data also be used for different purposes, especially when combined with other data sources? And what about data about the interaction between users and undertakings hosted by the platform? Is it used mostly to further improve matching or can it also help the platform operator get a leg up on competitors?

Finally, we also need to understand the extent of the competitive advantage conferred by the exclusive use of specific data sets. Search provides a good example in this respect. All known search engines process millions of queries every day. This generates much information about the search behavior of users very fast. Clearly, however, the larger players – and in particular Google – have information about many times more searches that smaller rivals. While it seems clear to a layperson that more experience and data about search make it possible to further refine the search algorithm, what is relevant for antitrust enforcement is the *size* of the advantage conferred by larger datasets. In other words, how large are the economies of scale in the gathering of search information? The unfortunate answer is that we still do not know much about this.

In the case of search, it seems that, even for a company like google, further data helps improve the accuracy of the search algorithm for "tail" queries, which represent a substantial part of an individual's daily interactions with the search engine. However, how much do consumers value such further refinements? Also, how durable is this advantage, i.e. how fast does past information become obsolete. Similar issues arise for data fed to advertising matching algorithms...or indeed any algorithm.

2. (Potential) Theories of Harm

Due to the dearth of actual data-based cases, we can only discuss what seem to be the more likely theories of harm in this area.

Essential Facility

Many policy makers and commentators are troubled by the amount of information that some companies, in particular Facebook and Google are amassing on various aspects of the characteristics and behavior of their users. Not only might such a large data advantage help these companies entrench their position in a number of markets where they already have significant market power, but there are also concerns that they might leverage their alleged data dominance into other markets. If the data advantage of some firms becomes indeed so large as to preclude the participation of rivals in a number of markets, one could consider building a theory of harm based on the control of an essential data facility. If such theory of harm were to be confirmed, a natural remedy would be to impose some sharing of data with potential rivals. As mentioned before, the existence of standards for data transferability would facilitate such remedies.

However, as explained above, the fact that we know so little about the marginal returns from ever bigger data sets and know even less about how the magnitude of the competitive advantage that the merging of data sets collected in several markets offer, would make it hard to demonstrate that any current data set should qualify as an essential facility. While such demonstration might become easier as we learn more about data-based competition, I believe that, in the short to medium term, encouraging interoperability and the emergence of markets for data is likely to be a more fruitful policy approach.

Privacy

Where a society stands on issues of privacy is not the province of competition policy. Moreover, as mentioned above, antitrust can only perform well if there are clear rules about property rights on various type of personal data. Nonetheless, it can be fruitful to think of privacy as, partly at least, an additional dimension of product or service "quality." In this view then, it would be entirely proper to ask whether a merger would lead to a substantial decrease in privacy for users and to impose appropriate remedies, such as data segregation or limitation on data use without the users' consent.

The implication of "privacy as quality" for antitrust are less clear. One could conceivably worry about conduct by a dominant platform that makes it harder for rivals – or indeed any undertaking operating on the platform – to compete with high-privacy services. I am not aware of any complaint about such conduct so far. Alternatively, it would be logical to consider exploitative theories of harm for lack of provision of adequate levels of privacy in the same way as one can pursue a dominant undertaking for excessive pricing. A problem with this approach (as exemplified by the German Facebook case) is that, while economics provide natural benchmarks for what would be a competitive price, establishing an equivalent benchmark for privacy can be challenging. Moreover, given the reluctance of antitrust authorities to pursue excessive pricing cases, one should not hope that theories of harm base on "insufficient privacy" are likely to flourish.

Raising Rivals' Costs

An interesting direction might be to look for conducts that deprive rivals or even platform users (potential competitors) from access to data generated by their own activity or conducts that force these undertakings to share these data with the dominant platform. Broadly speaking, both types of conducts could be construed as a manner of "raising rivals' costs" as they weaken its relative ability to compete.

Some Reflections on Algorithms, Tacit Collusion, and the Regulatory Framework

By John Moore, Etienne Pfister & Henri Piffaut[1]

Abstract

Whether algorithms do increase the risk of tacit collusion remains very uncertain. Yet, if this is the case, the consequences for the effectiveness of regulation and of competition policy could be important and regulators need to think on how to make sure that this risk of algorithmic collusion is reduced while simultaneously preserving firms' incentives to adopt such efficiency-enhancing mechanisms. This article reviews the latest experimental evidence of algorithmic collusion and its limitations. It then analyses some of the various solutions brought forward to adapt competition policy in order to tackle the issue of algorithmic tacit collusion, with a particular focus on possible complementarities between regulatory tools and competition enforcement.

I.   INTRODUCTION

A series of influential academic studies have highlighted the risk that algorithms may facilitate tacit collusion.[2] That has led to a growing interest of competition authorities and practitioners. Indeed, over the last couple of years, the UK, the French and German, and the Portuguese competition authorities have all published reports

---

1   Respectively economist, chief economist, and vice-president at the French Competition Authority. The views presented in this paper are those of the authors only. They are not meant to reflect those of the French Competition Authority.

2   See for instance Ezrachi, A. & Stucke, M. E. (2016). Virtual Competition: The Promise and Perils of the Algorithm-Driven Economy. *Harvard University Press*; Harrington, J. (2018). Developing Competition Law for Collusion by Autonomous Artificial Agents. *Journal of Competition Law & Economics*, Vol 14(3), pp. 331–363; or Calvano, E., Calzolari, G., Denicolò, V. & Pastorello, S. (2019a). Algorithmic Pricing: What Implications for Competition Policy? *Review of Industrial Organization*. Vol 55, pp. 155-171.

addressing this particular issue.[3] However, to the best of our knowledge, there is yet to be a case of purely algorithmic tacit collusion sanctioned by a European competition authority.

This notable absence of cases could be due to several, non-mutually exclusive, reasons. First, the risk of algorithmic tacit collusion may have been overestimated, at least in the short run. For instance, firms may be reluctant to use black-box pricing algorithms of the type used in the experiments showing that algorithms can lead to tacit collusion; real-life market conditions may also be too remote from the experimental settings where algorithm-supported tacit collusion was detected. Second, competition authorities could be ill-equipped to detect tacit collusion due to insufficient data monitoring. Furthermore, under the current legal framework (which requires either an agreement or a concerted practice to tackle collusion), it is not obvious that a purely tacit collusion, which would not involve any data exchange or any communication between firms, could be qualified as an anticompetitive practice.

Still, whether algorithms do increase the risk of tacit collusion remains very uncertain. Yet, if this is the case, the consequences for the effectiveness of regulation and of competition policy could be very important and regulators need to think about how to make sure that this risk of algorithmic collusion is reduced while simultaneously preserving firms' incentives to adopt such efficiency-enhancing mechanisms. After having reviewed the latest experimental evidence of algorithmic collusion and its limitations (Section 2), this article analyses some of the various solutions brought forward to adapt competition policy in order to tackle the issue of algorithmic tacit collusion (Section 3). In Section 4, we discuss possible complementarities between regulatory tools and competition enforcement as well as the obstacles that continue to lie ahead. Section 5 concludes.

II.   THE EXPERIMENTAL RESULTS ON ALGORITHMS AND TACIT COLLUSION

A. Presentation of the Results

Many papers that aim to assess the risk of tacit collusion due to algorithm pricing consider an experimental framework where algorithms "play" against each other in a setting that mimics a competitive environment. In their simplest form, the games consist of two identical algorithms, one per firm, each setting a price for a substitutable good or service given the firms' production function and the (estimated)

---

3   Competition & Markets Authority (2018), Pricing Algorithms: Economic working paper on the use of algorithms to facilitate collusion and personalised pricing; Autorité de la Concurrence and Bunderkartellamt (2019). Algorithms and Competition; or Autoridade da Concurrência (2019), Digital ecosystems, Big Data and Algorithms. Also see the paper by the President of the Bundeskartellamt in this issue.

level of demand. Very often, a certain degree of common knowledge is assumed, regarding demand conditions or competitors' prices for instance. The objective of the algorithms is to maximize the long-term profits of their respective firms. After setting its price, each algorithm then observes the outcomes: the price set by its competitor and the rewards earned from the fictive sales of the product given the prices set by the two firms. This experience is then repeated a certain number of times until the system stabilizes. In the end, the results of the experiment are generally compared with the perfectly competitive case to assess the degree of tacit collusion.

Experimental results have shown that, in such settings, tacit collusion, i.e. supra competitive prices or profits, is likely to be attained, at least after a given number of iterations.[4] However, these experimental settings have often been criticized for being too simplistic compared with real-life markets (see below). To address this issue, some researchers have tested whether their experimental results still hold when adding complexity to the framework. For instance, in a series of robustness checks, Calvano et al. (2019b)[5] consider stochastic (rather than a stable and perfectly known) demand for the good, the possibility of entry of a third firm during the experiment or the case of asymmetric companies. Their results show that the added complexity reduces the level of supra-competitive profits or increases the time span before a collusive outcome is reached. For instance, Klein (2019) show that the speed of convergence to collusion decreases as the number of discrete prices algorithms may use increases.[6] Yet, in spite of this complexity, algorithms still manage to reach some degree of coordination, as Calvano et al. (2019b)[7] show. Similarly, Hansen et al. (2020)[8] show that collusion is still likely to be attained even when algorithms do not observe each other's prices. All in all, it may be inferred from these various experiments that factors such as symmetry between firms, market stability, simple decision rules, market transparency, while not an absolute prerequisite to algorithmic collusion (at least in the experimental settings described above), may facilitate its attainment or the level of profits (and hence the consumer loss) it generates.

---

4 Tesauro, G. & Kephart, J. O. (2002), Pricing in Agent Economies Using Multi-Agent Q-Learning, *Autonomous Agents and Multi-Agent Systems*, Vol 5(3), pp. 289 et seq.; Calvano, E., Calzolari, G., Denicolò, V. & Pastorello, S. (2019a). Algorithmic Pricing: What Implications for Competition Policy? *Review of Industrial Organization*. Vol 55, pp. 155-171.

5 Calvano, E., Calzolari, G., Denicolò, V. & Pastorello, S. (2019b). Artificial Intelligence, Algorithmic Pricing and Collusion (https://ssrn.com/abstract=3304991).

6 Klein, T., Autonomous Algorithmic Collusion: Q-learning Under Sequential Pricing, Amsterdam Law School Research Paper, 2019.

7 Calvano, E., Calzolari, G., Denicolò, V. & Pastorello, S. (2019b). Artificial Intelligence, Algorithmic Pricing and Collusion.

8 Hansen, K., Misra, K. & Pai, M. (2020). Algorithmic Collusion: Supra-competitive Prices via Independent Algorithms, *CEPR Discussion Paper Series*.

B. Limitations of the Experimental Framework

In spite of these findings, a significant number of researchers and practitioners doubt that algorithms could end up colluding in real-life market settings (see for instance Kühn & Tadelis (2017),[9] Schwalbe (2018)[10]). They set forth five main criticisms:

- First, the comparison between the prices set by the algorithms during the experiments and the theoretical results concerning the level of prices in a perfectly competitive environment is uninformative. Absent pricing algorithms, managers would set firms' prices and such prices would likely be higher than the perfectly competitive benchmark if not higher than the prices set by the algorithms if managers also learn to tacitly collude. Unfortunately, the high number of iterations used in experimental studies on algorithms prevents researchers from replicating their studies with human players in order to assess the level at which the benchmark should be set. It is thus impossible to know whether, and to what extent, pricing algorithms enable to reach worse collusive equilibriums than human managers in the long run.

- Second, it is unclear whether firms would ever accept using the types of pricing algorithms considered in experimental studies. The algorithms used in the experimental literature are often black-box algorithms[11] whose actions cannot easily be understood or explained as opposed to descriptive algorithms. Firms may be reluctant to delegate their decision-making powers on prices to such algorithms. Furthermore, before potentially reaching any collusive outcome, Q-learning algorithms[12] such as the ones used in the experimental literature are likely to lead to losses for the firms, especially during the learning/training phase where the algorithms explore the rewards associated with different sets

---

9 Kühn, K.-U. and Tadelis, S. (2017). The (D)anger Behind Algorithmic Pricing, Mimeo.

10 Schwalbe (2018), Algorithms, Machine Learning, and Collusion, *Journal of Competition Law & Economics*, Vol. 14(4), pp. 568 et seq.

11 In their report, the Autorité de la Concurrence and the Bundeskartellamt distinguish descriptive algorithms, whose strategy and actions can be understood by analyzing the code or a description of the algorithm, from black-box algorithms, whose behavior is hardly interpretable for humans.

12 Experimental studies often consider Q-learning algorithms, a particular class of reinforcement learning algorithms that could be classified as a black-box algorithm.

of prices. These losses may not be negligible or short term as some time is needed before the firm is actually able to assess the level of profits associated with a given price. Firms may then be reluctant to accept such sacrifices, even in spite of the prospect of higher revenues due to tacit collusion in the longer run.

- Third, even if firms adopted pricing algorithms, these firms could want to exploit the data processing capabilities of algorithms to charge different prices to different (classes of) consumers using information collected on these (classes of) consumers. However, as underlined by the CMA in their report on pricing algorithms[13], tacit collusion and personalised pricing are very unlikely to occur simultaneously: *"without explicit communication and sharing of information, if there are many differentiated products and personalised prices, then it appears far more difficult to reach a common understanding of the terms of coordination."*

- Fourth, experiments on algorithmic collusion rely on strong assumptions on the economic environment. These settings usually consider only two players using the same algorithm each selling a single product, no risk of entry, a stable demand, discrete and uniform prices, etc. Calvano (2019b)[14] and Hansen et al. (2020)[15], among others, show that relaxing some of these assumptions individually may not decrease the risk of collusion to a great extent (see above). Yet, as argued by the Autorité de la concurrence & the Bundeskartellamt, *"a real-life market environment is likely to encompass several sources of complexity simultaneously. Their joint effect on the likelihood of collusion remains an open question for future economic research."*[16] Furthermore, in real life, algorithms may have to constantly re-learn how to price given the changing complexity of the environment.

---

13 Competition & Markets Authority (2018), Pricing Algorithms: Economic working paper on the use of algorithms to facilitate collusion and personalised pricing.

14 Calvano, E., Calzolari, G., Denicolò, V. & Pastorello, S. (2019b). Artificial Intelligence, Algorithmic Pricing and Collusion.

15 Hansen, K., Misra, K. & Pai, M. (2020). Algorithmic Collusion: Supra-competitive Prices via Independent Algorithms, *CEPR Discussion Paper Series*.

16 Autorité de la Concurrence & Bunderkartellamt (2019). Algorithms and Competition.

- Finally, it would seem that the positive effects of pricing software are often ignored or, at least, unaccounted for in these studies. There would need to be some analysis of whether these efficiencies are correlated to the collusive outcomes. In that case, the positive effects enabled by pricing algorithms, in particular, potential efficiency gains, could offset at least part of the costs that could arise from algorithms reaching collusive outcomes in some cases. Consequently, additional work should be done to inform on whether the net effect of pricing algorithms is negative or positive compared to a but-for world.

As a result, whether the increasing use of pricing algorithms by firms is likely to lead to more tacit collusion remains very debated.

III. POSSIBLE DIFFICULTIES FOR COMPETITION POLICY AND FOR THE REGULATORY FRAMEWORK

The relevance of the experimental framework used to demonstrate the risk of algorithm-based tacit collusion has important implications for competition authorities. If pricing algorithms are a risk for competition, competition policy has to address that risk. Conversely, if this risk is non-existent or over-estimated, such actions might only or mainly generate costs for companies and customers alike, and thus affect negatively economic efficiency as a whole. In addition, monitoring algorithms is also likely to increase the burden of regulatory agencies, thus requiring more resources or diverting existing resources from other tasks.

There is no consensus on the opportunity for competition policy to address algorithmic pricing. Some consider that the experimental framework is way too remote from the real world and that the higher risk of tacit collusion through algorithms compared to through humans is not sufficiently demonstrated. Advocates of this position often argue that no action should be taken. For instance, Schwalbe (2018)[17] considers that competition authorities should not waste important and finite resources on the topic: "*the limited resources of competition authorities should rather be devoted to more pressing problems as, for example, the abuse of dominant positions by large online-platforms.*"

While recognizing that the plausibility of algorithm-based tacit collusion is uncertain, some others insist that it cannot be ruled out, that only simple algorithms are used in the experiments and that more complex algorithms could certainly entail

---

17   Schwalbe (2018), Algorithms, Machine Learning, and Collusion, *Journal of Competition Law & Economics*, Vol. 14(4), pp. 568 et seq.

more collusion than is illustrated in these papers.[18] They argue that this issue, although now of uncertain relevance, will become more pressing in the future. Several regulatory tools to help address the risks associated with pricing algorithms have been discussed relying either on a new regulatory regime or on competition law enforcement.

A. Some Regulatory Solutions

Banning pricing algorithms altogether seems excessive.[19] Yet banning certain types of algorithms has been envisaged. For instance, descriptive algorithms, because they are easy to understand and thus to assess under competition law enforcement if needed, could be thus allowed. On the contrary, the effects of so called "black box" algorithms are harder to anticipate, monitor or interpret; the collusion that could stem from the use of such algorithms is thus more difficult to detect and to demonstrate – as a result, some could call for such algorithms be banned. However, compared to descriptive algorithms, black box algorithms are used because they present specific advantages that are unrelated to the possibility of tacit collusion. For instance, compared with descriptive algorithms, black-box algorithms usually automatically evolve, in particular regarding their pricing strategies, when faced with changing external conditions. Thus, banning them could generate costs that may exceed the benefits of reducing the risk of algorithm-based tacit collusion (Calvano et al. (2019a)).[20] Furthermore, less drastic solutions could also help reducing the risk of tacit collusion while preserving the efficiency gains associated with black box algorithms.

Hence, some propose to use an approach targeted on the design stage of an algorithm either through conformity by design or through sandbox testing. These are very much consistent with proposals in other public policy fields such as ethics.[21] Hence, following the "conformity by design" approach, competition rules should be integrated into the algorithms. While this is an attractive approach on paper, the competition rules that the design of algorithms should integrate are often unclear. Tacit collusion is not, by itself, anticompetitive and firms have the right to adjust their

---

18 See for instance the results from Crandall, J. W., Oudah, M., Tennom, Ishowo-Oloko, F., Abdallah, F., Bonnefon, J.-F., Cebrian, M., Shariff, A., Goodrich, M. A., & Rahwan, I. (2018). Cooperating with machines, *Nature Communications.* Vol. 9, 233.

19 See the discussion in Calvano, E., Calzolari, G., Denicolò, V. & Pastorello, S. (2019a). Algorithmic Pricing: What Implications for Competition Policy? *Review of Industrial Organization.* Vol 55, pp. 155-171.

20 Calvano, E., Calzolari, G., Denicolò, V. & Pastorello, S. (2019a). Algorithmic Pricing: What Implications for Competition Policy? *Review of Industrial Organization.* Vol 55, pp. 155-171.

21 See Fjeld J. & Nagy A. (2020). Principled Artificial Intelligence, Mapping Consensus in Ethical and Rights-based Approaches to Principles for AI. Berkman Klein Center for Internet & society.

prices to their competitors' behavior. A conformity by design approach would need to identify some key parameters embodied in the algorithm which may facilitate collusion such as speed of price changes, signalling attempts or information gathering.

The "sandbox testing" approach requires that tests are made before the algorithm is used in order to assess the risk of collusion (Ezrachi & Stucke (2016)).[22] These tests should be conducted in an environment that mimics the competitive environment. Competition authorities should then have the power to ban certain algorithms, which are prone to collusion,[23] or recommend changes to the code of the algorithms to limit the risk of collusion. This approach is fraught with difficulties. First, as already explained, it can be difficult to design a framework that mimics the real competitive environment; this framework may prove hard to design and hard to define *ex ante*, in guidelines for example. Second, tests should have to comply with some principles (to ensure integrity, verifiability, replicability, etc.) so that outcomes can be trusted and compared. Third, the number of these tests could be quite high if every algorithm is to be tested. Fourth, there is the question of who could undertake such tests: third parties, the companies themselves, etc. Finally, the results of the tests may also depend on the competitors' algorithms, which may not be known by the company that is testing its own algorithm and which may change or be adapted during activity.

B. Some Competition Enforcement Issues

The detection of algorithmic tacit collusion by competition authorities could be an arduous task. To facilitate detection, some authors have for instance suggested creating a whistleblower bounty program, where consumers could report potential cases of algorithmic collusion (Lamontanaro (2020)).[24] But even if detection could be simplified, proving the wrongdoing could also end up being strenuous if the competition authority lacks the necessary data. To alleviate this issue, a regulatory regime could require companies to keep a certain number of data on their past actions, their algorithm and a set of parameters (Marty et al. (2019)).[25] That would require that the algorithm be designed in such a way that its actions can be monitored. Data mining methods could also be used to detect abnormal algorithm

---

22 Ezrachi, A. & Stucke, M. E. (2016). Virtual Competition: The Promise and Perils of the Algorithm-Driven Economy. *Harvard University Press*.

23 For instance, based on the results of the experimental literature, Q-learning algorithms could be banned because they have been found to lead to tacit collusion. It should however be noted that Crandall et al. (2018) find that a lot of other types of algorithms have higher tendencies to cooperate than Q-learning algorithms.

24 Lamontanaro, A. (2020). Bounty Hunters for Algorithmic Cartels: An Old Solution for a New Problem, *Fordham Intellectual Property, Media and Entertainment Law Journal*, Vol 30(4), pp. 1259 et seq.

25 Marty, F., Harnay, S. & Toledano, J. (2019) Algorithmes et décision concurrentielle : risques et opportunités. *Revue d'Economie Industrielle*, Vol. 166, pp. 91 et seq.

decisions as well as to detect those companies whose price evolutions need to be investigated.

Some legal aspects are also important. Indeed, under current EU law, Article 101 can apply only when either an agreement or a concerted practice to be established. A concerted practice means a *"form of coordination between undertakings, which, without having been taken to the stage where an agreement [...] has been concluded, knowingly substitutes for the risks of competition, practical cooperation between them,"* in particular *"any direct or indirect contact between such operators by which an undertaking may influence the conduct on the market of its actual or potential competitors or disclose to them its decisions or intentions concerning its own conduct on the market."*[26] However, Article 101 *"does not deprive economic operators of the right to adapt themselves intelligently to the existing and anticipated conduct of their competitors."* In other words, when companies are acting unilaterally without an element of communication, Article 101 cannot apply. Hence, a competition authority can only condemn tacit collusion if it has shown that the pricing equilibrium is due to tacit collusion rather than to intelligent adaptation by the firms.[27] Drawing a line between communication and absence of communication is a difficult exercise, so the risk of false positive/false negative outcomes has led to an absence of cases targeted towards tacit collusion.[28] Practically, tacit collusion may only be sanctioned indirectly, if it is proven that the algorithms have used devices implying some form of communication (such as data exchanges between algorithms for instance).

Hence, if algorithms do increase the risk of tacit collusion, the fact that this kind of collusion is not currently forbidden by competition rules may constitute one of the most important obstacles faced by competition authorities when dealing with algorithmic collusion. Relying exclusively on competition law enforcement would thus require a change of competition rules or, at the very least, a change of stand by competition authorities on tacit collusion. It would appear that a dedicated regulatory regime would be required to enable any competition law enforcement. However, taking a different approach to tacit collusion would raise a number of arduous questions for competition authorities. For instance, should algorithmic tacit collusion and other types of tacit collusion be treated in the same way? In addition, an appropriate standard of proof concerning algorithmic-based tacit collusion may prove hard to determine.[29]

---

26   Case 40/73 *Suiker Unie*, ECLI:EU:C:1975:174, paras. 26 and 174.

27   European Commission (2017). Algorithms and Collusion – Note from the European Union. OECD.

28   It could be argued that a situation of tacit collusion could be covered by the concept of collective dominance. After all, the tests set out in the EU merger guidelines and in the case of an exchange of information are very similar. In the case of similar algorithms being used by competitors, it would make sense. However, an abuse still needs to be identified. There again, creatively, one could imagine that the reliance on pricing algorithms could lead to excessive prices and be captured by an exploitative abuse.

29   A few examples of questions: What level of supra-competitive prices/profits constitutes an abuse? Relative to which benchmark? For what period of time? What happens if tacit collusion is only reached by a small number of competitors active in the market?

IV. TOWARDS A UNIFYING REGULATORY FRAMEWORK? PRINCIPLE AND OB-STACLES

A. Principle

As appears from the discussion above, competition law enforcement and dedicated regulation as regards algorithmic pricing are not necessarily alternatives but rather complements. Both may be combined to increase the effectiveness of competition policy vis-à-vis algorithmic pricing. In order to overcome the limitations of either type of approach, one could envision a framework where firms could be required (or incentivized) first to test their algorithms prior to deployment in real market conditions ("risk assessment"), then to monitor the consequences of deployment ("harm identification"). In addition, a monitoring body may also be in charge of this two-stage assessment. Hence, when acquiring or developing algorithmic pricing software, a company would have to make an assessment of the risks that the use of this algorithm entails in terms of compliance with existing regulations (including the risk that the use of this algorithm may trigger parallel increases in prices). Alternatively, a monitoring body could be in charge of testing these algorithms or designing a system that would ensure proper testing of algorithms. During deployment and use of the system, the company would be required (or incentivized) to monitor the behavior of the system against some public policy objectives (such as the maintaining of competition on the markets).

Proving that parallel upwards price movements are tacit collusion rather than a mere adaptation to competitors' prices may turn out to be more feasible in such a setting. Indeed, if a dedicated regulation imposed that some testing were made before a given algorithm is deployed and if it were found that this pricing algorithm is highly likely to converge to a tacit collusion equilibrium, the burden of proof to demonstrate that there is tacit collusion on the market when the algorithm is deployed may be lowered as the risk of error (i.e. false positive) has, at least theoretically, been lowered. Also, once the algorithm is running the presence of monitoring mechanisms should help the company identify situations of tacit collusion. In such circumstances, the risks for a competition authority to adopt a false positive decision over the practices are decreased compared to the situation without algorithms. Alternatively, if the testing and monitoring do not show a risk of collusion, it becomes less likely that an authority would adopt a false negative decision (absence of collusion when there is actually one). Hence, one could argue that this would change the error cost since the potential harmful effect of algorithms could be flagged in advance.

Hence in such a setting, dedicated regulation would support competition law enforcement by helping to separate cases of tacit collusion from mere adaptations of prices. The benefits from both regimes would also be maintained: a higher flexibility is allowed yet the testing made before-hand and the monitoring made after the algorithm is deployed help ensure that cases of algorithmic tacit collusion can indeed be prosecuted and/or avoided. Yet, this basic theoretical framework still leaves several questions unanswered.

B. Limitations

First, the testing made during the "risk-assessment" phase should seek to replicate real life circumstances. This requires making assumptions in such a way that hypothetical market conditions and outcomes will approximate reality with minimum distance. The key parameters that should be reflected in testing would include market structure, transparency and stability and simplicity/complexness of decision rules. It is probable that an over-simplified sandbox testing leads to a frequent outcome of collusion as some of the papers discussed above have shown. Yet, as also discussed above, this way of testing algorithms does not reflect the economic reality of the industry where the algorithm will be used: the environment and its dynamics as well as the market interactions are often more complex than those captured in the model. Also, these tests must make a choice on whether all market participants use the same tested pricing algorithm or a mix of pricing methods. In addition, there is uncertainty on how the algorithm may evolve once it is fed with real life data.

Hence, more work should be undertaken to better understand whether a finding of likely tacit collusion under testing conditions would mean more likely collusion in real markets (i.e. to assess the extent of false positives). Such work would have to determine what would constitute proper testing conditions, and how close testing outcomes are to possible outcomes in real markets. Ultimately, there should be an objective line that would help to sort "bad" algorithms from "good" ones. In the same vein, more work should be undertaken to assess whether the absence of significant likelihood of tacit collusion in a testing environment would make the occurrence of tacit collusion a non-significant risk in real markets (i.e. to assess the extent of false negatives).

A second difficulty lies in the risk that the testing is done so as to lead to an outcome of "no risk of collusion." Indeed, the algorithm developers could internalize the testing so that there would be an appearance of limited likelihood of tacit collusion. There are various ways to try to address that risk beyond the institutional and regulatory setting already discussed: liabilities could be created, and auditing and explanation obligations could be created. It remains to be seen whether these are technically realistic.

Regarding the deployment phase, there are again two types of obstacles to the monitoring principle. The first obstacle is technical: that would require the design and operation of the algorithm to make it possible to track the decision making of the algorithm. The Commission has stressed the importance of auditing in its recent white paper.[30] It is not obvious that this could today be the case.

The second obstacle is one of identification. Indeed, while the *ex ante* testing may somehow alleviate the burden of proof that competition authorities must face when proving a tacit collusion, such cases of possible tacit collusions still need to be identified. As pointed out above, this is not an easy task and it cannot be excluded that as for classical tacit collusion, the error cost may be such that only extreme cases could be identified with enough certainty. Another route would be to get inspiration from the financial markets where the use of algorithms for trading instructions is routine. To avoid markets to get into some kind of resonance or being manipulated, market regulators have implemented a number of rules. For instance, MiFID 2 introduced rules on algorithmic trading and high frequency trading that aimed at avoiding the emergence of risks and facilitating their identification.

V. CONCLUSION

Although the extent of the risks that pricing algorithms entail for competition is still uncertain, possible ways to tackle this issue have to be foreseen in advance, in case this risk materializes. In this regard, despite their respective drawbacks, dedicated regulation and competition law enforcement adaptations combined could provide a competition policy answer. However, significant difficulties still lie ahead.

Hence, a first option would consist of mandating through dedicated regulation an accountability mechanism for algorithmic pricing. This would create an informational basis that would enable competition rules to possibly address algorithmic tacit collusion with a lower evidentiary threshold than the usual tacit collusion. If the uncertainty linked to the legal basis remains too high, then a dedicated legislation setting out principles-based rules or an authorization regime might be necessary – in case there is enough evidence that algorithmic pricing does facilitate tacit collusion of course. The choice between the two types of regimes should be based on the prediction value of the algorithm testing and the strength of monitoring tools. There remains significant work to be undertaken on these two aspects.

Of course, these thoughts are no substitute to the work that still needs to be done on how to build a testing procedure that is closer to real market conditions and on whether the risk associated with the use of algorithms in real markets is so high as to justify more regulation.

---

30 European Commission (2020). White Paper on Artificial Intelligence – a European Approach to Excellence and Trust. In particular the Commissions stresses that requirements for 'high-risk' AI applications should address: training data; data and record-keeping; information to be provided; robustness and accuracy; human oversight; and some specific requirements for certain particular AI applications.

Competition Law in the Digital Age: New Antitrust Standards or More Regulation? Blockchain a Solution from Markets and for Markets

By Antonio Capobianco[1] & Gabriele Carovano[2]

Abstract

This chapter analyses the effects and challenges that digitalization has caused for competition authorities ("CAs") and, more generally, the entire competition community. It provides a descriptive summary of the policy debate around digitalization and competition, analyzes the main challenges brought on by digitalization, and address some of the most significant open questions CAs are currently facing such as whether new laws, powers, standards, or regulatory interventions are needed. The chapter also suggests a greater consideration of new technologies, such as Blockchain, by CAs to counter tech-giants' market supremacy and offers some practical suggestions for CAs on how to best deal with digitalization and tech-markets.

I. INTRODUCTION

This chapter, through an international perspective, analyses the effects and challenges that digitalization has caused for competition authorities ("CAs") and, more generally, the entire competition community. The chapter, specifically, (i) provides a descriptive summary of the policy debate around digitalization and competition (Section 2); (ii) analyzes the main challenges brought on by digitalization and address some of the most significant open questions CAs are currently facing such as whether new laws, powers, standards, or regulatory interventions are needed (Section 3); (iii) suggests a greater consideration of Blockchain technologies by CAs to counter tech-giants' market supremacy (Section 4); and (iv) offers

---

1   Antonio Capobianco is the Acting Head of the OECD Competition Division. The opinions expressed and arguments herein are exclusively those of the author and do not necessarily reflect the official views of the OECD, the OECD Competition Committee, or its members.

2   Gabriele Carovano is a PhD Candidate at the Dickson Poon School of Law, King's College London.

some practical suggestions for CAs on how to best deal with digitalization and tech-markets (Section 5).

II.   DIGITALIZATION AND COMPETITION: THE CURRENT STATE OF THE DEBATE

Digitalization has recently grown in importance in the competition policy debate.[3] This reflects the rising relevance that digital firms have been acquiring in the global scene. In 2019, seven out of ten of the world largest companies by market capitalization were tech corporations.[4] One more compared to 2018.[5] Digital markets are also drawing the attention of CAs because, due to their specific features, they become increasingly more concentrated. In 2018, the OECD registered several broad economic trends that raised concern,[6] including the following: (i) firm entry rates have fallen, particularly in digital-intensive sectors;[7] (ii) mark-ups have increased; (iii) M&A activities targeting digital firms have accelerated; all that leading to (iv) growing concentration of revenues.[8]

---

3   To give a sense of the wide range of challenges digitalization presented for competition enforcers, see, among others, OECD roundtables on: (i) Merger control in dynamic markets; (ii) Digital disruption in financial markets; (iii) Quality consideration in the zero-price economy; (iv) Non-price effects of mergers (v) Personalised pricing in the Digital Era. The mentioned OECD roundtables are all accessible at the following link http://www.oecd.org/competition/roundtables.htm.

4   PriceWaterhouseCoopers (2019), "Global Top 100 companies by market capitalisation: July 2019," https://www.pwc.com/gx/en/audit-services/publications/assets/global-top-100-companies-2019.pdf.

5   PriceWaterhouseCoopers (2018), "Global Top 100 companies by market capitalisation: 31 March 2018 update," https://www.pwc.com/gx/en/audit-services/assets/pdf/global-top-100-companies-2018-report.pdf.

6   See OECD Ecoscope, Competition in the digital age, 31st March 2019, available at https://oecdecoscope.blog/2019/05/31/competition-in-the-digital-age/.

7   See Calvino, F. & C. Criscuolo (2019), "Business dynamics and digitalisation," *OECD Science, Technology and Industry Policy Papers*, No. 62, OECD Publishing, Paris, available at https://doi.org/10.1787/6e0b011a-en.

8   Among others, see Calligaris, S., C. Criscuolo & L. Marcolin (2018), "Mark-ups in the digital era," *OECD Science, Technology and Industry Working Papers*, No. 2018/10, OECD Publishing, Paris, available at https://doi.org/10.1787/4efe2d25-en.

Thanks to the role played by network effects,[9] economies of scale and scope,[10] big data,[11] switching costs,[12] intellectual property rights,[13] and consumers' inertia and inelasticity of "process innovation,"[14] tech-markets tend to be auto-preservative[15] and to lead to winner-takes-all or winner-takes-most situations. Because of these features, tech-markets are highly concentrated and competition, instead of in-markets, take place between-markets or ecosystems.[16] These tech markets' characteristics, as well as catching the attention of many academics, governments, and regulators worldwide, are also disorienting for them.

The competition policy debate on the digital economy is fragmented and multi-faceted. There is a wide and nuanced spectrum of opinions regarding actual (and would-be) problems, and the possible solutions to those problems. Some would like to see more competition;[17] others less.[18] Some argue that competition law is un-

---

9   Through network effects an increase in the number of users of a digital platform increases the value of the platform for existing users. Network effects, therefore, give greater competitive advantages to firms with a wider user base.

10   Strong economies of scale and scope are a consequence, for instance, of low variable costs and potentially high fixed costs.

11   Digital firms rely on large amounts of data that can be difficult to replicate.

12   For instance, users may have invested time and effort to create a profile on a social network or a reputation as providers on an exchange platform, which they may losing by switching.

13   Patents are an example. Notably, patents grant the owner a limited-term monopoly over the use of a technology or method.

14   Consumers' inelasticity of "process innovation" refers to that phenomena according to which the relative ratio between a "process innovation variation" (i.e. improvement in the process of producing a product or service) and the demand variation towards a given artefact (i.e. the concerned product or service) is (more or less) zero, if process innovation is not reflected on the final goods or services' prices. A zero ratio means that demand does not change as process innovation increases without causing a price reduction. In digital zero-price markets, process innovation is almost irrelevant. Innovation, to be significant, produce effects, and stimulate switches, must be capable of delivering 10X growth, so-called "10X Rule."

15   This makes the "first mover status" a key competitive advantage.

16   See OECD, Global Forum on Competition, Competition for the market, DAF/COMP/GF(2019)7, Paris, 2019, available at https://one.oecd.org/document/DAF/COMP/GF(2019)7/en/pdf.

17   See Herbert Hovenkamp & Carl Shapiro, "Horizontal Mergers, Market Structure, and Burdens of Proof," Faculty Scholarship, (2018); Stigler Center, "Committee for the Study of Digital Platforms," (2019); Tommaso Valletti, "A view from the Chief Economist," CRA Conference (2018); and Andrew Tyrie, "Is competition enough? Competition for consumers, on behalf of consumers," (2019).

18   See M.E. Stucke & A. Ezrachi, Competition Overdose, *Harper Collins Publishers*, 2020.

der attack as incapable of delivering the benefits expected from competition.[19] Some would like to curb competition assessment outcomes to protect national champions.[20] Some others would like to expand the scope of competition law (thus introducing new standards complementary to consumer welfare), stretching it inasmuch as to use it to solve other societal problems (environment, employment, privacy, etc.).[21] Others would go in the opposite direction, calling for a strict, traditional, purely economic-based antitrust enforcement. Some criticized the current "balancing of error costs,"[22] suggesting that the current balance is wrongly tilted in favor of under enforcement.[23] Consequently, they propose to reverse the burden of proof as well as revise the thresholds for antitrust intervention to support an enforcement boost. Others consider such reforms not a priority and condemn primarily the timing and quality of remedies

---

19 See Andrew Tyrie, "Is competition enough? Competition for consumers, on behalf of consumers," (2019); C. Pike & G. Carovano, "Competition Law under fire: responding to competing demands for change in the case of price parity clauses and loyalty rebates," *CPI September 2019 Antitrust Chronicle*, and the OECD, Global Forum on Competition, Roundtable "Competition under fire," 2019, available at http://www.oecd.org/competition/globalforum/competition-under-fire.htm.

20 See the proposal advanced in the afterward of the European Commission's prohibition decision in the *Siemens AG/Alstom* merger case by the Germany's Economy Minister, Peter Altmaier, and its French counterpart, Bruno Le Maire, who called for a reform of European Competition Rules, available at https://www.reuters.com/article/us-britain-eu/uks-may-to-promise-new-brexit-debate-in-push-for-more-negotiating-time-idUSKCN1PZ09S. Contrarily see Massimo Motta & Martin Peitz, Competition Policy and European Firms' Competitiveness, VOX CEPR Policy Portal, 20 February 2019, available at https://voxeu.org/content/competition-policy-and-european-firms-competitiveness.

21 O. Odudu, The Boundaries of EC Competition Law: The Scope of Article 81, *Oxford University Press*, 2006; O. Odudu, the wider concerns of competition law, *Oxford Journal of Legal Studies*, 2010, 30.

22 It consists in balancing the risk of under enforcement in terms of competition harms, with the risk of over enforcement that may hamper the manifestation of innovation.

23 Reports from the EU, the UK, and the U.S. suggested that the current balance errs too far in the direction of under enforcement. See UK Report Digital Competition Expert Panel (2019), "Unlocking digital competition," available at https://www.gov.uk/government/publications/unlocking-digital-competition-report-of-the-digital-competition-expert-panel; the EU report "Competition Policy for the digital era," available at https://ec.europa.eu/competition/publications/reports/kd0419345enn.pdf; the U.S. Stigler Center report, Stigler Committee on Digital Platforms, 2019, available at https://research.chicagobooth.edu/-/media/research/stigler/pdfs/digital-platforms---committee-report---stigler-center.pdf?la=en&hash=2D23583FF8B-CC560B7FEF7A81E1F95C1DDC5225E&hash=2D23583FF8BCC560B7FEF7A81E1F-95C1DDC5225E. Similarly, Valletti argued that *over and under enforcement are not symmetric and the balance is tilted in favour of over-enforcement.* See Paul Voorham, Vestager considers shifting burden of proof for big tech, GCR, October 31, 2019, available at https://global-competitionreview.com/article/1210348/vestager-considers-shifting-burden-of-proof-for-big-tech.

adopted in recent enforcement cases.[24] Some others, again, believe that there may be limits to what competition enforcement alone may achieve in digital markets and advocate for additional regulatory interventions, which would apply only to a specific subset of subjects with strategic market status.[25]

The primary results of this healthy, multi-faceted, and diversified debate have been a lot of interesting discussions but also some confusion due to the difficulties in answering some of the broad policy questions.

III. COMPETITION AUTHORITIES AND DIGITALIZATION: AN EXISTENTIAL DILEMMA

In the middle of the complexity of this debate stand CAs. Questions have been asked on their ultimate role, their institutional design and their powers,[26] and on the precise scope of their mission. What are competition authorities there for? Which interest or interests should they protect? In case of a plurality of interests and especially of conflicting interests, which should be the prevailing one? Should CAs take into account industrial policy considerations while carrying out their core duty to protect competition?

---

24   Damien Geradin in Paul Voorham, Vestager considers shifting burden of proof for big tech, GCR, October 31, 2019, available at https://globalcompetitionreview.com/article/1210348/vestager-considers-shifting-burden-of-proof-for-big-tech.

25   While the specific definition of firms with strategic market status or bottleneck power would need to be defined (the Stigler Report suggests this determination been done by a newly established digital regulator), this situation would generally arise if a platform has market power and acts as a gatekeeper, controlling the access of different sides of a market to one another. Contributing factors to this power could include high barriers to entry, substantial switching costs, and a tendency by consumers to use a single platform at a time (as opposed to multi-homing). By applying only to a subset of firms, the measures seek to address concerns about durable market power while avoiding the imposition of a regulatory burden on new entrants which may hamper competition.

26   See references above.

Faced with the pressure to provide answers, some CAs have commissioned external reports[27] and others have conducted studies of their own.[28] Moreover, the G7 competition authorities recently issued a "Common understanding" setting out their views on the challenges of digitalization for competition policy.[29] While the legal context, focus, and findings of each of these efforts varied significantly, some consensus for introducing digital regulators and subjecting tech-giants to greater and more tailored antitrust scrutiny have begun to emerge.[30]

---

27   This has been the case, among others, in the UK, the EU, the U.S., Germany, and Japan. See UK Report Digital Competition Expert Panel (2019), "Unlocking digital competition," available at https://www.gov.uk/government/publications/unlocking-digital-competition-report-of-the-digital-competition-expert-panel; the EU report "Competition Policy for the digital era," available at https://ec.europa.eu/competition/publications/reports/kd0419345enn.pdf; Michael Reich, Germany sets up body to lead modernisation of competition law, CPI, Sept. 2018, available at https://www.competitionpolicyinternational.com/germany-sets-up-body-to-lead-modernisation-of-competition-law/; the U.S. Stigler Center report, Stigler Committee on Digital Platforms, 2019, available at https://research.chicagobooth.edu/-/media/research/stigler/pdfs/digital-platforms---committee-report---stigler-center.pdf?la=en&hash=2D23583FF8BCC560B7FEF7A81E1F95C1D-DC5225E&hash=2D23583FF8BCC560B7FEF7A81E1F95C1DDC5225E.

28   This has been the case, among others, in in Italy, Canada, Australia, Portugal, France and Germany. See https://www.concurrences.com/IMG/pdf/agcm_-_autorita_garante_della_concorrenza_e_del_mercato-7.pdf?51760/e0bb8e15333a93d3f362c8b221d-3310d0ab89b55; https://www.competitionbureau.gc.ca/eic/site/cb-bc.nsf/eng/04342.html; the Australia Report by the Australian Competition & Consumer Commission (2019), "Digital Platforms Inquiry: Final Report," available at https://www.accc.gov.au/system/files/Digital%20platforms%20inquiry%20-%20final%20report.pdf; the Portuguese Report by the AdC, "Issues paper on Digital Ecosystem, Big Data and Algorithms," 2019, available at http://www.concorrencia.pt/vEN/News_Events/Comunicados/Documents/Digital%20Ecosystems%20Executive%20Summary.pdf; Bundeskartellamnt - Autorité de la Concurrance joint report on "Competition Law and Data," available at http://www.autoritedelaconcurrence.fr/doc/reportcompetitionlawanddatafinal.pdf; Bundeskartellamnt - Autorité de la Concurrance joint report on "Algorithms and Competition," available at https://www.autoritedelaconcurrence.fr/sites/default/files/algorithms-and-competition.pdf.

29   See http://www.autoritedelaconcurrence.fr/doc/g7_common_understanding.pdf.

30   See Valentina Pop, "She fined tech giants billions of dollars. Now she wants sharper tools," *The Wall Street Journal*, October 15, 2019, available at https://www.wsj.com/articles/she-fined-tech-giants-billions-of-dollars-now-she-wants-sharper-tools-11571131520; Paul Voorham, "Vestager considers shifting burden of proof for big tech," *GCR*, October 31, 2019, available at https://globalcompetitionreview.com/article/1210348/vestager-considers-shifting-burden-of-proof-for-big-tech; Stigler Center, Stigler Committee on Digital Platforms, 2019, available at https://research.chicagobooth.edu/-/media/research/stigler/pdfs/digital-platforms---committee-report---stigler-center.pdf?la=en&hash=2D23583FF8BCC560B7FEF7A81E1F95C1D-DC5225E&hash=2D23583FF8BCC560B7FEF7A81E1F95C1DDC5225E; Zuckerberg, M. (2019), "The Internet needs new rules. Let's start in these four areas," *Washington Post*, https://www.washingtonpost.com/opinions/mark-zuckerberg-the-internet-needs-new-rules-lets-start-in-these-four-areas/2019/03/29/9e6f0504-521a-11e9-a3f7-78b7525a8d5f_story.html?utm_term=.1c2c108fbc11.

A. Digital Regulation: Yes or No? Participative Antitrust?

The more traditional antitrust thinking aligns with those who consider regulatory intervention not to be particularly suited to address digital competition concerns. Indeed, both self-regulation[31] as well as public regulation would both be unsuitable. The former would be self-serving. The latter would be ineffective and limited in scope. Public regulation of digital markets raises difficult questions as to who should regulate, and how, to ensure that such regulation is effectively designed and enforced when jurisdictions have different policy approaches, and sometimes diverging political views on the scope of such regulation. Taking this perspective, some have suggested that CAs should consider working more closely with academia and business to develop new forms of so-called "participative antitrust," whereby the private sector, industry representatives and antitrust authorities jointly participate in the development of possible regulation.[32]

Such an approach is not totally new in Europe, where before the adoption of Regulation 1/2003 the European Commission ("EC") used to interact more with interested stakeholders on the enforcement of art. 101 TFEU and specifically of art. 101(3) TFEU (the so-called notification procedure). Similarly, the U.S. has had several experiences of designing participative antitrust solutions. The Department of Justice ("DOJ") review letters with regards to patent pools are another great example of participative solutions. The same is also true in Canada and China since both developed collective negotiation procedures to address the challenges presented by the online payments industry.

The supporters of this approach have submitted that these past experiences could inspire new forms of participative antitrust, which would ultimately result in evolving and principle-based guidelines, constantly subject to periodic checks. Such guidelines would: (i) minimize legal uncertainty and increase law predictability, (ii) make "regulation" adaptive, responsive, and fast evolving to market changes; and (iii) elicit industry information better than CAs could do by themselves using only their investigative tools. The obvious risk behind these participative solutions are risks of

---

31 Some of the largest digital companies (Apple, Facebook, Twitter, Microsoft, and Twitter) have also launched a project on their own initiative to promote data portability for consumers (see the Data Transfer Project available at https://datatransferproject.dev/), and Mark Zuckerberg has published an opinion article calling for regulation in this area (see Zuckerberg, M. (2019), "The Internet needs new rules. Let's start in these four areas," *Washington Post*, https://www.washingtonpost.com/opinions/mark-zuckerberg-the-internet-needs-new-rules-lets-start-in-these-four-areas/2019/03/29/9e6f0504-521a-11e9-a3f7-78b7525a8d5f_story.html?utm_term=.1c2c108fbc11).

32 See J. Tirole, OECD, Global Forum on Competition, Roundtable on "Competition under fire," Paris, 2019, available at http://www.oecd.org/competition/globalforum/competition-under-fire.htm.

anticompetitive coordinated conduct. That is why it is of vital importance that CAs spend their best resources to design collusion-proof participative procedures and constantly supervise and update these procedures when needed.

B. Competition Authorities and a Call for Change

Many of the criticisms moved against CAs flow from resentments and frustrations that are not (or mostly not) related to digitalization. Digitalization has merely opened a door through which all these criticisms could be channeled. The CAs' primary focus on a narrow understanding of consumer welfare, as well as its celebration, as the ultimate goal of antitrust enforcement may have inadvertently overly politicized the competition policy debate, causing a shift from a purely technical to a more political realm. This shift has exposed CAs to the general and acritical revisionism advocated by populist and nationalist parties and their narrative. As a result of politicians' inability to respond to complex social phenomena – such as (i) the financial crisis and slowdown of economic growth; (ii) the institutional crisis of democratically elected bodies; (iii) record unemployment levels; (iv) climate change; (v) rising inequality; (vi) job-erosion caused by technological progress – CAs are among those chosen as scapegoats, called to be accountable for the losses of many and gains of a few: the tech-giants.[33]

That is why the effectiveness and ability of CAs to deliver consumer welfare have suddenly been called into question, and several proposals have been put forward to reaffirm the primacy of politics in antitrust decision-making.[34] Significant in this sense have been some of the proposals advanced in Europe (i) to confer the European Council or the European Member States the authority to overrule DG Competition

---

33 Globalization and the digital revolution have greatly benefited the owners of firms, and particularly the wealthiest 1 percent, while delivering fewer benefits to consumers and workers. This has led to calls for a fundamental rethinking of the principles and purpose of competition law and policy. One area where competition law is particularly under the microscope concerns its ability to ensure that consumers obtain a larger share of the benefits generated by the rise of so-called tech giants and the digital economy. In this sense, among others, see Herbert Hovenkamp & Carl Shapiro, "Horizontal Mergers, Market Structure, and Burdens of Proof," Faculty Scholarship, (2018); Stigler Center, "Committee for the Study of Digital Platforms," (2019); Tommaso Valletti, "A view from the Chief Economist," CRA Conference (2018); and Andrew Tyrie, "Is competition enough? Competition for consumers, on behalf of consumers," (2019).

34 Revisionist phenomena are not only investing CAs but also other institutions, such as Central Banks. See The Economist, the independence of Central Banks is under threat from politics. That is bad news for the world, April 13, 2019.

or other National CAs' decisions to protect national champions and jobs;[35] and (ii) to expand CAs' mandate and mission to protect the environment, employment, privacy, etc.

A common element of these proposals is the attempt to reaffirm the primacy of politics over CAs' technical decisions, which many in the antitrust world have branded as an undesirable mistake. The reasons why independent CAs, independent especially from political whims, were established are still present. Notwithstanding that, in practice, even "independent" agencies are never fully independent.[36] Protecting and preserving CAs' independence, and ensuring that they have enough resources to attract high-expertise staff, is still key to ensure the quality of their decisions and, consequently, that markets function correctly and competitively. Abolishing or reducing such independence by introducing some form of political control over antitrust outcomes, while not solving current issues, would do nothing but revive old problems.

Additionally, these authors tend to believe that, to the maximum extent possible, CAs' mission should not be polluted by non-competition considerations, especially whether such non-competition interests can be dealt with other more appropriate instruments. This means that inequality, unemployment, global warming, privacy, health, trade distortions, etc., are important issues that government should be concerned with, but they should not be dealt with by CAs. Adequate and specific measures such as redistribution measures, carbon taxes, tailor-made economic incentives, taxation, etc. are better suited to achieve these important policy objectives than merger or cartel policy. That said, CAs can have a role to play in ensuring a better protection of interests such as inequality, unemployment, global warming, privacy, health, trade distortions, etc. But this is not their primary goal or their hardcore mandate. The protection of those interests by CAs is limited to the extent that their protection concurs with pro-competition considerations and measures.

CAs, therefore, should strive to preserve and strengthen their independence, budget, and mission as well as resisting being granted new objectives. Moreover, CAs could (should!) undertake some other uncontroversial measures to boost their effectiveness. Namely, they could improve and facilitate their co-operation with interna-

---

35 At the EU level, see the Franco-German proposal cited above file:///Users/ss/Downloads/ cited. At National level, instead, public interest considerations are included in many competition regimes and may take various forms, sometimes directly requiring CAs to consider public interest in their assessments or endowing different public bodies (usually government bodies) with the power to override competition decisions (this is the case, for instance in Germany, France, the United Kingdom, and the U.S.). While these powers have been used very rarely in the past, their utilization has increased in recent times. Instances of labor considerations influencing competition mergers decisions are the German *Edeka/Kaiser's Tengelmann* merger case (2016), the French *Financière Cofigeo/Agripole Group* merger case (2018) as well as the Dutch *PostNL/Sandd* merger case (2019).

36 Their mission, priorities, and guiding principles are still within political realm.

tional counterparts as well as other national regulators. Co-operation activities can take place with different purposes, forms, and modalities. International/national co-operation: (i) can aim at understanding certain markets' dynamics through means such as joint market studies; (ii) can be oriented to specific investigative actions such as mutual legal assistance in carrying out inspections or interviews on behalf and for the account of another CA, exchange information and use them as evidence;[37] (iii) can be used to design deterrent and geographically broader remedies or, finally, (iv) to ensure the enforcement of fines or periodic penalties where enforcement in the requesting CA's jurisdiction proved non-sufficient or fruitless.

New forms of co-operation should also be considered to increase the quality and authority of CAs' advocacy actions. Such international/national co-operation should also be considered when designing the new forms of "participative antitrust" suggested in the previous paragraph. Finally, such increased national co-operation would also help in drawing the line between competition, consumer protection, data protection law, etc. Indeed, increased co-operation will boost transparency and accountability for each authority involved and, consequently, will "re-politicize" the mentioned issues, shifting them from the merely "technocratic" domain.[38]

C. Competition Authorities and Their Mission: New Laws and Standards or a New Mentality?

So far, we have suggested that CAs should exclusively execute their primary mandate and do nothing but protect competition. Although this task seems clear in principle, it can be extremely complex in practice. CAs, indeed, while carrying out their enforcement activities are often required, especially in merger cases, to take into account other third party (often conflicting) interests as well as industrial policy considerations. With digitalization, the dimension of this industrial policy component within CAs' decisions has increased, since in digital market scenarios, due to their winner-takes-all or winner-takes-most features, also abuse of dominance or vertical restrictions decisions have the potential to influence or indirectly regulate an entire industry. This new dimension of competition enforcement, together with its increased politization, has sparked a debate around the standard or the standards that

---

37 There is a range of active enforcement investigations by competition authorities around the world seeking to grapple with the competition concerns identified in the introduction of this paper using existing legislation, with perhaps the most recent such investigation being the one announced in the U.S. by the Department of Justice (2019), "Press Release: Justice Department Reviewing the Practices of Market-Leading Online Platforms," https://www.justice.gov/opa/pr/justice-department-reviewing-practices-market-leading-online-platforms.

38 C. TOWNLEY, "Co-ordinated Diversity: Revolutionary Suggestions for EU Competition Law (and for EU Law too)," (2014) 33 Yearbook of European Law 1; King's College London Law School Research Paper No. 2014-13.

CAs should pursue. And on whether legislative interventions are needed to equip CAs with broader mandates and new powers.

According to some authors, legislative intervention is not needed. Competition provisions are broad enough to allow competition authorities to intervene any time they are needed. This is true both in the U.S. and the EU,[39] although in the U.S. – since the 1980s and following the Chicago School's influence – the interpretation of competition provisions with respect to refusal to deal, predatory pricing, and loyalty rebates, has been excessively focused around the "consumer welfare standard," narrowly interpreted as "consumer surplus." Therefore, whether a change is really needed, it is not so much in the law but in the CAs' approach to how they interpret market forces and competition enforcement. Namely, CAs should not interpret "market definition," "market dominance," "abuse," "restrictive practices," etc., as they used to.[40] Digitalization, indeed, introduced issues for CAs that although may not on their own be new, taken together pose novel challenges for competition policy. Digitalization, in other words, has changed the dimension, the speed, and the modalities of competition. CAs, consequently, must understand such change and reflect it in their enforcement actions.

---

39 In Europe, indeed, the European Court of Justice has recognized that EU competition law serve multiple standards such as: (i) Consumer welfare (EC Guidelines art. 101, para 33; EC Guidance paper art. 102, para 19), (ii) Consumer well-being (Joined Cases T-213/01 and T-214/01 *Österreichische Postsparkasse and Bank für Arbeit und Wirtschaft v. Commission* [2006] ECR II-1601, para 115), (iii) Effective markets' competitive structure (see Case C-501/06 P, *GlaxoSmithKline Services Unlimited v Commission and Others* [2009] ECR I-9291, Para 63; Case *T-Mobile*, AG Kokott opinion, para 71; Case T-286/09, *Intel Corp. v. Commission*, Para 105); (iv) fairness (Case 26/75 *General Motors Continental v. Commission* [1975] ECR 1367; Case 27/76 *United Brands v. Commission* [1978] ECR 207; Case C-177/16 Autortiesību un komunicēšanās konsultāciju aģentūra (AKKA)/ Latvijas Autoru apvienība (LAA) [2017] ECLI; *Deutsche Post AG* (Case COMP/C-1/36.915) Commission Decision 2001/892/EC [2001] OJ L331/40; Margrethe Vestager, "Fairness and competition" (2018), Speech delivered at the GCLC Annual Conference, Brussels, January 25, 2018); (v) market integration (Case C-52/09 *TeliaSonera Sverige* [2011] ECR I-527, para 22); etc. In this sense, see also A. Ezrachi, EU Competition Law Goals and the Digital Economy (June 6, 2018). Oxford Legal Studies Research Paper No. 17/2018.

40 On the opportunity to develop new forms of market definitions, see OECD Background paper on Quality considerations in digital zero-price markets, DAF/COMP(2018)14, Nov. 2018, available at https://one.oecd.org/document/DAF/COMP(2018)14/en/pdf. *"An often mentioned but rarely applied alternative to a SSNIP test is the small-but-significant non-transitory decrease in quality test (SSNDQ). Data availability can limit the range of circumstances in which it can be used. However, the test provides the framework for guiding even qualitative determinations of market definition. Indeed, in most cases, a qualitative approach will likely be needed, and a restrictive bright-line market definition may need to be avoided."*

Digital cases, so far, have been rare, long, and sometimes conflicting.[41] CAs, while engaged in the animated debate described above, either failed to act or, when acting, failed to understand the new dimensions of competition. For example, when assessing mergers such as *Google-DoubleClick*[42] or *Facebook-WhatsApp*,[43] CAs may have failed to fully recognize the "*fil rouge*" that links tech-giants' parent companies with the services provided by their subsidiaries. The new scope for competition in the digitalized world is to collect as many data points as possible and monetize them. What is relevant are not (or at least, not only) the individual services that tech-giants provide in themselves but the holistic ecosystem that they create to collect data.

In conclusion, these authors argue that a change in the law is not needed. CAs already have the means to be effective enforcers against this new dimension of competition. The real question is if CAs have the necessary expertise and skills to navigate this new "dimension of competition." The UK Competition and Market Authority ("CMA"), for example, seems to be going in the right direction with the creation of a new Data Unit, where it is hiring tech-engineers, data-scientists, behavioral-scientists, and data and technology strategic insight advisers. These new experts will help shaping the new enforcement approaches needed by the CMA to deal with digital competition issues. Similarly, the Australia Report endorses the creation of a "specialist digital platforms branch" within the Australian Competition and Consumer Commission ("ACCC") accountable for, among other things, "*proactively monitoring and investigating instances of potentially anti-competitive conduct and conduct causing consumer harm by digital platforms, which impact consumers, advertisers or other business users (including news media businesses)*."[44]

IV.   BLOCKCHAIN: A "MARKET-BASED" AND "PRO-MARKET" SOLUTION?

Because of digital markets' specific features, such as the role played by network effects and the importance of data as an asset, and thus as a barrier to entry, several international policy reports suggested the introduction of regulation aiming

---

41   See the *Booking.com* saga. On this see C. Pike & G. Carovano, "Competition Law under fire: responding to competing demands for change in the case of price parity clauses and loyalty rebates," *CPI September 2019 Antitrust Chronicle*; A. Capobianco & G. Carovano, Foreword – Cooperation between National Competition Authorities within the European Union, e-Competition Bulletin, *Concurrences* (forthcoming – June 2020).

42   *Google/DoubleClick*, Case COMP/ M.4731, 11 March 2008.

43   *Facebook/WhatsApp*, Case COMP/ M.7217, 03 October 2014.

44   Australia Report, "Digital Platforms Inquiry: Final Report," (2019), p. 31.

at ensuring consumers' data portability[45] and data interoperability.[46] Such regulation would seek to neutralize online platforms' network effects and boost market contestability by ensuring that firms compete fairly, rather than on firms' ownership of consumer data. The regulatory burden of each firm may vary depending on whether firms detain strategic market status or not. While the EU Report drew inspiration from the EU data protection framework to suggest the introduction of specific data portability requirements, and the UK Report proposes to go even beyond data portability and interoperability,[47] the U.S. Stigler Report, on the other hand, advocates for the utilization of "behavioral nudges" to boost consumers' awareness of their online decisions.[48]

Whereas significant practical challenges still need to be solved both regarding (i) when certain data must be considered essential so as to impose "data unbundling obligations," and (ii) how these "data unbundling obligations" should be designed (equivalence of input or output?[49]), the effectiveness of such "data unbundling obligations" is still opaque and questionable. In other words, it is still unclear to what extent these regulatory "data unbundling obligations" will be capable of reducing the entry barriers posed by data and network effects, and whether improving new entrants' access to incumbents' data would increase the number of competing firms in digital markets. Given this uncertainty and combined with the extra drawbacks related to regulatory interventions, we should consider regulatory interventions as a last-resort option. It would be preferable that solutions, instead, be "market-based" and "for-

---

45   It consists in consumers' ability to move their data among firms.

46   It consists in the creation of standards in the collation, storage, and utilization of data that could ensure that data are compatible across systems and firms. There are some examples of these efforts already underway. In the UK, the CMA has sought to promote competition in the retail banking sector by requiring firms in that sector to develop and implement "Open Banking" standards (for data, security, and application programming interfaces). On this last point, among others, see Roberts, B. (2019) "Celebrating the first anniversary of Open Banking," *Competition and Markets Authority Blog*, available at https://competitionandmarkets.blog.gov.uk/2019/01/11/open-banking-anniversary/.

47   See UK Report Digital Competition Expert Panel (2019), "Unlocking digital competition," p. 9.

48   Stigler Center, "Committee for the Study of Digital Platforms," (2019), pp. 19-20.

49   For an analysis of the pros and cons of both models in the telco sector, see Carovano G., Modelli di equivalenza nell'accesso e principio di non discriminazione al vaglio del Consiglio di Stato, *Giustizia Amministrativa*, 2015.

the-market." From this perspective, blockchain technologies[50] might be a technical innovation better capable of re-establishing competition in tech markets than regulators and regulation.

Blockchain technologies have the potential to achieve all the mentioned objectives (such as data access, data portability, data interoperability, etc.) that, according to the listed reports, justify regulatory interventions.

- **Search Engines:** Search enables consumers to search for information across the internet both from static and mobile devices. According to the European Commission, while Google (the main search engine worldwide) faces some sort of competition in this market,[51] it is by far the dominant player with a global market share in 2017 of 80 percent in desktop and around 95 percent in mobile.[52] A blockchain-based search engine ("BBSE") could better protects consumers' privacy, data portability, and increase consumers' benefits of their "search experiences" by disintermediating between value and personal data. A BBSE, indeed, while using consumer data, will not own or control them.[53] Consumers will retain ownership of their data and could monetize them. For example, consumers could earn "tokenized commissions" when receiving/seeing Ads. Such a new platform would establish a more balanced win-win situation between the BBSE and its users. A blockchain-based video platform ("BBVP") combined with smart contracts could better protect vid-

---

50 Blockchain is a multipurpose decentralized ledger technology capable of disrupting business models. It improves the trust, transparency, and democracy of markets' structures and dynamics as well as disrupting the concept of ownership in the data-economy. Technically, it consists of a decentralized P2P network protected by several cryptography techniques (blind signatures, hash functions, Merkle trees, etc.) and run through consensus algorithms. Blockchain could either be open (public permissionless) or closed (private permissioned) and adopt different consensus algorithms (proof of work, proof of stake, etc.) depending on the applications' needs. Note that for the purpose of this chapter, the word "blockchain: will be used interchangeably with "decentralized ledger technology" ("DLT"). Although the authors are conscious that the two are not coincident, their differences are not significantly relevant for this chapter.

51 Either by companies that use their own technology (Seznam or Microsoft (Bing)), or by companies that show results of a third-party general search engine with which they have an agreement (Yahoo, America Online, Ask80).

52 See European Commission's decision n. AT.39740, *Google Search (Shopping)*, available at https://ec.europa.eu/competition/antitrust/cases/dec_docs/39740/39740_14996_3.pdf; Table n. 1, Top 7 search engines (global average monthly market shares in February 2017), page 35.

53 This could be realized by combining the BBSE with an identity coin like Citizen. For further details, see Medium's official webpage available at https://medium.com/.

eo-creators *vis-á-vis* the platform, ensuring greater remunerations for the former. Steemit[54] and Mycelia[55] are two good examples of blockchain solutions threatening Google's YouTube business model.

- **Cloud Services:** Cloud platforms offer an app engine, hosting solutions, storage, domain name servers, and more. Everything is stored in cloud data centers. The cloud business could also be disrupted by blockchain solutions. Sia[56] and Storj[57] are good examples of blockchain-based cloud storage ("BBCS"). A BBCS encrypts and distributes individuals' files across a decentralized network. Peers can rent out hard drive space, without needing a centralized provider. Each individual controls its private encryption keys and maintains ownership of its data. No third party can access or control its files, unlike traditional cloud providers. Finally, each network member is incentivized to rent out its hard drive capacity, as it will earn "tokenized commissions." Such a decentralized approach would make BBCSs more secure and cost-efficient compared to traditional centralized cloud solutions.

These examples show how the future of competition may be "off-chain platforms" as opposed to "on-chain platforms." Because blockchain is still not a mature technology, CAs should pay particular attention to any tech-giants' initiatives and behavior aimed at either threatening the development of certain blockchain solutions or exploiting the evolution of such blockchain apps to boost their existing services. Similarly, as suggested by eloquent academics,[58] CAs may consider engaging in industrial policy. In this sense, CAs could stop being technology agnostic, and start supporting decentralized solutions to reduce concentration in tech markets. This does not mean picking winners and losers, or choosing a certain technology over another. Contrarily, it means creating incentives for certain decentralized technological solutions.

---

54   See Steemit official webpage available at https://steemit.com/.

55   See Mycelia official webpage available at http://myceliaformusic.org/#about. Among other, recently, musician Imogen Heap released her song Tiny Human on the Ethereum platform, and she used Mycelia's smart contract payment system to pay all contributors.

56   See Sia's official webpage available at https://sia.tech/.

57   See Storj's official webpage available at https://storj.io/.

58   Among others, see J. Tirole, OECD, Global Forum on Competition, Roundtable on "Competition under fire," Paris, 2019, available at http://www.oecd.org/competition/global-forum/competition-under-fire.htm.

V.   CONCLUSIONS

Digitalization has caused an unprecedented competition policy debate, which led to some questioning CAs' role and purpose and resulted in a number of reports, markets studies and many (sometimes conflicting) proposals for change. While the legal context, focus and findings of each of these efforts varied significantly, some consensus concerning the creation of digital regulators, and subjecting tech giants to greater and more tailored antitrust scrutiny have begun to emerge.

While supporting tougher antitrust scrutiny for tech-giants, regulatory intervention should not be a priority but a last-resort option to deal with concerns raised by digitalization. To relaunch the social and democratic role of CAs and to protect them from unwarranted populist revisionism, there are a number of initiatives that could be put in place:

- CAs' independence should be protected and preserved;

- Governments should carefully consider whether regulatory intervention is needed and suited to address digital competition concerns. Where deemed proportionate and necessary, regulatory interventions could benefit from stronger involvement by the private sector in the design and implementation of the new regulatory framework.

- CAs should improve and facilitate co-operation with their national and international counterparts. Co-operation activities can take place with different purposes, forms, and modalities. New forms of co-operation should also be considered to increase the quality and authority of CAs' advocacy actions.

- Simultaneously, to be more effective enforcers, CAs could (i) reconsider the utility of market definition in zero-price markets, or introduce new market definition methodologies as an alternative to the traditional SSNIP test;[59] (ii) increase

---

59   On the alternative to the SSNIP test, see OECD Background paper on Quality considerations in digital zero-price markets, DAF/COMP(2018)14, Nov. 2018, available at https://one.oecd.org/document/DAF/COMP(2018)14/en/pdf. *"An often mentioned but rarely applied alternative to a SSNIP test is the small-but-significant non-transitory decrease in quality test (SSNDQ). Data availability can limit the range of circumstances in which it can be used. However, the test provides the framework for guiding even qualitative determinations of market definition. Indeed, in most cases, a qualitative approach will likely be needed, and a restrictive bright-line market definition may need to be avoided."*

utilization of interim measures to ensure timely enforcement actions;[60] and (iii) better tailor remedies to restore competition (i.e. wider utilization of structural remedies);[61]

---

60   Interim measures are particularly suited to speed up enforcement actions when a given company behavior seems *prima facie* anticompetitive and there is urgency to act (due to the risk of serious and irreparable harm to competition if the infringement continues during the investigative procedure). Examples of interim decisions already adopted in practice are: (i) European Commission's interim decision on Broadcom in TV and modem chipset markets, Case AT.40608, available at https://ec.europa.eu/commission/presscorner/detail/en/IP_19_6109; (ii) Autorité de la Concurrences's interim Decision n. 19-MC-01, *Amadeus v. Google*, available at https://www.autoritedelaconcurrence.fr/sites/default/files/integral_texts/2019-09/19mc01_en_final.pdf.

61   See Damien Geradin in Paul Voorham, Vestager considers shifting burden of proof for big tech, GCR, October 31, 2019, available at https://globalcompetitionreview.com/article/1210348/vestager-considers-shifting-burden-of-proof-for-big-tech.

Current Reform Proposals for "Digital Mergers"

By Robert Klotz[1]

Abstract

Given the fast-paced evolution of the digital economy, the enforcement of competition law is facing new challenges. These include the need to take into account the value of data collection and the use of data sets. There is a perceived enforcement gap, especially for so called "digital mergers," which competition authorities are currently trying to fix with new tools, e.g. transaction-based thresholds. The main focus of this article however lies on the need for a more targeted substantive assessment of digital mergers. One way to deal with those transactions more effectively could be to apply the theory of innovative harm more broadly. This theory has often been criticized as too speculative, stifling innovation without relying on specific evidence. The European Commission's practice shows that the innovation theory of harm may not be best suited to address digital mergers more effectively in the future, especially because many tech companies cannot be compared to pharma and chemical companies as regards the relevance of such innovation. To face the rapid evolution of the digital markets and ensure predictability for mergers between tech companies, the European Commission is now looking into a possible review of the Notice on Market Definition and its Non-Horizontal Merger Guidelines (e.g. the chapter on conglomerate mergers). In addition, it is likely that "data advantages" and "data privacy" might be used more broadly as competition parameters. Overall, competition authorities can be expected to make use of such new tools or approaches to assess an increasing number of digital mergers in the coming years. However, any such changes, either to the enforcement practice or to the substantive merger rules themselves, should be made carefully, so as to avoid over-enforcement.

I. INTRODUCTION

The concept of "digital mergers," often referred to in enforcement practice and reform discussions, is not very precise, while digital technology is becoming ever more important in many sectors. For the purpose of this analysis, and in line with several recent expert reports, its scope should however be limited to those sectors and to companies whose main activities are the development and deployment of digital

---

1   Partner, Sheppard Mullin Richter & Hampton LLP, Brussels. With special thanks to Ms. Caterina Romagnuolo, Trainee at Sheppard Mullin Richter & Hampton LLP, Brussels, for her valuable assistance. A shorter version of this report was published in CoRe 2020, vol. 1, page VI.

technologies on B-2-B and B-2-C markets, as opposed to companies selling primarily other services, supported by digital technologies. It is being submitted that the assessment of such mergers may require new, more efficient and more intelligent tools in terms of processors and algorithms, but also amended substantive rules and/or procedures.

Under the existing rules, merger reviews are based on the definition of relevant markets in which the parties are active. This determines the assessment of the effects of the merger on competition, notably on price, quality, choice and innovation. However, the traditional approach followed by the European Commission ("EC") or the national competition authorities ("NCAs") is being increasingly challenged by the digital markets and the data economy. It is therefore necessary for the authorities to better understand how companies use data sets to modify the functioning of the markets in which they operate, the data being a resource conferring them a competitive advantage. It can be assumed that the big and fast-growing tech companies have indeed established their market power based on the collection of huge data sets.

This triggers the question whether the current merger rules are still adequate to address distortions of competition due to the takeover of smaller and promising start-ups by those tech giants. For such "digital mergers," a commonly shared perception is the under-enforcement of competition law, allowing (mainly non-EU) big tech companies to grow and become dominant, mainly based on data collection. Such mergers are being compared to "killer acquisitions," especially when the parties' main activities overlap, in which case they can lead to the elimination of future competitors. The purpose of this contribution is to examine whether such critical claims are justified, and if so, what changes can be made to fix the issue.

II. ECONOMIC VALUE OF DATA AS A SOURCE OF MARKET POWER

When assessing the extent to which the digital environment can be transformed into a factor of competitiveness for undertakings by providing them significant competitive advantages, two lead examples, often referred to, are *Facebook/Instagram*,[2] cleared by the Office of Fair Trading ("OFT") and the US Federal Trade Commission ("FTC") in 2012 without any conditions, as well as *Facebook/WhatsApp*,[3] cleared in 2014 by the EC.

In the *Facebook/Instagram* case, the OFT assessed the specific context of social networks and of the two-sided markets in question. Concerning the relevant market, the OFT mainly took into account that Facebook was active in the provision of social networking services to users, camera apps to users, and advertising space to advertisers. Ins-

---

2   UK Office of Fair Trading, *Facebook/Instagram*, ME/5525/12.

3   European Commission, *Facebook/WhatsApp*, M.7217.

tagram provided an app allowing users to take, modify and share photos. Consequently, the OFT reached the conclusion that no substantial competition concerns arose.

The OFT assessed the merger by considering horizontal issues, i.e. actual competition in the supply of photo apps and potential competition in the supply of social network services, as well as vertical issues, i.e. foreclosure of social networks and other photo apps. It was established that the parties overlapped in the supply of social networking services. Nonetheless, because of the existence of strong competitors, the OFT believed that Instagram would not be uniquely placed to compete against Facebook. Accordingly, the OFT concluded that the transaction would not give rise to a realistic prospect of a substantial lessening of competition within a market or markets in the United Kingdom, and the merger was not referred to the EC.

In the *Facebook/WhatsApp* case, the EC questioned the data concentration problems resulting from the transaction that could harm competition in the markets for online advertising services, consumer communications services and social networking services.

Regarding online advertising services, the EC considered that the transaction would only raise competition concerns in case the concentration of data were to allow Facebook to strengthen its position in advertising. However, the EC cleared the transaction as it recognized the presence of numerous and important operators capable of collecting consumer data, that would have prevented Facebook from controlling the price of advertisements, even if Facebook used WhatsApp for advertising purposes.

As observed, in the EU the cumulation of data has never been a sufficient reason to consider that a merger led to a substantial reduction of competition or to the establishment/strengthening of a dominant position. This also highlights the gaps within EU (and national) merger control, especially when start-ups with a very strong public visibility but generating little income are being taken over by digital giants. While the clearance of these deals was arguably the right decision under the existing rules at the time, in can be argued today that they may have significantly contributed to reduced competition and foreclosed market access, as well as incentivized or facilitated abusive conduct.

Likewise, it has been argued that the EC and the FTC/OFT failed to assess the anti-competitive consequences of the conglomerate effect. As a result of the combination of the parties' big data, the merged entity could acquire the power to derive more and better information about its users than the two companies, considered separately, would have inferred by working individually on their respective data sets. Consequently, the above-mentioned cases suggest that certain legal concepts are not well adapted to apprehend digital mergers. The key questions therefore are: can this be prevented/undone under the existing rules, or do they need to be amended to avoid such developments going forward?

III. IS THERE UNDER-ENFORCEMENT OF "DIGITAL MERGERS"?

While the ever-increasing market power of big tech companies, and the re-sulting difficulties for rivals and consumers to keep up, are undeniable, this may not primarily be due to under-enforcement of the merger rules, at least not in its legal dimension. If over-enforcement means stretching the given rules beyond their limits, under-enforcement must mean that the existing rules are not being properly applied by the competition authorities.

There are however no striking examples for this in the tech sector, because the reviews and (conditional) approvals of mergers were made in line with the relevant legal frameworks. Given the importance of predictable rules and their application in practice, any claims that the authorities should have been stricter on the merging parties by stretching the given rules beyond their limitations should be carefully assessed as to their pertinence.

Even in the broader economic/political context, it is not easy to accept the "under-enforcement" claims without reservations. This very much depends on the perspective of the parties: obviously the big tech companies will not share this claim, while rivals and consumer organizations might be tempted to over-emphasize it. But for the purpose of this debate, we can at least concede a perceived enforcement gap, which leads to the question how it could be closed, if we were to accept it as a given.

IV. POSSIBLE APPROACHES FOR UPCOMING REFORMS

A. Transaction Value Thresholds and Targeted Approach

One way to address this gap, which would lead to capturing more digital merg-ers when the target has no or little revenue but is of a high value, could be the introduc-tion of transaction value based thresholds, as it was done in Germany and Austria a few years ago. This would mean that the EU Merger Regulation ("EUMR") would have to be amended (Art. 1). However, this should not be done in any sector-specific manner, and so it would lead to applying a rather broad solution to a fairly specific problem.

Experience with the new German transaction value threshold shows that its impact is limited but the side-effects are significant. It would certainly be effective in bringing more Facebook/Instagram-type mergers under EU scrutiny, but it would also entail a difficult exercise to determine the value of a transaction at the time of filing and especially for digital transactions it could be complex to *"geographically allocate the transaction value (if such allocation were required as part of a deal-size test)."*[4]

---

4   See Summary of replies to the Public Consultation on Evaluation of procedural and juris-dictional aspects of EU merger control, July 2017, page 6, available at https://ec.europa.eu/competition/consultations/2016_merger_control/summary_of_replies_en.pdf.

Another way of addressing the gap would be to adopt a targeted approach, namely to list a number of undertakings that should be subject to a special regime. Similarly, it could be possible to look at the characteristics of the acquirer. This option was suggested by the UK report of the Digital Competition Expert Panel, released in 2019. The report recommends that digital companies identified as having a 'Strategic Market Status' (namely, those companies in a position to exercise market power over a gateway or bottleneck in a digital market, where they control others' market access) should notify all their acquisitions to the competition authority.[5]

However, in both cases, there is a risk of over-enforcement which would place additional burden, both on the merging parties and on the EC.

B. Substantive Test

More important is the question what substantive assessment shall be applied in the future to close the (perceived) enforcement gap for digital mergers, be it at EU or national level. Reform proposals will be high on the agenda in the next years and several recent reports advocate the adoption of a specific theory of harm. Such changes might be brought to the EUMR (Art. 2), but this may not be required for the definition and application of a novel theory of harm specifically geared towards digital mergers, and might thus lead too far.

One way to deal with such cases more effectively could be to apply the theory of innovative harm. Innovation is an important goal of competition enforcement, but it is not legally defined, and even economic research does not establish a clear link between competition and innovation. Innovation is mentioned (implicitly) in the EU Merger Regulation (Art. 2.1.b – technical and economic progress) and explicitly in the Horizontal Merger Guidelines (paras. 8 and 38) as a relevant factor among others to be considered for the competitive assessment of notified mergers.

However, the theory of innovative harm has faced a lot of controversies and may indeed not be the most useful one to assess digital transactions. This is also true, considering that competition authorities may also arbitrarily choose the types of innovation they want to promote.

In addition, in order to prohibit mergers or impose conditions, the finding of reduced innovation might have to be even more speculative in the tech sector than in the other sectors, like pharma and chemical, where the merging companies are usually based heavily on patents and/or R&D. This would not be a good outcome, because companies need a predictable legal framework above all.

---

5 Report of the Digital Competition Expert Panel, "Unlocking digital competition," March 2019, pages 55 and 95.

1. Elimination of Pipeline Overlaps

Usually, the effects resulting from mergers have an impact on two types of innovation, product innovation and process innovation. Process innovation would have as a result the reduction of costs of existing products, allowing for greater economies of scale, while product innovation refers to the increase in quality of the existing products. Therefore, both types of innovation allow the improvement of the efficiency of the merged undertaking compared to the individual companies.

As a consequence, merged companies that combine assets could create investment opportunities, and this can bring significant benefits to consumers. The merged undertakings could offer a higher level of investment in new technologies and network expansion than the individual entities, allowing for the diffusion of innovation and greater efficiency. As demand for data-intensive services grows and there is a requirement for more network capacity at higher speeds, it is critical that operators have incentives to continue to invest. Therefore, it can be concluded that the relationship between mergers and investment is extremely important.

The Commission applied this concept in its merger review practice for some time in different sectors, mainly with regard to overlapping patent portfolios or R&D activities of the parties. In a number of cases, this was done in a more "conventional" way, by showing, with concrete evidence, reduced competition among (or with) pipeline products of the merging parties, or reduced access to the parties' technology, in order to justify the imposition of conditions, such as divestments. In *General Electric/Alstom*,[6] the EC assessed the effects of the transaction from an innovation and technology point of view and concluded that the transaction would eliminate a significant competitive force in terms of innovation and technology in the market for 50 Hz heavy duty gas turbines. In particular, it was proven that after the transaction, the incentives and ability of General Electric to develop significant new upgrades for high power turbines would likely be limited compared to the incentives and capacity that Alstom would have in the absence of the transaction, so that General Electric would likely eliminate most of Alstom's R&D capabilities.

Therefore, according to the EC's assessment deriving from the unique nature of the market, there were high barriers to entry to innovation in the industry and the cancellation of overlapping pipeline products in certain segments was likely a result of the transaction. Consequently, the merged entity would result in less efficiency or/and output, having a negative impact on prices and choices available to consumers, and more importantly, on innovation investment, which would have lasted a long time, taking into account the high entry barriers on that specific market. The remedies imposed by the EC consisted in the divestment of Alstom's gas business to Ansaldo, to create a viable, independent and competitive activity that could allow to maintain the incentives for innovation.

---

6 European Commission, *GE/Alstom*, M.7278.

2. Vertical Foreclosure

Interoperability requirements were at the center of the remedies imposed by the EC in the *Intel/McAfee* case,[7] where the main risk was linked to conglomerate effects. Taking into account the existence of very complementary markets in which the parties operated, i.e. central processing units ("CPUs") and chipsets for Intel, and the IT security solutions market for McAfee, the EC found a technological and commercial link between the two products. In addition, Intel was dominant in the market for CPUs and chipsets. The EC assessed the risk of foreclosure by degrading interoperability between Intel's hardware and security solutions on the one hand, and the products of competitors on the other.

The EC's analysis concluded on the ability of Intel to favor McAfee's security software interoperability with its hardware in the detriment of competitors. Moreover, the EC considered as well that Intel is likely to degrade interoperability of its hardware with other security solutions than McAfee's products. The effects of such a transaction would be as well significant on the endpoint of the CPUs and chipsets and the security solutions market, having a negative impact on innovation. As a consequence, the investigation established that the degradation of interoperability would have the effect of strengthening the current dominant position of Intel on the relevant product market.

3. Innovation Incentives

The controversy over the innovation theory of harm arose in other cases where the Commission used this concept in a more "speculative" way, by assuming reduced innovation more generally (i.e. not in relation to existing or pipeline products), while not relying on specific evidence. This was particularly noted in the context of the merger between the American chemical giants Dow and DuPont, where the EC assessed the link between innovation and product market competition and raised not only economical concerns but also innovation issues, by profoundly revising its traditional analysis of innovation. The EC stated that " *innovation should not be understood as a market on its own right, but as an input activity for both the upstream technology markets and the downstream [...] markets. This however does not prevent the Commission to assess the impact of the Transaction at the level of innovation efforts by the Parties and its competitors.*"[8] The methodology refers to (i) "*the identification of whose companies which, at an industry level, do have the assets and capabilities to discover and develop new products which, as a result of the R&D effort, can be brought to the market*"; and (ii) the assessment of "*those spaces in which innovation competition occurs in the crop protection*

---

7   European Commission, *Intel/McAfee*, M.5984.

8   European Commission, *Dow/Dupont*, M.7932, para. 348.

industry."[9] Based on this clarification, the EC focused on measures of innovation output to assess innovation competition.

The decision rests on the presumption of harm to innovation and significant impediment to effective competition, even if it is admitted that the EC "*may not be able to identify precisely which early pipeline products or lines of research the parties would likely discontinue.*"[10] The assessment of the effect of the transaction on innovation competition focused on (i) the market features of the crop protection industry, characterized by high barriers to entry and likely to result in a decrease in the incentives to innovate; (ii) the important role of the parties as innovators; (iii) the parties being close competitors; and (iv) them limited number of alternative sources of innovation and the deriving negative effects.

In its competitive analysis, the EC took into account the fact Dow and Dupont were close competitors in terms of innovation, as illustrated by the ambitions and efforts that each of them devoted to R&D, by the numerous overlaps noted in the product pipelines under development and by the market segments on which their investments are concentrated. The EC also noted the existence of three other competitors, the innovation activity of which was generally less intense than that of the parties. Moreover, the overall innovation would be slowed down due to the loss of an independent innovator. Without even knowing when or how many products would be affected by the transaction, the EC stressed that the merged entity would limit the number of innovative products in the future. By doing so, the EC followed a dynamic analysis, by taking into account the future market and assessing product markets that do not exist yet. In order to approve the transaction, the EC ordered a divestment of almost the entirety of DuPont's global R&D organization.

A similar approach was adopted in the *Bayer/Monsanto* case, where the EC recognized, among other things, that the Horizontal Merger Guidelines expressly confirm that innovation competition is a criterion to assess the likely effects of a merger: "*effective competition may be significantly impeded by a merger between two important innovators, for instance between two companies with 'pipeline' products related to a specific product market.*"[11]

The EC found that the acquisition of Monsanto by Bayer was likely to lead to a significant reduction in innovation competition. In particular, the assessment of the effect of the transaction on innovation competition in the crop protection and traits markets focused on (i) the discontinuation and/or reorientation of R&D capabilities

---

9 *Ibid.* paras. 349, 350.

10 *Ibid.* paras. 3025.

11 Guidelines on the assessment of horizontal mergers under the Council Regulation on the control of concentrations between undertakings, OJ C 31, 5.2.2004, para. 38.

and projects; (ii) the parties' incentives to innovate; (iii) the parties being important and close innovators in several innovation spaces where few alternatives were available.[12]

The EC concluded that the transaction would have resulted in an immediate reduction of incentives to continue innovating in the case of overlapping lines of research and early pipeline products between the parties, and in reduced incentives to develop new products in the future.[13] To address the EC's concerns, Bayer proposed a divestment package that was accepted by the EC. By contrast to *Dow/DuPont*, the EC in this case made a specific reference to the products in respect of which the parties' R&D and assets should have been divested to ensure innovation competition.

Even though the approach adopted by the EC in these two cases was innovative, the decisional practice shows that the alleged harm to innovation was already a concern for the EC earlier on. In its decision *Deutsche Börse/NYSE Euronext*, the EC mentioned the *"European innovation space"*[14] and the fact that the *"parties compete at the level of introduction of new and improved contracts around their overlapping core franchises and were each other's closes competitors in this regard."*[15] The EC presented the approach as a plain application of the unilateral effects model. Subsequently it was widely criticized for defining a separate "innovation space" or "innovation market," besides the specific relevant markets identified based on the established criteria. This, according to the criticism, is not foreseen or permitted by the existing EU merger control rules. The result of this use of the innovation theory of harm therefore is a (perceived) over-enforcement of the merger rules.

V. TAKEAWAYS FOR THE REFORM DISCUSSIONS

As previously observed, there are good reasons to believe that the innovation theory of harm may not be best suited to address digital mergers more effectively in the future. Of course, if merging tech companies are based heavily on patents and/or R&D, and if there is clear evidence that this activity will be drastically reduced post-merger, the existing rules may be applied to block the merger or impose conditions. But many tech companies cannot be compared to pharma and chemical companies when it comes to the relevance of such innovation.

Tech mergers should therefore be assessed under a different, more specific theory of harm than innovation competition. In order to face these new challenges, not limited to tech mergers, but certainly with high relevance for them, the EC launched a public consultation on the functioning of certain procedural aspects of EU

---

12   European Commission, *Bayer/Monsanto*, M.8084, para. 78-80.

13   *Ibid.* para. 83.

14   European Commission, *Deutsche Börse/NYSE Euronext*, M.6166, para. 923.

15   *Ibid.* para. 601.

merger control, addressing mainly the simplification of the notification procedure, the system of referrals from or to Member States, other technical aspects of the notification procedure, as well as a new aspect on efficiency.

A. The Report "Competition policy for the digital era"

Following this consultation, the EC took stock of the challenges and possible solutions, in the report "Competition policy for the digital era."[16] In the report, it is established the importance of monitoring recent national legislation introducing transaction-based merger thresholds to analyze their practical effects. For instance, in France, it was concluded, that it was not advisable to provide an alternative threshold relating to the value of the transaction. At the same time, the report stressed that it is too early to modify the jurisdictional thresholds as defined in the EUMR. Instead, the cooperation between Member States should be improved, when mergers concern several Member states or trigger multi-jurisdictional filings.

The report also recognized the difficulty of defining the market in dynamic settings. In particular, it noted *"another problem [..] arises when a dynamic market environment leads to fluid, quickly-changing relationships of substitutability and possibly partial overlaps of varying significance between different services, sometimes combined with practices of multihoming and/or changing perceptions of consumer needs."*[17] However, even in less dynamic settings, when there is innovation, there is the risk that competition authorities would apply a static approach. For instance, if products can be differentiated not on the basis of their price but on the basis of their quality or performance, adopting a static approach would not be the best way to take into account the product's evolution and the customers' response to that evolution.[18] Indeed, when a product is free, competition mainly takes place on the basis of the quality of the product, as recognized also by the EC in the *Microsoft/Yahoo!* case.[19]

B. Reforming EU Rules

In light of the above, the EC is currently looking into a possible review of the 1997 Notice on Market definition.[20] The purpose of this exercise is to establish if the

---

16 European Commission, "Competition policy for the digital era," Final report, 2019.

17 *Ibid.* page 47.

18 See Decker C., Time matters: the temporal dimension of antitrust, *European Competition Law Review*, vol. 41, Issue 6, 2020, page 279.

19 European Commission, *Microsoft/Yahoo!*, M.5727, para. 101.

20 EU competition law – market definition notice (evaluation), available at https://ec.europa.eu/info/law/better-regulation/have-your-say/initiatives/12325-Evaluation-of-the-Commission-Notice-on-market-definition-in-EU-competition-law/public-consultation.

current way of defining the relevant market, including in merger cases, across different industries needs to be adapted to take account of the evolving scenarios, especially in the digital and tech sectors.

To ensure predictability for mergers between tech companies, the EC might also consider adapting its Non-Horizonal Merger Guidelines (e.g. the chapter on conglomerate mergers). Including "innovation markets" more generally into the substantive assessment of digital mergers may be a temptation in this context, but this might entail too much speculation (which the Courts tend not to overrule). The approach followed in the *Apple/Shazam* case,[21] where the EC considered that the Shazam user data does not appear to be unique and thus able to confer a significant data advantage to Apple post transaction which would impede effective competition, seems to suggest that the concept of "data advantages" might be used to block mergers in the future. Therefore, companies in the digital sector should consider their ability to use information as a tool to put competitors at a competitive disadvantage.

C. Concept of "Data Advantages"

Along this line, the UK Competition and Markets Authority ("CMA") has recently assessed the Google acquisition of Looker, a California-based data platform.[22] The purchase had already been approved by competition authorities in the U.S. and in Austria. However, the CMA decided to launch an inquiry and scrutinized the proposed transaction more carefully than it would have done in the past. The CMA considered whether Google could leverage its market power in online advertising and web analytics to drive competing business intelligence providers out of the market. The authority found that although Google could have made it difficult for rivals to access the data they need, it would not have had the incentive to do so. The CMA cleared the acquisition as it would have not resulted, or may be expected to result, in a substantial lessening of competition within a market or markets in the UK.

The concept of "data advantages" is clearly a relevant element also for the EC's assessment of the proposed acquisition of Fitbit by Google.[23] In particular, although Google has asserted that the "deal is about devices, not data," the EC is mainly concerned about the latter. The EC believes that the data collected via wearable devices would constitute an important advantage for Google in the online advertising markets and therefore it would be more difficult for rivals to compete with Google's online advertising services. To address these concerns, Google proposed to create a virtual storage of data ("data silo"), where certain data collected through wearable devices could be kept separate from other dataset within Google and could not be used for Google's advertising purposes.

---

21 European Commission, *Apple/Shazam*, M.8788.

22 Competition and Markets Authority, *Google LLC/Looker Data Sciences, Inc.*, ME/6839/19.

23 European Commission, *Google/Fitbit*, M.9660.

However, as the remedy proposed did not cover all the data that Google would access thanks to the transaction, the EC decided to launch a market test to gather comments from rivals and users. On the basis of the feedback received, the EC opened an in-depth probe to assess the impact of the transaction on three markets: (i) the supply of online search advertising services, in which Google holds a dominant position; (ii) the supply of online display advertising services, in which Google holds a strong market position; and (ii) the supply of "ad tech" services, namely analytics and digital tools used to facilitate the programmatic sale and purchase of digital advertising, in which Google holds a strong market position.[24]

This case attracts a lot of attention as it will be the occasion to see whether the EC's approach has changed, compared to the one it applied in the *Facebook/Whatsapp* case in 2014. A change in the EC's approach would not be a surprise as the EC's five-year digital strategy proposes that in the merger control field, "*the Commission will look closely at the possible effects on competition of large-scale data accumulation through acquisitions and at the utility of data-access or data-sharing remedies to resolve any concerns.*"[25] However, such approach should be fact-based and would have to be adopted on a case-by-case basis.

D. Privacy as a Competition Parameter

The Bundeskartellamt, in its decision against Facebook of early 2019, in which an abuse of dominance was found,[26] assessed the relation between competition law and the data protection principles, especially in the context where the General Data Protection Regulation ("GDPR") do not rule out the competence of a competition authority, and sets of rules take into account unbalanced negotiation positions. The competition law infringement was the result of Facebook's terms and conditions, as far as they refer to the collection of user and device data without their consent, and their use for purposes related to social network. On the same line, we could read the proposal made by the Monopolies Commission in Germany to introduce a new Platform Regulation that could provide for more stringent interoperability and portability obligations, which should be aligned with the experience in data protection law.[27]

Against this backdrop, the Bundeskartellamt's approach, which was recently

---

24   European Commission – Press Release IP/20/1446, August 4, 2020.

25   Communication from the Commission to the European Parliament, the Council, the European Economic and Social Committee and the Committee of the Regions, "A European strategy for data," COM(2020) 66 final, February 19, 2020.

26   Bundeskartellamt, B6-22/16.

27   Monopolies Commission, Biennial Report "Competition 2020," Summary, July 29, 2020, page 3.

upheld by the German Federal Court of Justice ("BGH")[28], after it had been overturned by the competent Higher Regional Court ("OLG Düsseldorf")[29], might possibly serve as a proxy for a future merger test for a closer vetting of transactions between data driven companies.

After all, the EC already found that privacy could be considered a competition parameter in its past decisions *Facebook/Whatsapp* and *Microsoft/Linkedin*. In particular, in the latter, the EC recognized that privacy *"can be taken into account in the competition assessment to the extent that the consumers see it as a significant factor of quality."*[30] However, it is also clear that any such changes would have to be crafted and applied with great care in any possible future merger reform process, so as to avoid over-enforcement.

---

28   Bundesgerichtshof, KVR 69/19 – Decision of June 23, 2020.

29   Oberlandesgericht Düsseldorf, VI-Kart 1/19 (V) – Decision of August 26, 2019.

30   European Commission – Press Release IP/16/4284, December 6, 2016.

Competition Issues in Digital Advertising: Views from Spain

By Lara Tobías-Peña,[1] Cristina Vallejo[2] & Pedro Hinojo[3]

Abstract

Digitalization is disrupting many economic activities and online advertising is no exception. Indeed, its impact on this sector is proving fundamental and includes relevant competition issues which are widely analyzed and debated at the moment. The Advocacy Department of the CNMC has actively contributed to this analysis in the past years from both horizontal and sectoral perspectives and is currently carrying out a market study on online advertising.

The general dynamics of digitalization and its potential effects on consumer welfare and efficiency are common ground in most analyses: economies of scale and scope, learning economies, and, more prominently, network effects are generally identified as key drivers to price reductions, lower transactions costs, and other benefits in terms of quantity, quality, or variety, but also as potentially harmful for competition, when it leads to horizontal and vertical integration. When it comes to online advertising, abuse of dominant positions in highly concentrated markets is a well-known risk, with "tying and bundling" and "self-preferencing" dynamics as common examples. Lack of transparency and data and privacy issues are also crucial concerns regarding the online advertising market, which leads to growing calls for more comprehensive solutions. The debate on the most effective ways to address those challenges, from a competition perspective, includes the need for flexible and faster responses, from both regulatory and enforcement standpoints. Some initiatives are already underway, which will contribute to further public reflection.

I.   INTRODUCTION

Digitalization is proving very disruptive to many economic activities. Transportation, tourist accommodation, financial services, and advertising are among the sectors most affected by this phenomenon.

---

1   Head of the Market Studies Unit at the Spanish Competition Authority ("CNMC"). The opinions expressed in this article are personal and do not necessarily reflect CNMC's views.

2   Advisor in the Market Studies Unit at CNMC.

3   Advisor in the Market Studies Unit at CNMC.

This disruption is changing the way in which many services are provided, and this is reflected in changing market structures. In the case of digital advertising, the final outcome that may result is particularly relevant from the point of view of competition.

A sound competitive environment is positive in every market because it means lower prices and a larger market size (and hence employment) and/or an increase in quality or variety. However, in advertising, a competitive environment is even more relevant because of two factors:

- Advertising is an intermediate input which firms need in order to convey marketing messages to actual or potential customers. More competition in advertising means that this communication reaches consumers more affordably and/or more efficiently. This is especially relevant for smaller, nascent, or innovative firms, which are more dependent on advertising to launch new products or ideas or to reach new clients in order to disrupt incumbent firms' positions.

- Advertising is very relevant for final consumers, since it gives them relevant information. Better advertisements mean more optimal decisions by economic agents, generating static and dynamic efficiency.

The changes that digitalization is bringing about have opened a debate on the opportunities and challenges presented by this new scenario. Part of this debate is whether public administrations, and particularly competition and regulatory authorities, have the necessary tools to address them.

II. THE CNMC'S RECENT ACTIVITY ON DIGITALIZATION

The Advocacy Department of the Spanish Competition Authority ("CNMC") has been very active in analyzing the disruptive effects of digitalization in the past years, both on the economy as a whole and on specific sectors.

In 2015, the CNMC launched a public consultation on new service provision models and the sharing economy,[4] with a special focus on transportation and tourist accommodation, to better understand the opportunities and challenges for public administrations and regulation.

---

4 CNMC, "The sharing economy and new models for providing services via the Internet," available at https://www.cnmc.es/en/ambitos-de-actuacion/promocion-de-la-competencia/consultas-publicas/the-sharing-economy-and-new-models-for-providing-services-via-the-Internet.

Sector specific studies on digitalization have followed in recent years. In 2018, the CNMC published a Study on the regulation of tourist rentals,[5] in which it reviewed and assessed regional and local regulations with the aim of advising regulators on the most procompetitive approach. The same philosophy was applied in the Report on the regulation of taxis and private hire vehicles published in 2019.[6] Also in 2019, the CNMC released a Study on the impact on competition of technological innovation in the financial sector (Fintech).[7] It analyses the Fintech phenomenon from a general perspective and focuses on specific innovations in the financial system, such as payment services, crowdfunding, or insurtech.

The CNMC's latest Action Plan renews its commitment to sectors affected by digitalization. The Advocacy Department is currently working on a new market study on online advertising,[8] the focus of which is the appraisal of the competitive environment in online advertising, zooming in on the Spanish market. To this end, a public consultation was launched last year in order to gather contributions from stakeholders and the study is expected to be published during the second half of 2020.[9]

All of the above show the efforts of the authority to grasp the changes that digitalization is bringing about, in order to guide regulators on how to approach this disruption and to make the most of it. An important part of this is understanding what digitalization entails and how it affects a particular market.

III. HOW DOES DIGITALIZATION AFFECT MARKETS?

New technologies and digital modes of service provision imply several changes, with potential effects on consumer welfare and on competition:[10]

---

5 CNMC, "La CNMC publica un estudio sobre la regulación de las viviendas de uso turístico en España," available at https://www.cnmc.es/node/371041.

6 CNMC, "La CNMC publica un informe sobre la normativa reguladora de taxis y vehículos de turismo con conductor (VTC)," available at https://www.cnmc.es/en/node/373207

7 CNMC, "Market Study on the Impact on Competition of Technological Innovation in the Financial Sector (Fintech)," available at https://www.cnmc.es/sites/default/files/editor_contenidos/Notas%20de%20prensa/2018/181009%20Market%20Study%20on%20the%20impact%20on%20competition%20of%20technological%20innovation%20in%20the%20financial%20sector.pdf.

8 See press release announcing the study, available at https://www.cnmc.es/sites/default/files/editor_contenidos/Notas%20de%20prensa/2019/20190425_NP%20Inicio%20Estudio%20Publicidad%20Online_EN.pdf.

9 See Press Release announcing consultations, available at https://www.cnmc.es/en/ambitos-de-actuacion/promocion-de-la-competencia/mejora-regulatoria/consultas-publicas/online-advertising.

10 Crémer, J., de Montjoye, Y.A. & Schweitzer, H. (2019), "Competition policy for the digital era," A report to the European Commission.

- Economies of Scale, due to low/negligible variable costs. This implies potential consumer welfare gains for consumers, due to the access to goods and services at low or zero prices. But at the same time, it generates a natural trend towards market concentration and winner-takes-most/all dynamics.

- Economies of Scope, which means that two activities can be carried out jointly relatively cheaper than separately. Firms which are very competitive in exploiting digital technologies can expand their outreach to different sectors (evidence of this is the increasing presence of Big Tech in financial services). Again, this is positive for consumers who value integrated services (e.g. they can receive targeted promotions while accessing financial products), although firms with market power in some sectors can leverage that position into other activities

- Learning economies, mostly due to the characteristics of big data, algorithms, and artificial intelligence. This increases the quality, differentiation, and personalization of services for consumers, but two risks loom. First, personalization can also mean price discrimination, so firms could appropriate welfare gains that would otherwise accrue to consumers. Second, learning economies have first-mover advantages and chicken-and-egg dynamics, reducing the contestability of the incumbents' positions.

But the most relevant effect of digitalization is the prominence of network effects/externalities, mostly indirect (crossed-group): agents on one side (e.g. buyers) value finding more agents on the other side[11] (e.g. sellers). This means that we are dealing with multi-sided markets so that platforms can add value by reducing transaction costs and facilitating match-making.[12]

When platforms are matchmakers (e.g. ad exchanges or platforms which connect buyers and sellers of advertising space, i.e. advertisers and publishers) or demand

---

11 Network effects can be direct too if users value finding more users on the same side. This can happen in matchmakers (where more users imply that the feedback systems work better, attracting other users), in demand coordinators or in some audience makers (like in social networks).

12 Evans, D. S. (2003), "Some Empirical Aspects of Multi-Sided Platform Industries," *Review of Network Economics*, 2(3).

coordinators (e.g. mobile ecosystems), indirect network effects are reciprocal. Buyers value finding more sellers (since they can more easily find transactions at lower prices), and sellers value finding more buyers (since that helps to increase revenues).

When platforms are audience makers (e.g. advertising-funded media, content creators/aggregators, social networks or search engines) these effects are not necessarily reciprocal. Advertisers (on one side of the market) value reaching more users (on the other side of the market), but users do not necessarily value finding more advertisers (although, indirectly, platforms with more advertisers are more attractive to users, since that platform is more likely to make more revenues to design better and more targeted advertisements).

The interest of the platform is to optimize market size. Since most digital intermediaries are funded through fees, an increase in transactions means a proportional jump in revenues in the short run. But, more importantly, platforms must safeguard indirect network externalities to maximize long-term revenues, bringing both sides of the market on board. Optimizing indirect network effects will imply maximum quantity/transactions sometimes, leading to price reductions for some agents (e.g. low/zero/negative prices for content/media, communication services, social networks or search engines, subsidized for price-elastic consumers). In other cases, optimizing network effects means ensuring optimal quality or variety (e.g. this can be very relevant in advertising, where ensuring a safe environment for the advertiser's brand can be more important than maximizing impressions of a given campaign).

In any case, network effects (mostly indirect) may yield potential price reductions, lower transactions costs, easier matching, and an optimal market size in terms of quantity, quality, or variety.

Nevertheless, multi-sided markets can also lead to winner-takes-most/all dynamics because of first-mover advantages. Despite apparently low barriers to entry, the position of dominant platforms is not so contestable. Small platforms will find it difficult to attract more users beyond a tipping point on one side of the market, and this will preclude growth on the other side of the market, falling into a chicken-and-egg trap.

There is another, subtler, type of competition problem. The fact that platforms could reduce the number of intermediaries is bound to be procompetitive in theory. This reflects a trend towards vertical integration, which can be a problem for smaller and non-vertically integrated competitors aiming at accessing the market at given points along the value chain.

Therefore, digitalization offers some promising features for consumer welfare and general efficiency: lower prices and cost (in theory), fewer barriers to entry and increased quality, variety and differentiation, with new or upgraded services for consumers. However, some competition issues may appear in the form of horizontal or vertical integration. And there is another source of concern for consumers (although not strictly related to competition), since digital modes of service provision rely much on consumer data and may imply a significant cost in terms of privacy and attention.

The analysis of these questions in the specific case of online advertising is presented below.

IV. A BRIEF OVERVIEW OF DIGITAL ADVERTISING

Advertising is an industry which, even before the adoption of digital technologies, already exhibited some of the above-mentioned characteristics. In particular, advertising-funded traditional media were a patent example of a multi-sided market with powerful indirect network effects. But digitalization has altered this environment in several ways.

First, new business models have appeared, with the capability of growing at a larger scale. On one side, the relevance of data and learning effects have facilitated the development of search engines and also content aggregators (since they have search functions too, apart from algorithms to suggest videos) or social networks (especially when including news and recommendations). On the other side, higher increasing returns and lower variable costs than in traditional media, together with other sociocultural changes, have implied the deployment of these services at a global scale compared to the national fragmentation of traditional media. With such an outreach, not only network externalities but also learning effects become more prominent.

Second, new modes of digital advertising enjoy much higher "targetability" than traditional ones, making it possible to tailor advertisements at the level of individuals[13] depending on past behavior (activity, browsing, purchases, revealed interests...) and all other information available, be it contextual (content/subject of the website or the words of the search, time, seasonal factors...) or personal (age, gender...). Sometimes, personal users' data are directly revealed when logging in an account (first-party data). In other cases, data are inferred (third-party data) using other characteristics and direct knowledge of other agents (i.e. first-party data can be used when extrapolating to the rest of users).

Therefore, getting the users' attention becomes crucial for any agent because of two things. On the one hand, increasing audience and time spent within the properties fosters marketing opportunities to place ads. On the other hand, and more importantly, growing users and time spent in the ecosystem allows for the accumulation of first-party data (which will be useful to improve third-party data too). And getting (the right) data

---

13 Goldfarb, A. (2014), "What is Different About Online Advertising?," *Review of Industrial Organization*, 44, 115–129.

is critical because advertising is becoming less contextual (less related to the content of the website where it is displayed) and consisting more and more in knowing what profile your users fit into, so that targeted ads can follow them along their browsing activity.

As a consequence, digital advertising is not only about reaching a wide audience but also about being able to segment your users. On the one hand, this can be positive for competition since even properties with small audiences can monetize their inventory. On the other hand, there are also risks of concentration, leaving only a few digital platforms given the interaction of scale, learning, and network effects.

Yet, there are other disruptive forces, such as the expansion of programmatic advertising.[14] This consists in the automatic matching of advertisements and space through real-time bidding ("RTB"), facilitating a bigger amount of transactions, easier placement, and checks on campaigns. The use of algorithms and artificial intelligence (without the need for direct human interaction) yields huge cost savings and scale economies compared to advertising in traditional media. Furthermore, the higher measurability of each advertisement's impact (or of the amount of impressions) can lead to performance-based remuneration schemes, improving static and dynamic efficiency.[15]

So new intermediaries specialized in this technology have appeared along the value chain, mostly exchanges (where supply and demand meet) or platforms and networks (which try to group the supply of advertising space or the demand orders of advertisement placement). But, at the same time, some agents have succeeded in vertically integrating some of these stages, especially when they are able to grease the wheels of transactions by using enriched databases and analytics.

All the above-mentioned factors and the transition to programmatic advertising have resulted in digital platforms (which are very competitive in these new technologies) taking a greater share of the advertising pie *vis-à-vis* traditional intermediaries, like advertising agencies, and traditional media.

To sum up, the disruption driven by new technologies has allowed the entry of new agents and new business models, which should boost competition and translate into higher consumer welfare, especially if we take into account the potential of the new environment, e.g. regarding targetability.

However, there is also a more complex environment, with some plausible risks which deserve some scrutiny.

---

14   Geradin, D. & Katsifis, D. (2019a), "An EU competition law analysis of online display advertising in the programmatic age," *TILEC Discussion Papers*, DP2019-031.

15   Marty, F. (2019), "From Demoting to Squashing? Competitive Issues Related to Algorithmic Corrections: An Application to the Search Advertising Sector," *CPI Antitrust Chronicle*, 1(2), 63-69.

V. POTENTIAL COMPETITION ISSUES IN DIGITAL ADVERTISING

The first issue is the trend towards market concentration because of the abovementioned forces (scale/scope/learning/network economies). However, the assessment of the degree of concentration warrants a reflection on market definition, which is a very controversial issue in digital markets due to various reasons. First, because their multi-sided nature makes it more difficult (if not impossible) to use conventional tests of price-elasticity (like the SSNIP test) to define markets. Second, because the degree of competition on one side of the market can be relevant when assessing apparent dominance on the other side. Third, because innovation in technology and business models implies that other sectors or firms (which were not initially considered within the relevant market) can suddenly become actual or potential competitors.

Nonetheless, some type of market definition is still necessary for typical competition cases. Some authors advocate for narrow market definitions,[16] both from a horizontal perspective (arguing that the different modes of online advertising, e.g. display vs search, are intrinsically different) and a vertical perspective (given that dominant intermediaries along the value chain can become indispensable). Others[17] suggest wider (if any) market definitions, given that different modes of advertising ultimately compete for advertising revenues and consumer attention.

Solving these dilemmas is a daunting but crucial task in mergers or abuse of dominance cases. Regarding the former, one tangible risk is the potential for "killer acquisitions," i.e. the purchase by a dominant platform of small, but still relevant, actual or potential competitors. Regarding the latter, abuses of dominance can take many forms. These include tying and bundling conduct or imposed or incentivized exclusivity, increasing dependence on dominant platforms and restricting the ability of competitors to grow. In other cases, the dominant position is not abused in the "primary" market, but it is leveraged from that market to distort competition in another.[18] It is important to recall that digital advertising is adjacent to many other markets: namely search engines, social networks, content aggregators or creators, mobile ecosystems, etc.

---

16 Geradin, D. & Katsifis, D. (2019), "Google's (Forgotten) Monopoly – Ad Technology Services on the Open Web," *Concurrences Review* 3-2019, Art. N° 90967.

17 Bitton, D., Pearl, D., Dolmans, M. & Mostyn, H. (2019), "Competition in Display Ad Technology: A Retrospective Look at Google/Doubleclick and Google/Admob," *CPI Antitrust Chronicle*, 1(2), 41-49.

18 Akman, P. (2018), "A Preliminary Assessment of the European Commission's Google Android Decision," *CPI Antitrust Chronicle*, 17-23; Banasevic, N. (2018), "The European Commission's Android Decision and Broader Lessons for Article 102 Enforcement," *CPI Antitrust Chronicle*, 12-16.

Other thorny conduct would include lack of transparency or an abrupt change in contractual conditions.[19] The consideration of an excessive loss of consumer privacy (which could be considered equivalent to an excessive price) as an exploitative abuse remains a controversial and unclear issue.[20]

Finally, the abovementioned trend towards vertical integration can also lead to cases of abuse such as self-preferencing. The consolidated company can favor its own services along the different stages of the value chain, foreclosing rival firms. This reduction in choice and competition can reduce innovation and increase prices in the long term, offsetting the potential efficiencies that vertical integration might yield in the form of lower intermediaries and transaction costs. This is very relevant in online advertising, with potential problems in the interoperability of the different platforms and exchanges on both sides of the market and the possible ordering or manipulation of the different bids in auctions ran by these intermediaries.

Of course, as is usual in competition policy, the assessment of these specific issues must be carried out case-by-case. We are already seeing many investigations and decisions by competition agencies dealing with those types of conducts. However, there are voices who call for the consideration of alternative approaches to safeguard competition in digital markets, ranging from an upgrade in competition authorities' resources and tools, to regulatory solutions. These proposals require a thorough assessment.

VI.   OPTIONS TO INCREASE COMPETITION IN DIGITAL ADVERTISING

The debates on how to increase competition in digital advertising are not sector-specific but are connected to the impact of digitalization. In principle, advertising is not an activity with a regulatory burden that could restrict entry or growth of new firms. Regulation in this case is rather horizontal, concerning consumer protection, data or privacy issues.

But the disruption driven by digitalization can also affect competition in advertising. Since digitalization is in essence horizontal, the many initiatives that are being debated touch upon many issues: mainly competition law, regulation, and consumer and data protection.

One of the first reports at the European level was the "Competition Policy for

---

19   Geradin, D. & Katsifis, D. (2019), "Google's (Forgotten) Monopoly – Ad Technology Services on the Open Web," *Concurrences Review* 3-2019, Art. N° 90967.

20   Botta, M. & Wiedemann, K. (2019), "Exploitative Conducts in Digital Markets: Time for a Discussion after the Facebook Decision," *Journal of European Competition Law & Practice*, lpz064.

the Digital Era,"[21] which called for stricter merger controls and proposed the shifting of the burden of proof in highly concentrated markets. It also recommended soft law guidance or data regulation, but leaving the question on how to implement it open.

In the UK, the so-called Furman Report (2019)[22] goes further and highlights the potential usefulness of creating a "Digital Markets Unit" either within the Competition and Markets Authority ("CMA") or operating as an independent body. The idea has been already implemented, after its public endorsement by the CMA within its recent report on online platforms and digital advertising (2020).[23]

The brand-new unit, called "Digital Markets Taskforce" ("DMT"), is led by the CMA in cooperation with the Information Commissioner's Office ("ICO") and UK's communications regulator ("Ofcom") aiming to providing advice to the UK's government on the potential design and implementation of pro-competitive measures for unlocking competition in digital platform markets.

CMA's proposals are included on the above-mentioned report, which has been recently released. The CMA agrees with the findings of the Furman Report, endorsing the idea of a new regulatory regime. In particular, the proposals relate to three main fields:

- Rules to govern the behavior of platforms with market power: an enforceable code of conduct for firms with "Strategic Market Status," based on fair-trading, open choices, trust and transparency.

- Pro-competitive interventions oriented to address specific sources of market power, Specifically it may include rules to give consumers greater control over data and to improve transparency, obligations on transparency, interoperability, access to "third party data" and data separation, as well as DMU's capability to impose vertical separation and portfolio access.

---

21   Crémer, J., de Montjoye, Y.A. & Schweitzer, H. (2019), "Competition policy for the digital era," A report to the European Commission, available at https://op.europa.eu/en/publi-cation-detail/-/publication/21dc175c-7b76-11e9-9f05-01aa75ed71a1/language-en.

22   An independent report for the UK Government, led by Jason Furman "Unlocking digital competition, Report of the Digital Competition Expert Panel: An independent report on the state of competition in digital markets, with proposals to boost competition and innovation for the benefit of consumers and businesses" (2019). See https://assets.publishing.service.gov.uk/government/uploads/system/uploads/attachment_data/file/785547/unlocking_digital_com-petition_furman_review_web.pdf.

23   CMA, "Online platforms and digital advertising market study," (2020). See https://www.gov.uk/cma-cases/online-platforms-and-digital-advertising-market-study.

- Pro-competitive interventions specifically addressed to Google and Facebook. As per the first one, the DMU may have the ability to restrict Google's capability regarding default tools and "quick and query data" obligations on the search market. As per Facebook, the CMA recommends interventions aimed to improve interoperability on the display segment.

As regards the U.S., the Report from the Stigler Center (2019)[24] also suggests governments should consider the creation of a "Digital Authority," with similar competences. Among other things, this institution could require the use of open standards, mandating the portability and accessibility of data, and assisting the Federal Trade Commission ("FTC") and the Department of Justice ("DOJ") – agencies in charge of antitrust action in the U.S. – in merger control reviews. In this case, it suggests that the Authority be a subdivision of the FTC, in order to avoid capture issues.

In a report released last year,[25] the Australian Competition & Consumer Commission also includes recommendations oriented to tighter merger controls, privacy legal framework reforms, and the idea of a holistic approach that would take account of the close links between competition, consumer and privacy issues.

Other institutions,[26] like the European Parliament, the European Data Protection Supervisor ("EDPS"), the Centre of Regulation in Europe ("CERRE") or the European Consumer Organisation ("BEUC") have called for increased cooperation between agencies in the fields of consumer and data protection and competition law.

---

24 "Stigler Committee on Digital Platforms, Final Report," Chicago's Stigler Center for the Study of the Economy and the State at the University of Chicago Booth of Business (2019), available at https://research.chicagobooth.edu/-/media/research/stigler/pdfs/digital-platforms---committee-report---stigler-center.pdf?la=en&hash=2D23583FF8BCC560B7FE-F7A81E1F95C1DDC5225E.

25 "Digital Platforms Inquiry," Australian Competition & Consumers Commission (2019), available at https://www.accc.gov.au/focus-areas/inquiries-ongoing/digital-platforms-inquiry/final-report-executive-summary.

26 See: http://www.europarl.europa.eu/doceo/document/TA-8-2017-0076_EN.html?redirect; "White Paper: Ambitions for Europe 2024. Digital Platforms, Data Governance, Artificial intelligence, Media & Content. Digital Infrastructure," CERRE (2019), available at https://www.cerre.eu/sites/cerre/files/cerre_whitepaper_ambitionsforeurope2024.pdf; and "The Role of Competition Policy in Protecting Consumer's well-being in the Digital Era," BEUC (2019), available at https://www.beuc.eu/publications/beuc-x-2019-054_competition_policy_in_digital_markets.pdf.

More recently, the European Commission has launched 2 public consultations[27,28] regarding these issues, within the framework of the European Digital Strategy.[29] The first one is part of the Digital Services Act package, an ambitious regulatory update in the digital field and includes the potential introduction of an *ex ante* regulation framework, considering different models: horizontal regulation or a specific one, addressing big platforms – called "gatekeepers." The second one considers the possibility of introducing a new competition tool ("NCT") aiming at addressing structural competition problems that the current competition toolkit may (allegedly) not address in whole or in part.

Therefore, the idea of a multidisciplinary response is on the table. Indeed, it is widely recognized that the boundaries between sectors, especially in the digital economy, are increasingly hard to draw. This is why calls for a holistic approach are on the rise. The nature of this disruption has revealed the increasing need for ever-faster and more flexible responses.

VII. CONCLUSIONS

There is growing concern regarding the challenges posed by the ongoing digital revolution in some markets. Some commentators advocate a comprehensive and effective new approach to tackle these challenges.

Competition enforcement tools are highly useful, since they allow for flexibility *ex ante* (they can be adapted to many different issues following a sound case-by-case approach) and *ex post* (since remedies can have a regulatory dimension). But some experts argue that they are not agile enough to redress harm to competition in some of these rapidly evolving markets, with winner takes-all dynamics that (allegedly) can sometimes be due to merger control under-enforcement. Furthermore, some cases (like interoperability issues affecting the connection of platforms and exchanges on both sides of the advertising market) are deemed to be very complex for non-specialist competition agencies lacking the needed technological skills.

The use of regulatory tools (potentially including a new independent digital authority/regulator in charge of these matters) are gaining momentum in the current debate. The objective would be to address some technical and economic concerns through the imposition of some obligations (e.g. ensuring interoperability or data

---

27 See press release at
https://ec.europa.eu/commission/presscorner/detail/en/IP_20_962.

28 See press release at
https://ec.europa.eu/commission/presscorner/detail/en/ip_20_977.

29 Full document, available at
https://ec.europa.eu/info/sites/info/files/communication-shaping-europes-digital-future-feb2020_en_4.pdf.

sharing by dominant undertakings) to ensure competition on the merits. However, a regulatory approach is more rigid (than competition law) and its appropriateness for dynamic digital markets must be carefully assessed.

Horizontal regulation, mostly dealing with consumer protection and consumer ownership over data, can address some of the concerns related to online advertising markets (like dominance in some segments or barriers to entry in access to data). However, a horizontal perspective may not take sufficiently into account market specificities that pose competition challenges in those markets.

To sum up, these alternative approaches (competition and regulation, including within the latter some horizontal issues) are complements rather than substitutes. Therefore, a combination of the different elements might be an option to consider, although more reflections on this topic are warranted in order to frame an optimal response that increases competition and consumer welfare in digital markets, including in online advertising.

The ACCC, Digital Platforms, and the Media in Australia

By Allan Fels AO[1]

Abstract

The Australian Competition and Consumer Commission ("ACCC") supported by draft Australian government legislation has proposed the establishment of a mandatory, arbitrated news media and digital platforms bargaining code under which, inter alia, Google and Facebook would pay media for content published on their platforms. The code has unique features including a final offer arbitration process to determine the payment and statutory powers to enforce its operation.

I.   INTRODUCTION

The Australian Competition and Consumer Commission ("ACCC") Digital Platforms Inquiry of 2019 and the subsequent proposed mandatory media bargaining code of 2020 is of special significance to media.[2] In this paper, I briefly provide an overview of the report as a whole, outlining its treatment of competition, consumer protection and privacy issues, but with a main focus on issues concerning the relationship of digital platforms (mainly Google and Facebook) and the media especially with respect to "public interest journalism." I then discuss significant events since the report of the inquiry in June 2019, most importantly the proposal to introduce a "compulsory" code of conduct and accompanying draft legislation regarding relationships between the major digital platforms and the media.[3]

---

1   Professor Allan Fels AO is Professor of Law and Economics at Melbourne and Monash University, and former Chair of the Australian Competition and Consumer Commission. He also chairs the Public Interest Journalism Initiative ("PIJI") an independent, not for profit body which conducts research and advocacy concerning the future of public interest journalism.

2   Australian Competition and Consumer Commission (ACCC), "Digital Platforms Inquiry. Final Report," June 2019.

3   Originally discussed in ACCC Mandatory News Bargaining Code: Concepts Paper, May 2020 and then formulated in CCC Draft News Media Bargaining Code: July 2022 and Treasury Laws Amendment (News Media and Digital Platforms Mandatory Bargaining Code) Bill 2020. See also ACCC Q and A's: Draft News Media and Digital Platforms Mandatory Bargaining Code.

II. ORIGINS AND TERMS OF REFERENCE OF INQUIRY

The decision by the Australian Government to hold an inquiry into digital platforms originated from an agreement by a minority group in the Australian Senate led by Senator Nick Xenophon to support Australian Government proposals to loosen some restrictions on cross media ownership i.e. co-ownership of TV, radio, and newspapers. Senator Xenophon and colleagues made it a condition of their assent to the legislation that there would be an ACCC inquiry into the platforms with a special emphasis on their impact and interrelationship with the media.

The Australian Government Terms of Reference ("TOR")[4] of the inquiry focused heavily on the media issues while leaving scope for the traditional "bread and butter" issues of competition and consumer protection that are usually the main focus of ACCC inquiries. Thus, the core TOR required the ACCC to inquire into the impact of digital of digital platforms on the state of competition in media and advertising services markets, in particular in relation to the supply of news and journalistic content and the implications of this for media content creators, advertisers and consumers.

The TOR reflects another important influence on the holding of the inquiry – the support of the media industry, especially of the powerful Murdoch media businesses in Australia operating under the News Corporation umbrella. The media has long complained about the adverse and unfair impact it says the digital platforms has on them and saw an ACCC inquiry as a way of advancing media interests in regard to their relationship especially financial relationship with the platforms.

One other background political feature is that Google, Facebook, and other global digital giants do not enjoy the amount of political influence and support in Australia that most big businesses such as banks, retailers, mining companies and others do. This has made the Coalition government (a government of the Right) more willing to take action in relation to the platforms and in doing so to take considerable account of the interests of traditional media businesses (including but not exclusively News Corporation interests). At this time, it is unclear how much notice the Australian government and the ACCC will take of threatened withdrawals of their news services from Australia and of any accompanying pressures from the government of the United States.

III. COMPETITION

Australia's competition law approach is often located in the middle between Europe and the United States. In relation to the digital platforms the European com-

---

4 Set out in ACCC Final Report 2019 (see above).

petition authorities have been more concerned about and more interventionist while the United States authorities have been more cautious in their assessment, and more standoffish in their actions.

The Australian report takes the view that Google and Facebook have "substantial market power" (a pre-condition to trigger intervention under the abuse of market power provisions of the competition law) but is cautious in the actions it proposes in that field. The report noted that the TOR did not require the ACCC to focus on whether the digital platforms have misused their market power (although it notes that if they use their power in a way that contributes to "market failure" this is within scope).

As a result, the inquiry merely recommends some tightening of the merger law framework and some reducing of "default bias" by providing consumers a wider choice of search and internet providers. It also flags potential concerns over issues of data portability and of the operation of them and of the tech supply chain (this chain is now the subject of a follow-up ACCC inquiry).

Subsequent to the inquiry, there has been no competition law litigation concerning Google and Facebook comparable to that in Europe e.g. regarding self-preferencing, though there has been some litigation concerning consumer issues. Some merger proposals are under consideration.

IV. CONSUMER PROTECTION, DATA PROTECTION, AND PRIVACY

The ACCC has long combined the roles of being a competition and consumer protection and public utility access regulator. It also has powers to apply codes of conduct to deal with unequal bargaining power between businesses e.g. franchisors and franchisees, retailers and suppliers etc. Hence the report addresses consumer and unequal bargaining power issues, and although the ACCC has never previously had a role in privacy law and policy, it includes a substantial discussion of privacy issues, noting their interaction with consumer protection issues, but generally referring them to other bodies.

Thus, noting that there is a lack of informed and genuine choice by consumers in their interaction (or "bargain") with digital platforms, the ACCC calls for a range of strengthened protections under the Privacy Act including provisions regarding consumer consent to utilization of personal information. It also proposes a Privacy Code of Practice relating especially to the provision of information to consumers about the data practices of the platforms. This would be developed by the Office of the Australian Information Commission ("OIAC").

Finally, additional protections under consumer law are recommended, including the application of unfair trading practices law.

While the report did not make any specific recommendations for enforcement action or litigation, the ACCC has subsequently taken legal action against Google in regard to alleged misleading and deceptive conduct. The case relates to allegations that Google has falsely led consumers to conclude that geospatial information was not being collected about them when it was.[5]

V.   FUTURE SCRUTINY

The draft recommendations of the inquiry report suggested that future detailed scrutiny of the platforms was required and that this should be done by a new specialized government body. The draft recommendation was criticized – why was yet another government body needed? Would it be as well-equipped and forceful as the ACCC? The final report proposes that future scrutiny should rest with the ACCC for which additional resources would be required. (This has been accepted and resources provided by the Australian Government).

VI.   THE MEDIA

As noted a major and internationally distinctive feature of the inquiry was its focus on the relationship of the digital platforms and the media.

There are two key matters emphasized. The first is the decline of traditional media, especially newspapers. The decline is driven especially by their loss of advertising revenue to digital forms of advertising. Traditionally the revenue received from advertising ("the rivers of gold") has not been as large as in the past, to fund ("cross-subsidize") journalism, especially "public interest journalism" (a term addressed below).

The ACCC took the view that public interest journalism was a "public good" i.e. a product valued by the market but unable to be adequately supplied by the normal operation of market forces. (A better term might have been a "merit good" i.e. a good or service of greater value than the market was willing to pay for, even if technically there was no market failure). The diminished supply of public interest journalism was of detriment to the public and there needed to be a set of government policy steps to support public interest journalism such as direct grants and various tax concessions. There was a special emphasis on the decline of regional and rural media, and some suburban newspapers, and new forms of media.

On this first key matter there are two points to note here. First, the decline of public interest journalism due to digital disruption occurred largely prior to and was

---

5   Concise Statement: *ACCC v. Google Australia Pty Ltd and AMOR*, NSW Registry, Federal Court of Australia, File No. NSD1760/2019.

largely unrelated to the advent of Google and Facebook. Second, following the report, widespread bushfires in country Australia and the impact of COVID-19 has led to a massive decline in advertising, and the widespread contraction of media, most notably in regional and rural Australia, accentuating the pressure for government intervention in regard to the media.

The second key matter emphasized in the ACCC report concerned the balance between the bargaining power of platforms and the media. Essentially the media argued that the publication on the digital platforms of "snippets" or headlines of stories taken from them was unfair and exploitative, reflecting unequal bargaining power and that they should be compensated for use of their product. Digital platforms responded that the publication of these snippets brought a substantial net benefit ("referral traffic") to news publishers by drawing the attention of platform readers to news stories and potentially attracting them to view the relevant content (sometimes for free, sometimes on a priced basis). It is not easy to determine who is right or wrong on this matter of "exchange value" let alone the net dollar value of the exchange. One reason is that there is little information about how the platforms operate. There is no opportunity to "look under the bonnet" of the platforms as to how they operate. Moreover, if data were available, it would still be a difficult question to resolve.

Notwithstanding this the ACCC came down on the side of the media and concluded that there was unequal bargaining power and that it was being used to the detriment of the media. It proposed that there should be a code of conduct established to deal with the matter.

As noted above, the Australian Competition and Consumer Act, unlike many pieces of comparable legislation overseas, makes provision for the establishment of codes of conduct. Although the legislation says very little about the nature, scope and content of codes they were originally established mainly to deal with "vertical tensions" that is situations where some business enterprises seem to have unequal bargaining power with respect to downstream or upstream businesses with which they interact. Examples included: oil companies and service stations; cinema distributors and exhibitors; retailers and suppliers; and franchisors and franchisees. Codes play a role in dealing with some shortcomings in their bargaining dimensions. Codes are mainly based on a voluntary agreement between the businesses concerning their behavior. Some codes have a higher legal status: the voluntary agreement about conduct can be enforced in courts by the ACCC. The code can also be compulsory that is that the government or the ACCC specifies required conduct, makes it legally obligatory and empowers the ACCC to enforce it.

Following the publication and broad endorsement by the government of the Digital Platforms Inquiry including a recommended code, the ACCC commenced work in 2019 on establishing a voluntary code but after some months reported to the government that it was not making progress on reaching an agreement. At that point the government stepped in and stipulated that there would be a compulsory code of conduct and made it clear that it would be backed by legislation and that the legislation would be enacted quickly. It referred the nature of the code to the ACCC to determine.

There was an early perception that although the code would in part be used to resolve some non-monetary bargaining imbalances in relationships between media and the digital platforms in fact the outcome of the code and associated legislation would be that Google and Facebook would be required to provide substantial funds which would be used to pay some of the big providers for the alleged exploitation of vertically imbalanced bargaining power and/or to support the development of public interest journalism. News Limited (the Australian arm of News Corporation) proposed that a billion dollars should be set aside for the industry and Channel 9/Fairfax proposed six hundred million (about ten percent of Google and Facebook revenue). There was a clamor by regional and rural publishers and commercial telecasters for some funding support. There have been similar claims by small media innovators.

How would the ACCC determine how much of an impost there should be on Google and Facebook? Three approaches suggested themselves: there should be a general levy perhaps of ten percent on advertising revenue of the digital giants and then it should be distributed in accordance with arrangements comparable to those of the copyright collecting societies. Another approach is that there should be amounts related to the investment that was needed to ensure the continuation of public interest journalism. Finally, another approach suggested by the Public Interest Journalism Initiative ("PIJI") research was to build on its survey work in estimating how much the public was willing to pay for news (being between $400M and $800M).[6] Once an amount was determined this would be then allocated between bigger commercial interests but also with a significant portion being set aside for the promotion of regional, rural and small public interest journalism. In the event, none of these approaches was adopted: instead a bargaining approach was adopted by the ACCC. One reason was that the ACCC and the government did not want to be seen to levying a tax as that could conflict with international tax agreements.

VII. THE DRAFT NEWS MEDIA AND DIGITAL PLATFORMS MANDATORY BARGAINING CODE

The ACCC backed by the Australian government released a draft code and related legislation for public consultation on July 31, 2020. The aim was for a final code and the enactment of legislation before the end of 2020. The code would then commence.

---

6 Public Interest Journalism Initiative ("PIJI") and the Judith Neilson Institute for Journalism and Ideas Joint Submission to the ACCC Mandatory News Media Bargaining Code Concepts Paper, June 2020. (The author is Chair of PIJI an independent, not for profit entity).

A. The Code

The code seeks to "address the fundamental bargaining power imbalance between Australian news media businesses and major digital platforms. This imbalance has resulted in news media businesses accepting less favourable terms for the inclusion of news on digital platform services than they would otherwise agree to."[7]

The ACCC asserted that while bargaining power imbalances exist in other areas of the economy, the bargaining power imbalance between news media businesses and major digital platforms was being addressed as a strong and independent media landscape is essential to a well-functioning democracy.

The code would allow news media businesses to bargain individually or collectively with Google and Facebook over payment for the inclusion of news on their services.

The code also includes a set of "minimum standards" for:

- providing advance notice of changes to algorithmic ranking and presentation of news;

- appropriately recognizing original news content; and

- providing information about how and when Google and Facebook make available user data collected through users' interactions with news content.

B. Roles and Responsibilities

The draft code has been developed by the ACCC in close consultation with the Australian Government's Department of the Treasury and the Department of Infrastructure, Transport, Regional Development and Communications.

The ACCC would be responsible for administering and enforcing the code, and would have a role in providing submissions as part of compulsory arbitrations conducted under the code. The Australian Communications and Media Authority ("ACMA") would be responsible for determining eligibility of news media businesses to participate in the code.

C. Platforms Covered

---

7   ACCC, draft news article and digital platforms mandatory bargaining code, July 2020.

The government and the ACCC have stated that digital platforms must participate in the code if the Treasurer makes a determination specifying that the code would apply to them. The code would initially apply only to Facebook and Google. Other digital platforms may be added to the code if they hold a significant bargaining power imbalance with Australian news media businesses in the future.

D. News Media Businesses Covered

News media businesses wishing to participate in the code would apply to the ACMA. News media businesses would nominate which of their "news sources" they would like included in the code. These can include news websites, newspapers and other print publications, television programs, radio programs, and other audio or video content made available online.

Based on the news sources they nominate; news media businesses can participate in the code if:

- **They *predominantly* produce "core news," and publish this online.** The draft code defines "core news" as journalism on publicly significant issues, journalism that engages Australians in public debate and informs democratic decision making, and journalism relating to community and local events. Some examples of this kind of journalism are political reporting, court, and crime reporting.

- **They adhere to appropriate professional editorial standards.** These can include editorial standards set by the Press Council or the Independent Media Council, editorial standards set in relevant media industry codes, or equivalent internal editorial standards.

- **They maintain editorial independence from the subjects of their news coverage.** News sources are unlikely to meet this test if they are owned or controlled by a party that has a direct commercial interest in the coverage they produce — such as a magazine that mainly produces sponsored or "advertorial" content, or a publication reporting on a local council owned by that council. News sources are also unlikely to meet this test if they are owned or controlled by a political advocacy organization, such as a political party or a union.

- **They operate primarily in Australia for the purpose of serving Australian audiences. This excludes foreign media such as the New York Times.**

In addition to the criteria above, an eligible news media business's annual revenue must exceed $150,000.

In order to be eligible to participate in the draft code, a news media business must nominate one or more of its news sources that mainly produces "core news." The draft code defines "core news" to include journalism about publicly significant issues; journalism that engages Australians in public debate and informs democratic decision making; and journalism relating to community and local events. Some examples are political reporting; court reporting and reporting on crime. Once a news media business is eligible to participate in the code, it would be able to negotiate with digital platforms over *all news* produced by its nominated news sources — not just the "core news" described above. The code's minimum standards for dealing with news on digital platform services would apply to all news on participants' news sources, rather than just "core news."

Some examples of content that is not "core news" but would still be covered by the code when reported by an eligible news media business include:

- reporting about sport, such as interviews with coaches and players or investigative journalism focused on sports administration;

- reporting about entertainment and the entertainment industry, such as news about new film releases or television shows.

The code is not intended to capture any non-news media content, such as:

- broadcasts of sports games or printing of sports results and scores;

- entertainment content such as drama or reality television programming;

- product reviews;

- talkback radio;

- academic publications; and

- documentary films.

E. Did the ACCC Consider Other Models for the Code?

The ACCC considered a range of potential bargaining frameworks. These frameworks were based on collective boycott of digital platforms by news media businesses, and on "collective fee arrangements," a subset of which could have required digital platforms to pay fixed fees into a funding "pool" to be shared between news media businesses.

The draft code adopts a model based on negotiation, mediation and arbitration "to best facilitate genuine commercial bargaining between parties, allowing commercially negotiated outcomes suited to different business models used by Australian news media businesses."

Further, ACCC noted that the outcomes of negotiations conducted between a digital platform and one news media business (or a collective of news media businesses) under this model would not affect the outcomes secured by other news media businesses – which is not the case for a "zero sum" or "one-size-fits-all" framework such as a collective funding "pool."

It also emphasized that the implementation of any "funding pool" arrangement would require the government to make complex upfront decisions on value of news content, and on the distribution of funds between news media businesses; it contended that such decisions are best left to the parties themselves.

Another unstated reason may be that the government and the ACCC may have wanted to avoid the appearance of levying a tax or quasi taxi as this could ruffle feathers with the U.S.

F. Compulsory Arbitration

Should news media businesses not reach commercial agreement with a digital platform within three months of commencing bargaining, the code provides for compulsory arbitration on payment within reasonable timeframes, and a set of minimum standards that improve on the *status quo* currently available to Australian news media businesses.

The bargaining power imbalance between news media businesses and the digital platforms is particularly acute for smaller, regional, and rural news media businesses. The draft code would allow news media businesses to bargain with digital platforms either individually or (more likely in the case of smaller media) as part of a collective. Bargaining as part of a collective would allow smaller news media businesses to negotiate from a stronger position than negotiating individually. Collective bargaining is likely to also reduce costs for individual news media businesses, and allow groups to pool resources and expertise during the negotiation process.

The draft code would see news media businesses benefit from minimum standards applying to their dealings with digital platforms. For example, these minimum standards would require digital platforms to provide news media businesses with clear information about the nature and availability of user data collected through users' interactions with their content on digital platform services. The ACCC contended that this would particularly benefit smaller news media businesses who may not be aware of the type of information currently available to them, and how they can seek to use this data to better serve their audiences online.

The minimum standards would also require digital platforms to give news media businesses at least 28 days' notice of algorithm changes likely to materially affect referral traffic, to affect ranking of news behind paywalls, or to result in substantial changes to the display and presentation of news, and advertising directly associated with news, on their services. This advanced notice would give all news media businesses the opportunity to implement strategies to maintain or increase audience reach and engagement with their news on digital platform services.

The draft code would require major digital platforms and news media businesses to negotiate in good faith over all issues relevant to news on digital platform services.

If negotiation and mediation does not result in an agreement within three months, news media businesses can elect to bring the dispute to compulsory arbitration.

Once arbitration has been triggered through either of the methods above, it is compulsory for the digital platforms to participate in the arbitration. The outcomes of arbitration would be considered binding on both parties.

The ACMA would appoint a register of arbitrators to resolve disputes under the code if required.

By default, arbitration under the draft code would only consider the inclusion of news on the following digital platform services:

Facebook

- Facebook News Feed (including Facebook Groups and Facebook Pages);

- Instagram; and

- Facebook News Tab (when launched in Australia).

Google

- Google Search;

- Google News; and

- Google Discover.

G. Final Offer Arbitration

Arbitration under the code would be performed through "final offer arbitration." The digital platform and news media business (or a collective of news media businesses) must each submit a final offer on the remuneration to be paid by the digital platform within 10 days of the commencement of arbitration. Parties would then have a further 5 business days to provide comments on each other's offer.

The ACCC may on occasion make a non-binding submission to the arbitrator to assist with consideration of the parties' submissions or to provide guidance on the application and interpretation of the code.

The arbitrator would then have 30 business days to choose one or the other of the parties' "final offers," which would form a binding agreement between the parties.

If the arbitrator forms the view that both offers raise significant public interest concerns related to consumer welfare or the provision of public interest journalism, they may adjust the more reasonable of the two offers. However, this mechanism is expected to be rarely used.

The draft code requires that in deciding between the two parties' final offers, the arbitrator must consider:

- the direct and indirect benefit that the content of the news business (or news businesses) provides to the digital platform's service;

- the cost to the news business (or news businesses) of producing news content; and

- whether a particular payment amount would place an undue burden on the commercial interests of the digital platform.

The ACCC contends that the code's use of final offer arbitration recognizes the significant challenges involved in setting a price for the inclusion of Australian news on digital platforms services. According to it while digital platform services such as Google Search and Facebook News Feed do derive some direct monetary value from showing advertising alongside news, much of the benefit that these services derive from Australian news is indirect. Such indirect benefits include: the public perception benefits of being known as a provider of Australian news; the ability to attract and retain digital platform users on the basis of featuring Australian news; and the value of user data collected through the presence of Australian news, which can be used to improve the services digital platforms provide to users and advertisers.

Given these challenges, final offer arbitration leaves it to the parties to determine a suitable price through their final offers. The fact that the arbitrator or arbitration panel would be choosing from one of two offers rather than attempting to determine a price would discourage ambit claims and provide a strong incentive for both parties to submit their most "reasonable" offers.

Final offer arbitration would also provide much quicker outcomes than conventional commercial arbitration would allow, with the arbitrator required to make a decision within 30 business days of receiving offers and comments from the parties ⊠ a maximum of 45 business days after arbitration commences.

H. Minimum Standards

As indicated above, in addition to the obligation to bargain in good faith, the draft code introduces a series of "minimum standards" for digital platforms to meet in their dealings with news media businesses. These would require digital platforms to:

- give news media businesses at least 28 days' notice of:

  o algorithm changes likely to materially affect referral traffic to news;

  o algorithm changes designed to affect ranking of news behind paywalls; and

  o ubstantial changes to display and presentation of news, and advertising directly associated with news, on digital platform services;

- give news media businesses clear information about the nature and availability of user data collected through users' interactions with news on their services;

- publish proposals to appropriately recognize original news on their services;

- provide flexible user comment moderation tools for news media businesses; and

- allow news media businesses to prevent their news being included on any individual digital platform service.

These minimum standards reflect terms that Australian news media businesses may have been able to secure in commercial negotiations with major digital platforms in the absence of the existing significant bargaining power imbalance.

The draft code's minimum standards require digital platforms to provide clear information about the data they currently collect through news content. However, the code does not include any requirements for digital platforms to increase sharing of user data with news media businesses. Accordingly, the code does not have an impact on the privacy protections currently applicable to digital platform users.

The code would give news media businesses more control over their content and advertising to a certain extent.

News media businesses would be able to "opt out" of having their news content featured on individual digital platform services against their will. News media businesses would also have more control over user comments made against stories they post or publish to digital platform services, with digital platforms required to provide flexible moderation tools that allow:

- removing or filtering user comments;

- disabling user comments against individual news items; and

- blocking user comments or accounts.

The draft code would prohibit digital platforms discriminating against the news content of news media businesses on the basis of their participation in the code.

Broadly, such discrimination would occur if a digital platform disadvantaged the content of a news media business that participated in the code when compared to another news media business that did not. For example, this may occur by a digital platform artificially lowering the ranking of a news media business's content in search results or a social media feed.

A decision by digital platforms to place more reliance on international news and lower the ranking of, or cease carrying, Australian news content on the basis of participation in the code would also be considered discrimination.

The ACCC may decide to take enforcement action for non-compliance with certain aspects of the draft code, including:

- not bargaining in good faith during negotiations, including refusing to participate in negotiation, mediation or arbitration;

- breaching minimum commitments; and

- breaching non-discrimination provisions.

The ACCC can issue infringement notices of 600 penalty units ($133,200) where it has reasonable grounds to believe a party that has contravened the code. Should the ACCC commence court proceedings, the maximum penalties would be the greater of either:

- $10,000,000;

- three times the benefit obtained from the conduct (if calculable); or

- 10 percent of a digital platform's annual turnover in Australia in the last 12 months.

The penalties would apply to the digital platforms for all contraventions of the code, and also apply to news media businesses if they are found to have not acted in good faith in their negotiations with the digital platforms.

VIII. CONCLUSIONS

The ACCC has proposed a mandatory media bargaining code backed by legislation to resolve the consequences of what it sees as unequal bargaining power between media organizations and the digital platforms.

The code provides for certain minimum standards and for methods of determining payments to be made from the digital platforms to the media companies for publication of their content.

The ACCC claims that the proposed adoption of the code is not a major departure from what it usually does. It is a multi-function regulator which applies competition and consumer law, regulates telco, energy, and other utilities especially via the operation of "access to essential facilities" type laws, conducts market studies, and does advocacy. In particular it also prescribes and oversees codes of conduct between big business and small business where there is unequal bargaining power.

The code is in draft form and there will be some changes before the law goes through Parliament and comes into effect in 2021.

The most novel element is that pursuant to its conclusion that there is unequal bargaining power between digital platforms and media organizations the ACCC has proposed a commercial bargaining/arbitration process to address the inequalities. It has avoided resolving the differences between the media businesses and the digital platforms by means of a levy or tax or by direct regulation. A levy could have been seen as conflicting with international tax agreements and could have attracted the ire of the United States Government as well as the fierce opposition of Google and Facebook. A commercially negotiated and arbitrated code is more in accordance with standard ACCC regulation. This approach also means that the ACCC does not have to make difficult decisions about payment amounts and other matters. These are left to bargaining and independent arbitration.

Arguably the code will have the effect of evening out the imbalances of bargaining power between large media organizations and the digital platforms. It is not so obvious, however, that it will do the same in relation to smaller media organizations with less capacity to bargain, lesser information about the platforms, and weaker bargaining power. This matter may receive more attention before the code is finalized.

There is also considerable uncertainty about how revenue payments will be determined. There are some criteria in the proposed legislation but they give little specific guidance. Moreover, the final offer arbitration process is capable of generating a very wide range of outcomes. It is possible that the criteria will be elaborated in the final version, but it is not clear how greater certainty can be created about such contentious matters as the "exchange value" which occurs when media content appears on digital platforms.

The final offer arbitration process may prove to be an ingenious solution to resolving the differences between the media companies and the digital platforms. It arguably will force each party to make "reasonable" final offers. On the other hand, while this is possible it needs to be noted that this form of arbitration differs from some other kinds of final offer arbitration used in labor bargaining and in bargaining between sports organizations and media organizations. In those markets bargaining occurs in the context that all parties, including arbitrators, have a great deal of information and general understanding of the surrounding circumstances (e.g. prices for comparable sports offerings on other TV or media outlets). The less certain ACCC proposal may generate "unanticipated consequences." However, as the ACCC contends, the big gap between the views of the opposing sides of the bargaining process, the uncertainty and wide range of possible outcomes makes the reasons for final offer arbitration all the stronger and the code provides that in some circumstances both final offers can be rejected if the public interest or consumer protection requires it. And the outcomes will be reviewed every year or two.

The code excludes the public broadcasters, principally the Australian Broadcasting Commission ("ABC") from inclusion in the revenue bargaining although it would be covered by the other minimum standard practices of the code. The government excluded the ABC (broadly similar to the BBC) on the grounds that it does not broadcast advertisements and so it is not adversely affected by platforms in the same way as commercial broadcasters. Also, to the extent that there is "market failure" in the provision of public broadcasting it is already dealt with by direct government funding. One complication is that there is some concern that the digital platforms might as a result preference ABC content if it is "free." However, a number of provisions, especially those relating to anti-discrimination, are designed to prevent this. If they are inadequate, the possibility of ABC inclusion may be considered.

Finally, there has been a strong negative reaction from Facebook and Google. Facebook in particular has said that it will leave the market and there are precedents from Spain and France when there were attempts to make the platforms pay for news content. However, some elements of the drafting of the legislation e.g. the anti-discrimination clauses make this look more difficult than in Spain and France. Moreover, the government holds in reserve the possibility of using its power to impose a tax of say ten percent on the revenue of the digital companies. The exercise of such a power has its own considerable complications including international repercussions but it highlights that Google and Facebook could avoid this dire outcome by settling for the potentially cheaper solution of a world first code.

Do Digital Platforms need Updated Merger Laws?

By Stephen P. King[1]

Abstract

Mergers involving large digital platform companies, such as Google and Facebook, create unique challenges for competition law and competition authorities. Are existing laws capable of dealing with mergers involving digital platforms, or do they need to change – either broadly or by having "digital economy specific" merger laws?

This chapter draws on the experience of a range of countries including the U.S., EU, UK, and Australia, to argue that, while existing merger laws may need some refinement, they are more than capable of dealing with the issues raised by digital platforms. Further, where refinements are needed, they involve raising existing processes to "best practice" for all merger analysis. There is no case for specific rules to deal with digital platforms.

I.   INTRODUCTION

Large digital platform companies, such as Google and Facebook, have been involved in a substantial number of mergers and acquisitions. Between 2008 and 2018 "Google has acquired 168 companies, Facebook has acquired 71 companies and Amazon has acquired 60 companies."[2] This volume of mergers by some of the world's largest companies,[3] raises questions about the efficacy of existing competition laws – and particular merger laws – when dealing with large digital platform companies.

The acquisition of the assets of one commercial entity by another entity is usually illegal if the acquisition will result in a "significant" or "substantial" reduction in (effective) competition.

---

1   Productivity Commission, Melbourne, Australia. I would like to thank Catherine de Fontenay for comments on an earlier draft of this paper. The views expressed are those of the author alone and should not be attributed to the Productivity Commission.

2   Argentesi, E., P. Buccirossi, E. Calvano, T. Duso, A. Marrozzo & S. Nava (2019) "Merger policy in digital markets: An *ex-post* assessment," Discussion Paper, DIW Berlin at p. 14.

3   Amazon.com; Alphabet Inc (Google's parent company) and Facebook are regularly three of the ten highest value public companies by market capitalization.

Details differ between countries. For example, in the European Union ("EU"), the reduction in competition must be related to the creation or strengthening of a dominant position.[4] In the United States ("U.S."), a merger is illegal if it may have the effect of substantially lessening competition or tend to create a monopoly.[5] However, the overall test is similar, based on whether or not an acquisition will, or is likely to, significantly reduce competition compared to the "counterfactual" situation(s) without the acquisition.

Competition concerns have been raised regarding digital platform mergers, but few acquisitions – and none of the Google, Facebook, or Amazon acquisitions – have been ruled illegal on competition grounds. Some competition concerns relate to "traditional" economic issues. For example, it is claimed that some acquisitions aim to buy out potential rivals before they can grow to become a competitive threat.[6] It is also claimed that digital platforms are buying businesses in separate but related markets to leverage their power between the markets (for example, the acquisition of LinkedIn by Microsoft[7]). Other theories of harm relate directly to the nature of digital platforms, such as the importance of data in reinforcing market power (for example, Facebook's acquisition of the messaging platform, WhatsApp[8]) or the potential of a market to "tip" to a winner-takes-all situation due to an acquisition (for example, the acquisition of the Trading Post by Carsales in Australia[9]).

These competition concerns, together with the lack of intervention by competition authorities, has led to a debate about the efficacy of existing merger laws. In this chapter, I review the state-of-play in merger law and whether or not current competition laws are able to deal with the unique aspects of digital transactions. In particular, I focus on four aspects of the merger clearance process – the relevance of notification thresholds; the use of market definition to make competitive inferences about a merger; the need to update theories of competitive harm; and the "hurdle" that competition authorities face when trying to show a "likely" significant anti-competitive effect of a merger.

---

4   Council Regulation (EC) No 139/2004 of 20 January 2004 on the control of concentrations between undertakings (the EC Merger Regulation) Article 2(3).

5   Clayton Antitrust Act of 1914, Section 7.

6   For example, see the discussion on acquisitions and "nascent" competitors by Hoffman, D.B., (2019) "Antitrust in the digital economy: A snapshot of FTC issues," Remarks at GCR Live Antitrust in the Digital Economy, U.S. Federal Trade Commission, May, p. 5-7.

7   See the discussion in Argentesi *et. al.* (2019, p. 10-11) *Op. Cit n.1.*

8   The European Commission cleared this acquisition in October 2014, but in 2017 fined Facebook for providing misleading information to the Commission on the ability to "link" Facebook and WhatsApp data. See European Commission (2017) "Mergers: Commission fines Facebook €110 million for providing misleading information about WhatsApp takeover," Press Release, Brussels, May 18.

9   The ACCC opposed the acquisition and it did not proceed. See ACCC (2012) "ACCC to oppose Carsales acquisition of Trading Post," Canberra, December 20.

II.   BACKGROUND – THE MERGER CLEARANCE PROCESS

While the specific wording of merger laws differs between countries, the process of analyzing the competitive effects of a merger are similar, and can be summarized in four steps:

- Notification of the acquisition to the competition authorities. In some countries, it must also be determined whether competition authorities have jurisdiction to intervene in the transaction.

- Determination of the relevant market or markets impacted by the transaction (market definition);

- Identification of any potential theories of harm that could arise due to the merger; and

- Analysis of the size and probability of any competitive harm that could arise due to the merger (relative to the "counterfactual" situation(s) where the acquisition does not occur).

If a competition authority determines that a merger would, or is likely to, lessen competition beyond the relevant legal threshold, then it may, depending on the legal structure in its country, engage with the merger parties to see if there are any "remedies" or "undertakings" that the merger parties can put forward in order to offset the anti-competitive effects of the merger. Such remedies may be structural, for example where the merging parties agree to divest certain assets. Or the competition authorities may accept behavioral remedies, where the merging parties agree to engage in certain conduct into the future, such as submitting to price regulation.

If the competition authority considers that the competitive harms of the merger exceed the relevant legal threshold, regardless of any proffered remedies, then it will oppose the merger. The decision of the competition authority will usually be subject to appeal to the courts. In this sense, the legal precedent established by the courts will, at a minimum, guide the decisions of the competition authority and, in many situations, will effectively bind the competition authority.

III.   NOTIFICATION AND JURISDICTION

Most countries have notification criteria which, if met, require that merging parties inform the competition authorities in advance of an acquisition.

For example, in the U.S., the Federal Trade Commission ("FTC") updates the (Hart-Scott-Rodino) notification thresholds each year in line with the growth in the size of the U.S. economy. For 2020, this meant that transactions exceeding $94m had to be reported to the FTC.[10] The merging parties are then subject to a waiting period before they can "consummate the deal."[11]

Regardless, the competition authorities in the U.S. can legally oppose an acquisition whether or not it meets the notification threshold. Such a broad jurisdiction does not apply to all competition authorities. For some competition authorities, the jurisdiction to oppose an acquisition may also depend on legal thresholds. In the EU, the coverage of the European Union Merger Regulation ("EUMR") depends on the combined turnover of the merging entities.[12] Similarly, in the UK, the Competition and Markets Authority ("CMA") can only intervene in acquisitions that meet jurisdictional thresholds based on either the target's UK turnover or combined sales or purchases.[13]

In contrast, Australia has no formal notification or jurisdictional threshold. Businesses have no legal obligation to inform the Australian Competition and Consumer Commission ("ACCC") about a merger.[14] The ACCC, however, may oppose any acquisition that it considers will, or is likely to, substantially lessen competition, regardless of the size of the relevant businesses.

There has been concern that existing merger thresholds in some jurisdictions, such as the UK and the EU, may fail to "catch" acquisitions by a digital platform of a small start-up that, while currently under the reporting threshold, has the potential to grow into a viable long-term competitor.

The concern covers both notification and jurisdiction. For notification, the concern is that a potentially anticompetitive acquisition may not be subject to timely scrutiny because it is not brought to the attention of the authorities. For example, when Grab acquired the operations and assets of Uber in South-East Asia, "[t]he parties did not notify the competition agencies in the countries involved because the transaction did not meet the mandatory notification thresholds or because there was

---

10   See https://www.ftc.gov/news-events/blogs/competition-matters/2020/01/hsr-threshold-adjustments-reportability-2020 for details.

11   See https://www.ftc.gov/tips-advice/competition-guidance/guide-antitrust-laws/mergers/premerger-notification-merger-review for details.

12   The thresholds are set out in article 1(2) and 1(3) of the EUMR.

13   Competition and Markets Authority (2014) "Mergers: Guidance on the CMA's jurisdiction and procedure" CMA2, January, at paragraph 4.3. Formally there is no legal requirement on parties to notify the CMA of an acquisition, even if it meets the jurisdictional thresholds.

14   Australian Competition and Consumer Commission (2008, amended 2017) *Merger Guidelines* Canberra, November, at paragraph 1.7.

no merger notification requirement, for example in Singapore."[15] This concern is reflected in the ACCC's view that "it is critical to establish processes that ensure the ACCC is notified early of potential acquisitions" by large digital platforms.[16]

For jurisdiction, the concern is that, in relevant countries, competition authorities may be unable to prevent an anti-competitive acquisition by a digital platform because the jurisdictional thresholds may not be met. For example, Cremer *et. al.*, in their work for the European Commission, note that "the acquisition of start-ups which still have very low turnover … may not be "caught" by traditional merger control."[17]

Concerns about jurisdictional thresholds, however, appear to be a solution searching for a problem – at least when applied to large digital platforms.

Most mergers involving large digital platforms that are likely to raise competition concerns will involve businesses that operate over multiple jurisdictions. This means that relevant mergers will usually come under the jurisdiction of *some* competition authority. This includes the U.S., where there are no jurisdictional thresholds, and the EU, where different thresholds between countries can see a relevant merger referred to the European Commission by a member country.[18] For example, the acquisition of Shazam by Apple and the acquisition of WhatsApp by Facebook, did not meet the EUMR jurisdictional thresholds. However, these acquisitions were analyzed by the European Commission after referral by the Spanish authorities, who have jurisdictional thresholds based on market share or turnover. Indeed, it is difficult to identify relevant mergers, including those that might be viewed as "problematic" in hindsight, which would not have fallen under the jurisdiction of *any* relevant competition authority. For example, while the acquisition of Instagram by Facebook fell outside the EUMR thresholds, it was analyzed by the UK's CMA. The CMA's decision not to intervene to prevent the merger has been criticized with hindsight.[19] But this is an issue of competition authority competence, not jurisdictional thresholds.

Even where a digital platform merger may only involve one or two countries and the competition authorities in those countries are constrained by jurisdictional

---

15   UNCTAD Secretariat (2019) "Competition issues in the digital economy" Note for 18th session of the Trade and Development Board, Intergovernmental group of experts on competition law and policy, United Nations Conference on Trade and Development, Geneva, July 10-12, at page 10.

16   Australian Competition and Consumer Commission (2019) "Digital platforms inquiry: Final report" Canberra, June at p.110. See also Recommendation 2.

17   Cremer, J., Y-A de Montjoye & H Schweitzer (2019) "Competition policy for the digital era: Final report," European Commission, Brussels, at p. 110. At p. 115, they note that neither the Facebook/Instagram merger or the Google/Waze merger met the EU jurisdictional thresholds and were not considered by the European Commission.

18   Cremer *et. al. Op. Cit n.17* at pp. 113-116.

19   Argentesi, *et. al. Op. Cit n.2.* at pp. 20-28.

thresholds, those thresholds may be "flexible" and "open to interpretation." For example, the UK's Digital Competition Expert Panel noted the CMA's view that the current "share of supply" test for jurisdiction "is characterised by a considerable degree of flexibility."[20] Put simply, if a competition authority really considers that it should investigate a particular acquisition then it usually will.

Notification thresholds raise slightly different issues. Competition authorities have faced situations where they only find out about a potentially anti-competitive acquisition after it has been consummated, such as the Uber-Grab merger noted above. This is a problem if there is a significant lessening of competition. Once a merger has occurred, it may be difficult, if not impossible, to "unscramble the egg" and return competition to the pre-merger state.

That said, the failure to notify competition authorities of potentially anti-competitive mergers is not limited to acquisitions by large digital platforms. For example, in July 2018 the New Zealand Commerce Commission announced that it had commenced proceedings over a completed merger involving car parks. It had not been notified of the acquisition.[21]

The real question is whether digital platform mergers have particular features that make *ex post* merger enforcement less viable, so that they should be subject to different notification thresholds to other industries.

Once a merger is completed, it can take considerable time for systems (including IT systems), capital and workers to become integrated. There is often a significant window where a competition authority can act, for example, by seeking a ruling from a court to prevent further integration of the merging parties and, if necessary, requiring that the acquisition be unwound.

In contrast, mergers that involve data and intellectual capital may be significantly more difficult to "unscramble." It can take only a matter of seconds for merged entities to share software, product designs or customer lists. Once this is done, it can be difficult, if not impossible, for a court or competition authority to order that the merging parties return to their original competitive states. In such situations it can be reasonable to require that competition authorities are notified of a potential acquisition before it is completed.

A number of competition authorities and commentators appear to believe that this is the case for acquisitions involving digital platforms. For example, the UK

---

20   Digital Competition Expert Panel (2019) "Unlocking digital competition" (the Furman report) Report to the UK government, March, at paragraph 3.64.

21   See Commerce Commission (2018) "Proceedings filed against Wilson Parking over acquisition of Wellington car park," Media Release, Wellington, July 20.

Digital Competition Expert Panel recommended that "[d]igital companies that have been designated with a strategic market status should be required to make the CMA aware of all intended acquisitions."[22] Similarly the Australian government recently announced that "[l]arge digital platforms [are] to work with the ACCC to develop a voluntary notification protocol."[23]

These digital platform specific approaches, however, have two problems.

First, expanding notification thresholds, even for one group of companies, is not costless. These costs are not theoretical. Indeed, the recent draft *Act on Digitisation of German Competition Law* will double one of the domestic turnover thresholds that is required for merger notification. The aim is to reduce the number of notified mergers – and hence the workload of the German Federal Cartel Office ("FCO") – by approximately 20 percent. Overall, the changes to the German merger regime will allow the FCO to apply a more detailed competition analysis to fewer mergers.

By contrast, it is far from clear that those calling for broader notification thresholds have carried out the cost-benefit analysis needed to justify such changes.

Second, it is far from clear that digital platform mergers generally satisfy the criteria for enhanced notification. Indeed, some other areas involving data and intellectual property, such as pharmaceuticals, may raise greater concerns about unnotified acquisitions. While digital platform mergers may involve data integration and transfer, it is far from clear that this can occur quickly (e.g. Facebook and WhatsApp). Further, the acquisition of small start-ups may involve long periods to integrate software or may even involve the applications operating side-by-side over the long term (e.g. Google and Waze). In either case, there is adequate time for competition authorities to intervene once the acquisition is public, even if it has been completed.

In summary, there is a real issue of unnotified acquisitions when integration and value transfer between the merged entities can occur quickly. But the blanket tightening of notification thresholds only for digital platform mergers may impose excessive costs on competition agencies while failing to address the underlying problem.

IV.   MARKET DEFINITION AND COMPETITIVE INFERENCE

From one perspective, market definition should be a relatively innocuous part of merger analysis. Under this view, the role of market definition is to highlight relevant competitive constraints on the merged entity. For example, for a horizontal

---

22   *Op. Cit n.20*, Recommended action 8.

23   Commonwealth of Australia (2019) "Regulating in the digital age: Government response and implementation roadmap for the Digital Platforms Inquiry," Canberra, December 12 at p. 15.

merger, what are the substitute products that consumers can turn to if the merged entity seeks a small but significant and non-transitory increase in prices? Market definition, under this approach, is a way of focusing the competitive analysis but does not replace this analysis. It is not definitive of the impacts of a merger on competition and often it is unnecessary to precisely define a unique market for competition analysis. Broadly speaking, this is the approach taken under Australian competition law.[24]

Alternatively, market definition may be used as a tool of inference in merger analysis. For example, market shares – which necessarily depend on the definition of the relevant market – may be used to infer market power. In this situation, market definition can have significant legal implications. In the U.S., following the court decision in *United States v. Philadelphia*

National Bank,[25] high market shares for the merging businesses are used to shift the burden of proof onto those businesses. Market definition is also relevant in the analysis of any merger efficiencies by competition agencies in the U.S. In general, to be relevant to any competition analysis in a market, the efficiencies must arise in the same market as the anticompetitive effect.[26] This is a critical issue for digital platforms where there are multi-sided interactions and benefits can arise on one-side of the platform that might offset anticompetitive harm on another side of the platform.[27]

There has been considerable debate about whether it is appropriate to use structural presumptions based on market definition.[28] Indeed, some authors have questioned whether such inferences make logical sense or, indeed, whether market definition is even required for merger analysis.[29]

As a matter of economics, inferring the competitive effects of a merger from the definition of the relevant market is fraught. There are no simple short-cuts to

---

24   See Australian Competition and Consumer Commission (2008, amended 2017) *Op. Cit. n.14* at paragraphs 4.1-4.4.

25   374 U.S. 321 (1963).

26   See U.S. Department of Justice and the Federal Trade Commission (2010) "Horizontal merger guidelines" Washington D.C., August 19, at footnote 14.

27   While not a merger case, this issue was central to the 2018 decision of the US Supreme Court in *Ohio, et al., Petitioners v. American Express Company, et al.* In this case, restrictions on the "merchant side" of the platform led to a loss for merchants but there was a simultaneous gain to participants on the "consumer side" of the platform. The majority decision was that there was a single market that covered both merchants and consumers.

28   For a recent defense of this approach, see H. Hovenkamp & C. Shapiro (2018) "Horizontal Mergers, Market Structure, and Burdens of Proof," Yale Law Journal, 127(7), 1742-2203.

29   For example, see L Kaplow, (2015) "Market definition, market power," National Bureau of Economic Research Working Paper 21167, May; and L Kaplow (2010) "Why (ever) define markets?," Harvard Law Review, 124, 437-517.

competitive analysis. Inferring competitive impact from, say, market shares may sometimes help to winnow mergers that are *unlikely* to be anti-competitive. In this sense, using (rough) market shares may be a useful screening device for competition agencies. However, once a merger is subject to competition analysis, market shares, at best, are simply a small part of the relevant information that is required. More broadly, market definition can help to inform competition analysis by focusing on relevant products and theories of harm, but it can do no more than this.

When inference from market definition has significant legal implications, as in the U.S., merger analysis can become centered on market definition rather than focusing on competition analysis. The definition of a "specific market" can become central to the analysis and market definition can gain a degree of importance far beyond simply establishing "the relevant 'field of inquiry' for merger analysis."[30]

The problems of competitive inference from market definition are heightened by large multi-sided digital platforms. For example:

> for multi-sided platforms, the product that a platform provides to one side of the market does not compete with the product it provides to another side. ... [T]he question of how many markets to define cannot be answered within a market definition exercise ...[31]

Indeed, where the complexities of defining relevant markets for digital platforms are significant, the OECD notes that "[t]he first best solution ... would be to leave the market undefined."[32] Of course, this is not possible where the legal structure means that the relevant market is used as a tool to infer the competitive effects of a merger. In such situations, markets may be defined poorly, leading to incorrect inferences and erroneous merger decisions.

For the U.S., there are two potential solutions. The first would be to retain the use of competitive inferences from market definition for most mergers, but explicitly not to apply such inferences to digital platforms. The alternative would be to reduce the role of market definition by limiting, in all merger analysis, the competitive inferences that competition authorities and courts can draw from the relevantly defined markets. The former is unlikely to be workable. It would lead to significant debate about whether a merger was or was not covered by "competitive inference." The latter would require either formal legislative change or high-level court decisions that overturn long standing legal precedent.

---

30 Australian Competition and Consumer Commission (2008, amended 2017) *Op. Cit. n.14* at paragraph 4.1.

31 Directorate for financial and enterprise affairs (Competition committee) (2017) "Hearing on rethinking the use of traditional antitrust enforcement tools in multi-sided markets," Organisation for Economic Co-operation and Development, Paris, 22 June, chapter 1 at p. 5.

32 *Ibid.* at pp. 8-9.

Unfortunately, some suggested approaches to digital platform mergers in the U.S. appear to reinforce, rather than reduce, the role of "competitive inference." For example:

> Mergers between dominant firms and substantial competitors or uniquely likely future competitors should be presumed to be unlawful, subject to rebuttal by defendants. This presumption would be valuable, not because it would identify anticompetitive mergers with precision, but because it would shift the burden to the party with the best access to relevant information on issues of competitive effects and efficiencies from the merger.[33]

This recommendation takes the process of inference well beyond market definition. If implemented, it would see merger analysis for digital platforms dominated by esoteric and often irrelevant debate about whether or not the platform was dominant (which would rest on market definition) and whether the business to be acquired was somehow "uniquely" placed. Rather than focusing on competitive analysis, which should be at the heart of the merger decision, it would focus on particular aspects of the merger that may or may not be important.

Fortunately, outside the U.S., the problem of competitive inference is less serious.[34] In general, if competition agencies take the lead and reduce their reliance on competitive inference from market definition, for example in their merger guidelines, then this will refocus merger analysis. Academic debates about whether or not the sides of a digital platform are in the same or different markets will continue. But if both competition authorities and the courts make it clear that these questions are largely irrelevant for competition analysis, then the problem of inappropriate competitive inference from market definition will disappear.

V. THEORIES OF HARM AND DIGITAL PLATFORM MERGERS

Determining whether or not a merger will, or is likely to, substantially lessen competition depends on the theories of harm that apply to the merger.

The growth of digital platforms means that existing theories of harm will often need to be modified to allow for the specific economics of platforms. For example, if a market can "tip" to monopoly once a platform reaches a specific size, then a horizontal aggregation that may raise few concerns in a "standard" market, may raise

---

33 Stigler Committee on Digital Platforms (2019) "Final report" Stigler Center for the Study of the Economy and the State, Booth School, University of Chicago, Chicago at p. 98.

34 That said, "[t]he ACCC considers it may be worthwhile to consider whether a rebuttable presumption should also apply, in some form, to merger cases in Australia." Australian Competition and Consumer Commission (2019) *Op. Cit. n.16* at p. 109.

considerable competition risk when it involves digital platforms. Digital platforms may also raise unique theories of harm. For example, the importance of data and the commonality of zero (monetary) prices may raise competition concerns that are absent from most other mergers.[35]

Many of these potential theories of harm are being actively researched in economics.[36] In this sense, legal analysis of digital platform mergers under competition law will often depend on cutting edge, and potentially controversial, economic research. The interaction between competition research and competition law, however, is not new. Indeed, the symbiotic relationship between competition research and competition cases has a long and productive history.[37] While the emergence of digital platforms has led to a new path for this research, the need for competition authorities and the courts to be kept up to date on this research is not new.

In some countries, however, there is a view that the courts are "falling behind" and that this is leading to under-enforcement of competition rules and incorrect judgements. For example, in the U.S., the Stigler Committee on Digital Platforms argued that "[a]pparent under-enforcement is in part due to courts' reliance on so-called Chicago School assumptions that do not have a sound theoretical or empirical basis."[38] When commenting on the American Express decision by the Supreme Court, the Committee stated that:

> … [T] he case does suggest that the five-Justice majority on the Court is hostile to antitrust enforcement (at least in vertical and exclusion cases), does not understand multi-sided markets very well, and might be more influenced by ideological preconceptions than by evidence in the case or fact-finding by district court judges.[39]

---

35   For example, see UNCTAD Secretariat (2019) "Competition issues in the digital economy" Note for 18th session of the Trade and Development Board, Intergovernmental group of experts on competition law and policy, United Nations Conference on Trade and Development, Geneva, July 10-12, at paragraph 18.

36   For example, C. Choe, S. King & N. Matsushima (2018) "Pricing with Cookies: Behavior-Based Price Discrimination and Spatial Competition," Management Science, 64(12), 5461-5959, considers how data can alter pricing decisions by competitors. For an economic analysis of zero pricing, see J. Gans, (2020) "The Specialness of Zero," (January 14) available at http://dx.doi.org/10.2139/ssrn.3486964.

37   Indeed, most modern economics texts on Industrial Organization are dominated by issues of competitive harm such as tying, bundling, integration and the like.

38   Stigler Committee on Digital Platforms (2019) *Op. Cit n.33* at p. 64.

39   *Ibid.* at p. 70.

While less direct, the ACCC has noted that:

> [t]he ACCC is increasingly concerned about the hurdles it faces in opposing anticompetitive mergers in court, and these hurdles are likely to be even greater in digital markets where market dynamics are particularly fast-moving and predicting the future direction is more challenging. … Recent cases … suggest that there can be undue confidence placed by the [Australian Competition] Tribunal and the courts in the ability of market forces or behavioural commitments to overcome increased barriers caused by an acquisition – a view which the ACCC does not always share.[40]

The Stigler Committee note that one way to overcome this problem is to establish a specialized antitrust court.[41] An alternative approach, used in New Zealand, is to have an independent competition economist employed by the Court to assist the judge. The use of such "lay members" has been an effective way to ensure that the court is able to deal with the complex economic evidence presented to it.[42]

VI. WHEN IS A SUBSTANTIAL LESSENING OF COMPETITION "LIKELY"?

Competition analysis of a merger is predictive. It requires the authorities to consider what will happen in the future in the relevant market(s) both with and without the acquisition that is being analyzed.[43] Competition authorities do not have "crystal balls" that allow them to predict the future, so competition analysis – comparing multiple uncertain future scenarios – can be controversial. While this is not unique to mergers involving digital platforms, the level of innovation, fast-moving nature of the relevant markets, and the uncertainties about how competition will develop over time, mean that the difficulties of competitive analysis are magnified for digital platforms.

For example, Argentesi *et. al.* (2019) systematically reviewed the merger decisions of the UK Office of Fair Trade ("OFT") for the acquisition of Instagram by Facebook and the acquisition of Waze by Google. The authors note "a number of gaps in the Authorities' assessment of the *Facebook/Instagram* merger."[44] Many of these relate to the competition analysis and whether or not Instagram would have emerged

---

40 Australian Competition and Consumer Commission (2019) *Op. Cit. n.16* at p. 108.

41 Stigler Committee on Digital Platforms (2019) *Op. Cit. n.33* at p. 78.

42 For details, see https://www.courtsofnz.govt.nz/the-courts/high-court/cases-to-court/#lay-members-of-the-high-court.

43 The analysis of what will occur in the market without the acquisition is sometimes called "counterfactual" analysis.

44 *Op. Cit n.2* at p. 26.

as a viable social-network competitor to Facebook absent the acquisition. However, at the time of the acquisition, it would have been difficult, if not impossible, to determine whether Instagram, which was one of many "mobile photo applications," was uniquely placed to challenge Facebook as a social network. In hindsight, specific characteristics of Instagram can be highlighted and compared to the characteristics of other potential social-network competitors. But competition authorities do not have the benefit of hindsight.

The *Facebook/Instagram* merger illustrates the problem of changing merger laws to prevent large digital platforms from acquiring start-ups that might be future potential competitors. It is difficult, if not impossible, to predict, in advance, whether or not a particular start-up, absent a take-over, is likely to be a competitive rival for a large digital platform.

Nonetheless, some parties have called on competition authorities to be given more power to pursue such acquisitions.[45]

Given the difficulties, competition authorities, understandably, can be cautious in predicting the future success of a relatively small company such as Instagram. However, the degree of confidence that a regulator requires in order to prevent an acquisition also depends on legislative constraints and legal precedent. Simply showing that an acquisition would possibly result in a substantial lessening of competition is generally not enough to rule that acquisition unlawful. Rather the competition authorities must show that the probability of the substantial lessening of competition actually arising is high enough to pass a legal hurdle.

The relevant hurdle differs between jurisdictions. For example, in the UK, "[i]n order to block a merger, the CMA must conclude that there will be, on the balance of probabilities, a substantial lessening of competition. In other words, it must find that a substantial lessening of competition is more likely than not."[46]

This is a higher benchmark than in the U.S. The Clayton Act makes illegal a merger where the effect may be substantially to lessen competition or to tend to create a monopoly. "Congress settled on "may be" to mean "reasonable probability" of anticompetitive effects."[47]

---

45 For example, see H. Schweitzer, J. Haucap, W. Kerber & R. Welker, Robert, (2018) "Modernising the Law on Abuse of Market Power: Report for the Federal Ministry for Economic Affairs and Energy (Germany)," September 17 available at http://dx.doi.org/10.2139/ssrn.3250742 at pp. 4-5.

46 Digital Competition Expert Panel (2019) *Op. Cit. n.19*, at paragraph 3.80.

47 Feinstein, D. (2014) "The Clayton Act: 100 years and counting," Bureau of Competition, Federal Trade Commission, October 15, available at https://www.ftc.gov/news-events/blogs/competition-matters/2014/10/clayton-act-100-years-counting.

In Australia, it is unclear exactly how "likely" a substantial lessening of competition needs to be before it can be considered by the Courts.[48] One view is that, like in the UK, a merger is only illegal if it is "more likely than not" to substantially lessen competition.[49] In contrast, legal precedent in New Zealand goes further than the U.S. and makes clear even a 30 percent (but possibly lower) chance of the merger substantially reducing competition compared to the situation without the merger is sufficient to make the merger illegal.[50]

Having to show that a substantial lessening of competition due to a merger is "more likely than not" sets a high bar for merger enforcement. It downplays the uncertainty associated with forward looking merger analysis and is a likely source of considerable under-enforcement. It also fails to recognize the asymmetric nature of mergers. A merger will only be pursued if the acquiring firm believes that it will be profitable. Often, a significant source of an increase in profitability is market power created by the merger. This market power will be antithetical to competition and usually against the interests of consumers.

This does not mean that all mergers are anti-competitive. Rather, it means that the simple fact that a merger is pursued by a large digital platform (or any other large business) should raise the possibility of competitive harm. This possibility can be offset by the evidence. But the "starting point" for merger analysis should be "weighted" towards a finding of competitive harm. Requiring that a merger be "more likely than not" to lessen competition based on the information and evidence gathered during a merger investigation, sets the bar too high.

In summary, merger enforcement in general, as well as for large digital platforms, would be improved if the courts and competition authorities used a more sophisticated approach to the probability of harm. This approach indicates that requiring competition authorities to show that a substantial lessening of competition is "more likely than not" will tend to allow anti-competitive mergers to proceed.

It is also important for competition authorities and the courts to appropriately deal with the uncertainties that can arise *absent* a merger. The "counterfactual" to a merger may be the *status quo*, but this is unlikely to be the case in many rapidly evolving digital platform markets. Rather, the exact way that a market will evolve absent a particular acquisition will be unclear. In general, there will be multiple specific alternative futures that can play out. Some of these may imply that the merger raises

---

48   For example, see Australian Competition and Consumer Commission (2011) "ACCC responds to Metcash decision" Release NR 228/11, December 5.

49   See S. Chubb & C. Cadd (2011) "Why the Metcash case will continue to trouble the ACCC," Herbert Smith Freehill LLP, December 16, available at https://www.lexology.com/library/detail.aspx?g=30157ce6-4d20-4de5-83bd-1dc89caa58de.

50   See *Woolworths Ltd v. Commerce Commission* (2008) 8 NZBLC 102.

competitive concerns (i.e. the merger will lead to a significant loss of competition compared to the specific alternative future). Others may not. But the issue before competition authorities and the courts is not to identify each counterfactual in detail. Nor is it to come up with a single alternative future that is both likely and leads to a substantial lessening of competition.

The aim of competitive analysis is to determine whether the acquisition, is likely (or more likely than not) to be anti-competitive. This implies that authorities should focus on the overall probability of a substantial lessening of competition rather than the likelihood of specific alternative counterfactuals in order to avoid downplaying the potential for competitive harm.

For example, suppose that competition authorities identify four alternative anti-competitive situations that may arise in the relevant market absent the acquisition. Individually, each of these situations may not be "likely." But the relevant question is whether absent the merger a substantial lessening of competition is likely (or more likely than not). This means that the authorities should focus on the overall probability of *any* of the four alternative anti-competitive situations arising. The fact that each does not individually meet the threshold of "likely" is irrelevant.

Similarly, if each of the anti-competitive situations fits into a broad category of harm, detailed individual analysis of each situation may be unnecessary or counterproductive. For example, if a business is not acquired by a large digital platform then it may be acquired by some other business that does not raise anti-competitive concerns. In general, it will not be necessary to identify the exact potential buyers and their likelihood of purchase. This detail will be irrelevant to the core question of competitive harm. What matters are broad questions. Absent the current merger, will the relevant business continue to grow and become a potential competitor in the future? Or, absent the merger, will the relevant business need to be acquired by another party to prosper and, if so, what is the likelihood of a future pro-competitive acquisition?

This approach differs from the "balance of harms" approach advocated by the UK's Digital Competition Expert Panel.[51] The Panel's approach would "weigh up both the likelihood and the magnitude of the merger. This would mean mergers being blocked when they are expected to do more harm than good."[52] Similarly it differs from an "error-cost" approach.[53] Both of these approaches require significant specificity on explicit counterfactual futures, as they require both an evaluation of the likelihood of a particular alternative future and a quantification of the level of harm that will arise if the merger proceeds, relative to that future. In my opinion, such

---

51 *Op. Cit. n.20* at paragraphs 3.88 – 3.108.

52 *Ibid.* at paragraph 3.88.

53 For a summary of this approach, see *Op. Cit. n.17* at p. 50.

specificity will rarely if ever be available. Implementing either a "balance of harms" or an "error-cost" approach to merger evaluation would simply focus the attention on an unattainable level of detail.

In contrast, I consider that there needs to be two clear reforms. First, the threshold for merger analysis should not be too high. The competition test should be whether or not there is a real chance or a reasonable likelihood that an acquisition will substantially lessen competition. Countries that require that the authorities to meet a "more likely than not" threshold face too high a hurdle. Second, the legal test should focus on whether a substantial lessening of competition *overall* is likely to occur. Authorities should avoid trying to focus on a level of detail – for both likelihood and harm – in competition analysis that, at best, will obscure the underlying competition questions and, at worst, will lead to incorrect decisions based on misplaced confidence.[54]

VII. CONCLUSION

Many of the competition issues raised by digital platform mergers are novel. However, this does not mean that existing competition laws are unable to deal with these new challenges. Indeed, the bottom line from the quick review of merger issues presented in this chapter is simple: Good merger review legislation and practices are more than capable of dealing with the competition concerns raised by mergers and acquisitions by large digital platforms.

Where change is needed, those changes are not unique to digital platforms. The issues raised by these platforms have been raised by other rapidly innovating, fast growing industries in the past. This means that specific "digital platform laws" should be avoided.

For example, notification thresholds may need to be re-examined to ensure that competition authorities have the time and resources to focus on the most important mergers. But this may involve raising those thresholds, as in Germany, rather than lowering them.

Similarly, using market shares or other "quick and easy" shortcuts, for example, to alter the burden of proof in merger analysis, is likely to derail serious merger analysis. Rather than focusing on competitive effects, merger analysis can be led down esoteric and ultimately unproductive discussions on the specifics of market definition or the determination of whether a takeover target is or is not "unique." However, this is already a problem in some countries such as the U.S. Digital plat-

---

54 In this sense, I agree with Cremer *et. al.* who "propose that competition law should not try to work with the error cost framework case-by-case, but rather should try to translate general insights into legal tests" (*Ibid.* at p. 51).

form mergers highlight the unproductive nature of such shortcuts and indicate that they should be avoided.

While digital platform mergers raise novel forms of competitive harm, merger laws are generally flexible enough to deal with these issues. There may be an issue of capability in some countries, either with the merger authorities or the courts. However, the key for effective merger enforcement is not to set the burden of proof too high for competition authorities. Merger investigations are prospective. They consider potential future states of the market and any merger decision will necessarily shape the future of the market. Requiring merger authorities to prove that a merger is more likely than not to significantly reduce competition allows too many anti-competitive mergers to proceed.

Vertical Restraints in Digital Markets: The *Google* Case in Brazil

By Alexandre Cordeiro Macedo [1]

Abstract

Due to constant growth and a strong tendency towards concentration and dominant market positions, the digital economy is appearing more and more on the radar of antitrust agencies around the world, which, since the first cases, have been confronted with significant challenges. The digital economy is characterized by rapid change, constant innovation, and an increased level of interdependence between its participants. This any regulation authority to acquire technical knowledge as well as cautious and well-considered proceedings, given that a premature intervention can cause vast consequences. Relatively new concepts have to be taken into account, like multiple-sided markets, network effects, and new forms of profit making, so instruments and concepts that function in the traditional economy need to be adjusted. The present article describes some of these challenges, as demonstrated in the recent Google Shopping case - the first unilateral conduct case in the digital economy investigated by Brazil's antitrust authority, CADE, which dealt with allegations concerning discrimination against competitors on Google's search results pages.

I.   CONTEXT

Few issues are more controversial in the field of antitrust prosecution than the treatment of digital markets by regulatory bodies. Since the emergence of the first tech giants in the computer industry – Apple, Microsoft, and IBM, in the 1960s and

---

1   Alexandre Cordeiro Macedo is the current General Superintendent and Former Commissioner of Cade. He has two degrees in Law and Economics. He holds a Master's degree in Constitutional Law from the Law School of Brasilia/IDP and a postgraduate degree in Administrative Procedure from the University of Brasília. He is a Visiting Scholar at the Antonin Scalia Law School - George Mason University in Washington-DC. He has been a career auditor of the Union's General Comptroller Office since 2006, where he was an advisor and chief of staff of the Union's General Comptroller. He is former Vice-minister of the Cities in Brazil. He is a professor of Competition Law, Compliance at the Law School of Brasília/IDP. He is a visiting professor at the University of Brasilia- UNB, University of Campinas-Unicamp/SP, Federal University of Rio Grande do Sul, Law School of Vitória - FDV. He is the organizer and author of the book, Special Topics of Competition Law, published by Editora Cedes. Author of several articles in books, magazines and newspapers. Lecturer at various events and universities in Brazil and abroad, such as Harvard Law School – Cambridge, Northwestern University - Chicago, American Bar Association - ABA, International Bar Association - IBA, International Competition Network - ICN, Global Competition Review – GCR and Concurrence.

1970s – the market's tendency to concentrate and form monopolies due to network[2] or intellectual property effects,[3] with the subsequent abuse of dominant position through unilateral conduct in some cases has drawn the attention of the US antitrust institutions. Due to the global growth and impact of these companies as well as the rise of new business models and big players on the digital economy, this trend reached antitrust institutions worldwide, just like in Brazil.

However, because of the unique design of digital markets, they create some challenges and important questions for regulation authorities. First of all, the digital economy is characterized by an unprecedented velocity of innovation cycles and high-pitched competition in the fight for market penetration and consumer attention, leading to highly dynamic markets with the appearance of new and disruptive technical solutions and the emergence and disappearance of big players in no time. Consequently, standard investigation patterns for traditional industries, broadly examined by economic literature, cannot be applied to cases in this market environment.

The present chapter analyzes the implication of these market specificities for antitrust investigations, based on the 2019 case E-Commerce Media Group *Informação e Tecnologia Ltda. v. Google Inc. e Google Brasil Internet Ltda.*[4] First, it outlines the basic circumstances of the case. Then, it examines the challenges, difficulties and diversities of evaluation during the investigation phase. Finally, it presents the answers and motivations given by the different votes of the final judgment.

II. BACKGROUND OF THE CASE

In 2011, the Brazilian *E-Commerce Media Group*, owner of the price comparison websites *Buscapé* and *Bondfaro*, filed an action against *Google Brazil*, accusing the latter of granting its own price comparing system, Google Shopping, a privileged position on the top of Google's Search Engine Results Page ("SERP"). This would allegedly harm the plaintiff by deteriorating its market position in terms of audience, number of clicks and return, thus causing higher prices for the consumer. In an amendment to its complaint, in 2013 the plaintiff charged Google with using data from competitors' web pages to boost traffic to its own pages (a practice called "scraping"). CADE´s Superintendence decided to create a separate investigation to analyze this alleged conduct. Google rejected the accusations in question, alleging that the

---

2   VAN GORP, Nicolai; HONNEFELDER, Stephanie. Challenges for Competition Policy in the Digitalized Economy. Communications & Strategies, Montpellier, Ed. 99, 3rd quarter 2015, pp. 149-162,191-192: "(…) *digital markets have a tendency to tip into a winner-takes-all outcome due to network effects.*"

3   POSNER, Richard A. Antitrust in the New Economy. John M. Olin Program in Law and Economics, Chicago, Working Paper No. 106, 2000, p. 3-4.

4   CADE. Administrative Process nº 08012.010483/2011-94. Plaintiff: E-Commerce Media Group Informação e Tecnologia Ltda. Defendant: Google Inc. e Google Brasil Internet Ltda.

prominent position of Google Shopping on the SERP was an innovation that benefitted the consumer and did not violate any competition rules.

For a better understanding of the case, it is necessary to comprehend the functioning of online search engines and the landscape of the online product search and price comparison market.

A. The Mechanics of Search Engines

With the popularization of the world wide web, search engines emerged to allow users easier user access to information available on websites. These engines allow access to websites even when the user does not know its domain name or even of its existence. Initially, two different search models emerged: search directories (also called "ranked lists") and search engines or tools ("query-based tools").

Unlike search directories, search engines do not display links in a predefined list: they work in response to free queries made by users. This is the case of Google's search engine, which displays responses to users using a threefold process: First, automated software (crawlers or spiders) visit websites on the web, generally by navigating through links to sites that have been visited before, or for which a "visit" has been requested by a site administrator; then the information from the visited page is saved in a Google index; finally, when a user makes a search query, search engine algorithms select the pages with the most appropriate content as a search response and rank them in a Search Engine Results Page ("SERP").

Nowadays, Google is the undisputed leader in search in many western countries. Basically, it is a tool that emerged in 1998 amid the various search engines created at the time. Its success, however, is attributed to a differentiated algorithm for page ranking, called PageRank.[5] Inspired by academic citation practices, PageRank attaches greater importance to sites that are referenced by other sites. This system was already used by other search engines, but Google improved it differently. Among the innovations implemented in the tool is the greater importance the algorithm attributes to referrals by websites that are frequently referenced themselves.[6] In addition, Google's own indexing was innovative: The tool was able to store not only textual information about pages, but also information about text placement, font, capitalization, etc. The text of a link is also indexed as indicative of the content of the page to which it links.[7]

---

5 Seymour, T., Frantsvog, D., & Kumar, S. (2011). History Of Search Engines. *International Journal of Management & Information Systems (IJMIS)*, 15(4), 47-58. https://doi.org/10.19030/ijmis.v15i4.5799.

6 PAGE, Lawrence et al. The PageRank citation ranking: Bringing order to the web. Stanford InfoLab, 1999.

7 BRIN, Sergey; PAGE, Lawrence. The anatomy of a large-scale hypertextual web search engine. Computer networks and ISDN systems, v. 30, n. 1-7, p. 107-117, 1998.

Google currently uses over 200 factors to rank sites in response to a search query. This search service, which is offered by Google for free, is called organic search. Factors and their importance are constantly changing and, according to testimony made in the context of the case, with hundreds of changes in the algorithm per year.[8]

The demand for techniques to adjust websites to meet criteria that guarantee a good ranking in Google's search pages has given rise to the provision of SEO – search engine optimization services.[9] Any company willing to increase its brand awareness and scope via online marketing has the opportunity to do so by augmenting their webpage's conformity with Google's algorithms, with the purpose of entering the potential customer's field of vision through an appearance on a top position on the results page.

B. Google Ads

Despite its widely known function as a free online research tool, Google's main source of revenue is its ad business.[10] Among Google's oldest ad business is Google AdWords, which inserts "sponsored links" (also referred to as "sponsored search") into the SERP presented to the searcher.[11] Any firm can participate in an auction and bid for specific keywords, so that its website will appear in some designated area in the interface of Google's SERP, when a user executes a search query employing these specific words.

In the course of time, aiming for constant improvement of the user experience by increasing the accuracy and usefulness of the search results, Google significantly enhanced its results page in terms of design and functionality. A central aspect in this process was the goal to answer to users' multiple intentions at the same time. Concretely, if someone types the word "iPod" in the search field, the SERP should show suitable results for a person who wants to get news about recent product developments, as well as for someone who just wants to buy the music player. Considering the limited space on the SERP, there is a tradeoff between showing an elevated diversity of topics to be relevant to as many user's interests as possible, or presenting a

---

8 Seymour, T., Frantsvog, D., & Kumar, S. (2011). History Of Search Engines. *International Journal of Management & Information Systems (IJMIS), 15*(4), 47-58. https://doi.org/10.19030/ijmis.v15i4.5799.

9 See Google's Support Page about contracting eternal SEO services: https://support.google.com/webmasters/ answer/35291?hl=en.

10 "*We generate revenues primarily by delivering advertising on Google properties and Google Network Members' properties*," Annual Report delivered to the Securities and Exchange Commission (SEC) for the fiscal year ended Decemeber 31, 2018, https://www.sec.gov/Archives/edgar/data/1652044/000165204419000004/goog10-kq42018.htm#s3A72DA419 3545F4B849FF498BB9C1EAA.

11 MARVIN, Ginny. Google AdWords Turns 15: A Look Back At The Origins Of A $60 Billion Business. Search Engine Land, 28/10/2015, https://searchengineland.com/google-adwords-turns-15-a-look-back-at-the-origins-of-a-60-billion-business-234579.

greater amount of detailed information about a specific topic, for example indicating a greater number of stores that are selling iPods.

The first kind of online research is called "horizontal/general search" and the second "vertical/topical search." Another issue to be solved was the estimation of the relevance of vertical and horizontal search results in order to evaluate their placement among the search results.

Putting this in practice, between 2001 and 2006 Google implemented a mechanism called "OneBox" in its SERP in the United States. This box would appear above the organic results list and in its final version included search results for news, products, books, local information, maps, videos, blogs, weather, sports scores, and financial information.

In 2007, also in the United States, Google launched "Universal Search," a technique that allowed it to compare the relevance between vertical and general results to properly rank them within the SERP. Thus, instead of a box with some thematic results being displayed only at the top of the page, thematic results were displayed at the middle or bottom of the page, within the so-called "Universal Box," according to their relevance for the user and the quality provided by the thematic search results.

With the launch of Universal Search, thematic search results for products and items to sell were also featured differently on the generic search results page. Around the same time, Google's price comparison service, Google Product Search (the predecessor of the Google Shopping site) gained space in the standard search page and their product results (i.e. information sent by both retailers and crawled information from Google) started to be displayed within the SERP with images, pricing, and links to merchant sites where products could be purchased. The respective box with Product Search results, which ranked the distinct products according to relevance and usefulness, was called the "Product Universal."[12]

In 2009, in the USA, Google started charging for the display of thematic product results in a system called "Product Listing Ads" ("product listing ads"; "PLAs"). As explained by Google, "PLAs are ads that display an image of a particular product, the price at which a particular retailer is selling the product, and the name of the retailer. PLAs are generated through standardized data feeds from retailers provided to Google. The feed may be uploaded directly to Google, via FTP (a specific file transfer protocol), by indicating the location of the feed on the retailer's website (in which case Google downloads the file) or by an API (an application programming interface).

---

12   In Brazil, the implementation of new Google mechanism took place with some delay, so that in 2011, when E-Commerce Media Group pressed charges, the Product Universal just has been launched. The PLAs and the shut down of Product Universal occurred in 2012 and 2013, respectively.

In 2012, Google stopped displaying the (free of charge) Product Universal, and concentrated its product presentation in the PLAs, that are shown as of today on top of the SERP in cases where the algorithm considers the presentation of online shops and retail store websites to be adequate for the user´s search request. According to Google, the main condition to be fulfilled for an online seller to be displayed in the PLAs box, in addition to the successful participation in the corresponding auction for the ad space, is that the link connected with the announcement has to lead to a website with a one-click opportunity to purchase the article. This measure aims to facilitate the user experience and at the same time guarantee a certain quality of the ad in the matter of accuracy of the information (e.g. price or product features) and availability of the product.

C. Price Comparison Services

As described above, services like Google allow users to conduct general searches across the Internet. Later, some general search engines created pages specialized in product searches, such as Google Product Search. However, some specialized search services for products not related to general search engines also appeared in the late 1990s. These services ("price comparison services" or, in the acronym in English, "PCSs") allowed, for example, price comparison of different vendors. In Brazil, one of the first sites to offer this service was Buscapé, created in 1999.

Buscapé has gone through different business models. The initial idea was to sell software to be installed on retailers' computers that would search for products and prices in the local system and then send them to Buscapé via BBS (computer connection system prior to the Internet). After that, the system was structured to be similar to that of a search engine, that is, with the use of crawling and indexing. As a source of revenue, sites that would like to be featured could choose to be listed in special positions on the SERP and pay for the click on the link displayed. Today, retailers always need to pay to be listed on Buscapé. Bondfaro, the other comparison service belonging to the plaintiff, is another example of an established Brazilian company in this segment.

III. THE ACCUSATION

The *Google Shopping* case was one of the main unilateral conduct investigations in the digital economy judged by CADE. The administrative proceeding was initiated by E-Commerce Media Group Informação e Tecnologia Ltda. against Google, alleging that the "privileged positioning of Google Shopping in the top positions on Google's organic search results page would violate the search algorithm's neutrality and cause rivals of Google Shopping to lose audience, clicks and revenue, resulting in higher prices for the final consumer." Further, the plaintiff claimed that

"Google would be using content from competing sites to leverage traffic from its own specialized search sites (scraping)." Google has claimed that "the display of Google Shopping results is a beneficial innovation for the consumer which does not violate the Antitrust Law."

IV. THE INVESTIGATION

During the investigation, CADE identified various complex questions that, as part of a global analysis applying the rule of reason, had to be answered over the course of the process. First, it had to clarify whether a search engine had to be neutral, following pre-established rational criteria, or whether it could be manipulated to favor its own products, like the Google Shopping website, weakening any potential competitor. This discussion goes further than any debate about the right of a company to deliberately design its product. Instead, it deals with questions of the transparency of rules for users and companies that purchase the products and to whom a certain parameter is disclosed, while a different standard is actually applied by the vending company. This process clearly can generate anticompetitive reflexes by opening the possibility of Google using its dominant position in the market of online searches and leveraging it to the market of price comparison services. As a result, competitors can be harmed or forced out of the market, which would lead to less choice, less innovation, and less price competition for the consumers.

CADE's General Superintendence concluded, nevertheless, that the search algorithm of any company does not have to be neutral in terms of equal treatment between its own services and competitors, because this neutrality would imply non-personalized, non-directed search results, which would strongly compromise the quality of the product. Following the rationale of the rule of reason, it also has to be considered that in various customer surveys the launch and distinguished placement on the SERP was well received by users. Therefore, it can be stated that the innovation implemented by Google enhanced the consumer experience and the quality of the product.

In the context of the analysis of the practice engaged in by Google, a crucial point was the proper definition of the relevant market in order to try to identify the defendant's dominant position. The delimitation of the market usually happens in two dimensions: geographical and product. While the first one, dealing with search engines and online shopping sites, services that are naturally limited by language barriers, logistics and local content, coincided with the national territory of Brazil, the second one, the product dimension, required a closer look.

First of all, CADE considered the Google Shopping site, the Product Universal with its PLAs, price comparison services like the plaintiffs' and, indirectly affected by the case, online marketplaces that offer differentiated products with unique characteristics and functions. Even though they are different products they exert competitive pressure on each other, which means that they are imperfect substitutes, and therefore part of the same relevant market. The plaintiffs used exactly this competitive pressure as an argument for their case, and even Google admitted in a deposition that they developed the product search function as a direct response to the growth rates of Amazon in the United States.

Above this lies Google's generic search, which executes a kind of gateway to the internet function, taking into consideration the fact that most internet users don´t access websites via the address bar of the browser, but by typing keywords into Google search. In this separate market, Google has to compete with other search machine suppliers like Yahoo or Bing.

However, Google didn´t share the Superintendence's view on market classification, considering that its generic and topical search services form part of one and the same market, together with all specialized services, like hotel reservation portals, flight comparison sites, and news portals, competing with Google and with each other. This seems, in the case of specialized online service providers, a bit constructed. In fact, as presented by CADE's Superintendence, they should be seen as different markets, one for online travel accommodation booking, one for flight reservation, and one for consumer product price comparison, offering different services and information to the customer.

Nonetheless, another particularity that had to be taken into account in this case and which is quite common in the digital economy is the fact that Google functions as a platform that matches different groups of users in the form of advertisers and private consumers, so its two-sided structure has to be considered for an adequate market definition. As a result, the afore described separation gets a bit softened from the perspective of the advertisers, who normally act on one big market for targeted online advertisement, competing for user attention.

Altogether, the investigation came to the conclusion that Google held a dominant position on each side of the market, which is reinforced by the impracticality of using multiple generic search engines ("multihoming"), both on the side of the final customer, due to familiarization, and on the advertiser´s side, caused by Google's market share of more than 90 percent in generic online search. Besides, platforms like Google benefit from virtuous growth cycles due to network effects: The more user traffic the platform has, the more interesting it is for companies to buy ad space on Google, which can use the revenue to improve the user experience and win more market share.

In relation to the accusation of loss of traffic and clients on the side of the plaintiff, which in fact should be seen as an effect and not as a form of conduct, the investigation didn't find evidence that would prove causality between the development of the traffic of the price comparison sites and Google's innovations. Also, in light of the emergence and growth of online marketplaces like Amazon and others in Brazil, which offer direct buying opportunities on their own webpages instead of just giving price information, alterations in user traffic of the price comparison services could be explained by a shift in consumer preferences.

Referring to the privileged position of the PLAs on top of the results page, Google adduced the argument that the plaintiff could acquire PLA space by itself, if it would comply with the requirements of sharing its statistically relevant user data and implementing a direct link to a seller's webpage. However, the sharing of data that included information about the structure of the website and customer behavior and surfing habits was found not viable by the plaintiff because of their competitive sensitivity. Another point is that access to PLAs is considered to be vital because it represents the only possibility to have picture-based ads on Google, taking into account that the sponsored search is completely text based and that Google's free Product Universal was discontinued (the paid version, except for its placement on the SERP, is different from PLAs); and this access is granted to Google's price comparison service, Google Shopping, but not to the plaintiff's services, which could lead to discrimination against competitors based on abusive terms and conditions, and may thus have to be justified by the defendant.

Weighing the different arguments, the Superintendence did not see enough negative elements that would justify a condemnation in the light of the rule of reason. Although some negative consequences could arise for price comparison sites, due to their diminished visibility on Google's SERP and, by implication, the higher visibility of online marketplaces, web shops, and other competitors of the plaintiff, the positive effect for the clients, consumers as well as advertising online sellers, have to be taken into account. On the one hand, online product search has become less time consuming and more comfortable, giving the user already on the results page an overview about prices and vendors by just typing a term like "iPod" in the Google search bar; on the other hand, advertisers won with the PLAs a new and creative way of product presentation that communicates visually with potential clients. In short, matching in online sales became more efficient.

All in all, CADE's General Superintendence suggested closing the administrative process, noting "the inexistence, according to the analysis of the rule of reason, of robust elements to condemn Google for the practices denounced. On the other hand, it stressed that it would be advisable for the company to start accepting price comparison services ("PCSs") in its PLAs."

V. THE JUDGEMENT

Antitrust authorities around the world have faced problems when it comes to cases involving digital markets, dealing for example with the complexity of defining the relevant markets or identifying the exact product or service offered. A frequent challenge also lies in the need to understand the business model represented on multisided platforms in highly dynamic markets.

At CADE's plenary session, amid the disagreements, the counselors who decided the Google Shopping case dealt with important concepts involving the digital economy, when analyzing Google's conduct regarding the placement of Google Shopping, via PLAs, in a privileged position within the search results. The case involved the markets for general search engines and price comparison services, an extremely technological and innovative market. The discussions encompassed the existence of evidence of the competitive harm caused, as well as the efficiencies achieved and the creation of procompetitive innovation on the corresponding market.

CADE's Court decided to close the case by a majority, with reference to the verification of efficiencies and the lack of proof of the harmful effects allegedly caused by the conduct attributed to Google. The arguments of the reporting council member were that: (i) Google did not deny access to an essential facility, especially considering that there are effective substitutes for PLAs and for the SERP, and that price comparison sites have access both to Google's results page and to PLAs, as long as they present the required compatibility features; (ii) there was no refusal to sell to competitors, since price comparison sites can even buy and bid for PLAs, provided that the essential functionalities for this product are met; (iii) neither was "tying" found to exist, because the data feed requested for the placement of PLAs on the Google platform is essential for its functioning, and without which it would not be possible to provide an efficient service to users and online marketplaces. The requirement for this data is part of the functioning of the market and does not form part of any type of abuse.

Likewise, the possible effects of the practice, such as reduced visibility of competing sites, reduced organic traffic, increased CPC value and limited number of products advertised by retailers / marketplaces, have not been proven. It is noteworthy that, in these types of conduct, companies could not be punished for merely potential negative effects.

As for eventual efficiencies, the evidence in the case file showed benefits to consumers and advertisers arising from the advertising rules in PLAs. The whole context led a pro-competitive scenario, with an increase in value of the Google platform for facilitating matching between users and advertisers. It was also emphasized that the effects of the practice lead to product improvements to the benefit of consumers, and thus, together with stimulating innovation and economic development, the practice could not be rejected.

On the other hand, the defeated opinion of the court noted that "the mere potential for damage is sufficient to constitute a violation of the economic order, especially in cases where the determined conduct is still in progress at the time of its administrative judgment." In addition, it proposed remedies such as to "(i) prevent the display of any link that leads directly to the Google Shopping page; (ii) require that any link that leads directly to the Google Shopping page also offers, under sufficiently similar conditions, the option for the user to be directed to another price comparison site."

In short, CADE's Court concluded that there was a lack of sufficient elements of proof of the anticompetitive conduct resulting from supposed discrimination and the privileged positioning of the Google Product Search (and price comparison service) via PLAs and in the organic search results. It is recalled that for the defense of competition, conducts that generate damage only to competitors and not to final consumers should not be considered illegal.

Digital markets are characterized by a higher degree of interrelation between each other and their participants than in traditional sectors of the economy, so intervention against one company can have indirect beneficial effects on others, altering the competitiveness between apparently distant players, but who compete for users, for advertisers, or for traffic, regardless of the product that generates those results.

The case demonstrated that the Brazilian antitrust authority has faced the challenge of analyzing conduct in the digital economy market, based on international experiences of other authorities, but without neglecting traditional antitrust analysis and the specificities of the Brazilian market. In the future, what will undoubtedly be taken into account is the power of digital platforms, considering the volume of data and the velocity with which they are processed. CADE has been careful to analyze these new business models, while maintaining incentives for innovation. It is also expected that more interaction will occur with other competent bodies for investigating cases involving the digital economy, such as, for example, the recently created National Data Protection Authority ("ANPD").

Data in Antitrust: Conceptions and Misconceptions

By Alexander Elbittar & Elisa V. Mariscal[1]

Abstract

Digitization has not only changed the physical means by which we capture commercial information but also its scale, scope and detail. Registering individual's information now involves capturing preferences while noting their heterogeneity. Now consumers not only consume data but generate or produce large amounts of data (prosumer). Digitization has allowed companies to have direct contact with their consumers, thus opening the possibility for them to mine data directly, catered to their immediate and changing needs. This is only possible when algorithms are built to reap the information contained in a universe of zeros and ones. As algorithms become more effective at unravelling information from Big Data, reaching equilibrium in a market may be possible with a lower variance, thus enhancing the allocation process in terms both of welfare and speed. The central question for any antitrust analysis is not really whether large volumes of data exist associated to a conduct, merger or market, but how it can be specifically exploited and analyzed. Whether there are endogenous and exogenous conditions in place that affect competition in a market and make it relatively easy or hard for economic agents to behave in anticompetitive ways, or for markets to tip, or to become increasingly less efficient.

I. INTRODUCTION

> *A new medium is never an addition to an old one, nor does it leave the old one in peace. It never ceases to oppress the older media until it finds new shapes and positions for them.* Marshall McLuhan, 1964, Understanding Media

Digitization has allowed us to technologically move the information capture of commercial transactions from analogue media to digital media. We have moved

---

1 Elbittar is Professor of Economics at CIDE (Centro de Investigación y Docencia Económicas), Mariscal is Adjunct Professor of Economics and Law at CIDE and Director at Global Economics Group. We are indebted to Isabel Davara and Ruben Guerrero for comments to a draft of this paper. The views expressed in this paper belong to us alone, as do any mistakes. Corresponding author is Mariscal, emariscal@globaleconomicsgroup.com.

from atoms to bits. This technological transition has not only changed the physical means by which we capture information but also its scale, scope and detail.

Paraphrasing McLuhan (1964), the new digital medium has not been an addition to the analogue medium, it is a new medium of information capture and content creation, but it has not left the analogue medium the same. The digital medium continues to transform and pressure the analogue medium pushing it to find new forms to present its products and services, and to position, expose and compete itself vis à vis the digital economy.

A clear example is the newspaper business, which has not disappeared in its analogue form but has instead used its new digital transmission medium in a way that allows it to interact with the reader. Through this process, it has completely and irrevocably changed. Sections and choices no longer follow a pre-established and fixed format but are tailored to individual readers, and the digitized portion of the business now specializes in gathering this intelligence to strengthen the core "analogue" business which continues to function, regardless of the consumer habits and preference data that it now generates.

> *If you're not paying for it; you are not the consumer, you're the product being sold.* - Commenter on Metafilter, 2010

Digitization has deepened and expanded the type of information captured about consumers: registering an individual's information now involves capturing individual preferences while noting, not their homogeneity, but their heterogeneity, as individuals, as a group, as a pack, as a herd. While each individual consumes a branded product, he or she might still have differentiated preferences with respect to their "ideal" product. Thus, in terms of economic analysis, we have moved from product differentiation models that emphasized obtaining data based on the characteristics of products,[2] to models where the location, habits, preferences and any other information relating to the consumer of these or similar products becomes the centerpiece and most valuable information to capture.[3]

This data is obtained by accessing information on the habits and preferences of consumers with the intent of bringing us closer to what his or her "ideal" product choice would be, as opposed to simply observing realized transactions which only

---

2 For a summary of articles that use these traditional approaches see Bresnahan, Timothy (1989), "Empirical Studies of Industries with Market Power," in Handbook of Industrial Organization, eds. R. Schmalensee and R. Willig, vol. 2 North Holland.

3 Examples of these include Berry, Steven (1994), "Estimating Discrete-Choice Models of Product Differentiation," The RAND Journal of Economics, Vol. 25, No. 2 (Summer 1994), 242-262 and Berry, Steven, James Levinsohn and Ariel Pakes (1995), "Automobile Prices in Market Equilibrium," Econometrica, Vol. 63, No. 4 (jul., 1995), 841-890.

provided information on a consumer's "revealed preference." However, it is relevant to make a distinction between "usual" consumers and the so called "prosumers," which not only consume data but generate or produce large amounts of data. The following phrase can sum up this distinction when we refer to a consumer (vs. a prosumer).

I cannot make a market with detailed information from <u>one</u> consumer.
- An entrepreneur, regarding the limits of digitization in business

In some cases, digitalization allows the supplier to reach the customer without intermediation — that is, resolving the problem of access to the last mile, whereby a wholesaler or manufacturer of any product or service can now access a final consumer directly, with no retailer but himself as intermediary. Hence, the supplier can "see" for himself not just what and how much is bought, but also purchasing habits and patterns: where and when things are purchased (places, dates, times), how they are paid for and, if becoming a little more inquisitive, the supplier can also see by whom — age, gender, education, location, probable income, products viewed before purchase, etc. In addition, if we consider that browsers and search engines can track a customer's browsing history, then there is a lot more information to gauge from a simple online transaction between two parties.

The logical conclusion of this is that a simple sale now is not only limited to a monetary exchange between one party and another, but intelligence can be obtained from the habits of a consumer to better serve all customers; this is the logic behind exploiting Big Data. Thus, a firm can rationalize or adjust its offer of products, its market strategy or brand positioning, uncover and exploit different market niches, or have a general idea of possible improvements, or changes in the product, and even consider complementary, substitute or new products. In this train of thought, observing a large number of consumers and exploiting Big Data allows the supplier to use the information as predictive analytics of user behavior and to extract value from data to discover all kinds of sales and production possibilities. For those who sell in the digital world, having access and ability to exploit Big Data can be vital to compete.

Consequently, following this narrative, consumer information can become much more valuable than the actual product — at least the basic product — and a supplier of the product is willing to "give it away" provided he can exploit this information. The key, of course, is whether all these possibilities of exploiting Big Data can in fact be realized, including whether industry characteristics do not conspire to reduce the potential benefits from gathering and exploiting data to obtain useful information.

Our emphasis here is on the usefulness, the value that exploiting Big Data creates, rather than the problems that arise from use of Big Data. While most of the public discussion surrounding Big Data have focused on the problems that exploitation of large quantities of information will create, the fact remains that we have embarked on this analysis precisely because of the benefits that it can generate—which does not negate potential costs. However, Big Data is not a panacea either. While its analysis may rely on the design of sophisticated algorithms based on artificial intelligence/ machine learning and deep learning, it does not substitute for the market mechanism as a decentralized form of allocating resources and gathering useful information for parties to exchange goods by using prices as a signal of production value and agents' preferences.

We can think of markets as mechanisms, "algorithms" that receive and transmit information by means of a price system. The digitalization of consumer data — and the use of algorithms to structure and obtain intelligence from it — returns us to the heart of a discussion on whether society, or some "benevolent central planner," has the expertise and knowhow of information-processing capabilities that allows it to assign resources "to each according to their needs" and "from each according to their abilities." This is related to the problem posed by Hayek, almost 80 years ago, on the use of knowledge in society.[4]

Hayek states that any physical exchange between people is ultimately an exchange of information, regardless of what product, service or good is being bought or sold. He stressed that we never really know the circumstances under which these exchanges take place — be they concentrated or integrated — since these are really scattered fragments of incomplete and frequently contradictory knowledge possessed by separate and uncoordinated individuals. Therefore, the economic problem of society is not simply a problem of allocation of resources, but the problem of how solve and better ensure the use of the resources known by any member of society; in other words, the problem is "how to use knowledge that is not given to anyone in its entirety."

Taking this idea from Hayek, perhaps we can reflect on the likelihood of the omniscient nature of data and the wealth of information generated from it, which after considering Hayek's paper seems highly unlikely. It may be partly possible to relieve the market of some of its tasks as a decentralized mechanism for allocating resources efficiently by using data organized by algorithms, but it is almost impossible to think that they can be a substitute. Hayek's view can be thought of as micro (individual), macro (an aggregate of identical individuals) and meta (resolving the aggregate for different types of individuals): to truly allocate resources in the best possible way we need to know what each individual involved in an exchange desires; to resolve the problem for a group of people; we need to know what members of society want; and all members need not agree on a solution or aggregation of each person's desires.

---

4 Hayek, F. A., "The Use of Knowledge in Society," (1945). American Economic Review, Vol. 35, Issue 4, p. 519-530.

It is unclear whether algorithms and IA as they currently stand can lead to the same result as a market. Big Data analytics would have to resolve contradictory information at the micro and macro level and then solve the social problem in its totality, entirely. Hence, obtaining individual data — or handling ever more data from an increasing number of transactions (Big Data) — is not the entire solution to the problem of efficient allocation. Therefore, while more precise information and its processing might bring us closer to "*a solution*," it is not necessarily "*the solution*" to society's resource allocation problem or the optimal solution for all firms or individuals.

While we are still far away from thinking that the market mechanism can be substituted by large scale data analytics, data algorithms can substantially improve information completeness in a market, thus improving its efficiency. In an experiment, Gode & Sunder (1993) show how zero-intelligence traders with differing levels of rationality and information converge to market equilibrium in a similar fashion as human traders.[5] The only difference is the profit dispersion across different groups of individuals with differing levels of information but, on average, profit remains the same — in the words of the authors "Adam Smith's invisible hand may be more powerful than some may have thought; it can generate aggregate rationality not only from individual rationality but also from individual irrationality."

Hence, to the extent that data can be used to improve the amount of information in a market, the variance of profits for any trader, rational or irrational, should decrease and market equilibrium can be reached faster. We present this example as supporting a view of data algorithms as being complementary to the market mechanism. We will discuss next conditions that may weaken this result.

II. ALGORITHMS, LEARNING AND THE SPEED OF LEARNING DECLINE

Additional data currently being used and the advantages that it promises to confer are not automatic or identical. Data *per se* does not confer a firm with any competitive advantage. It requires **data-enhanced-learning** to fully exploit the information that is constantly gathered for every consumer, and this is attained through the design of **algorithms** that can provide additional value to the basic data inputted and the capacity to analyze the new output in such a way that the product or service is improved.

In addition, the speed of learning can vary depending on the speed at which the marginal value of additional data decreases: a faster decreasing marginal value of additional data will require less data to gather the same amount of information, while

---

5 Gode, Dhananjay K. & Shyam Sunder, "Allocative Efficiency of Markets with Zero-Intelligence Traders: Market as a Partial Substitute for Individual Rationality," Journal of Political Economy, Vol. 101, No. 1 (Feb. 1993), pp. 119-137.

a slower decreasing marginal value of additional data will require greater amounts of data.[6] This situation is illustrated in Figure 1.

Figure 1 illustrates these two types of speed of decline of MVAD, each of which has differing implications on the order and speed of entry, the use of open vs. closed systems, and the ability to exploit network effects, among other possible elements that are endogenous to the type of good or service using data intensively. We take these three elements and elaborate further on the different implications that they have on competition based innate industry structure in the next section.

Figure 1

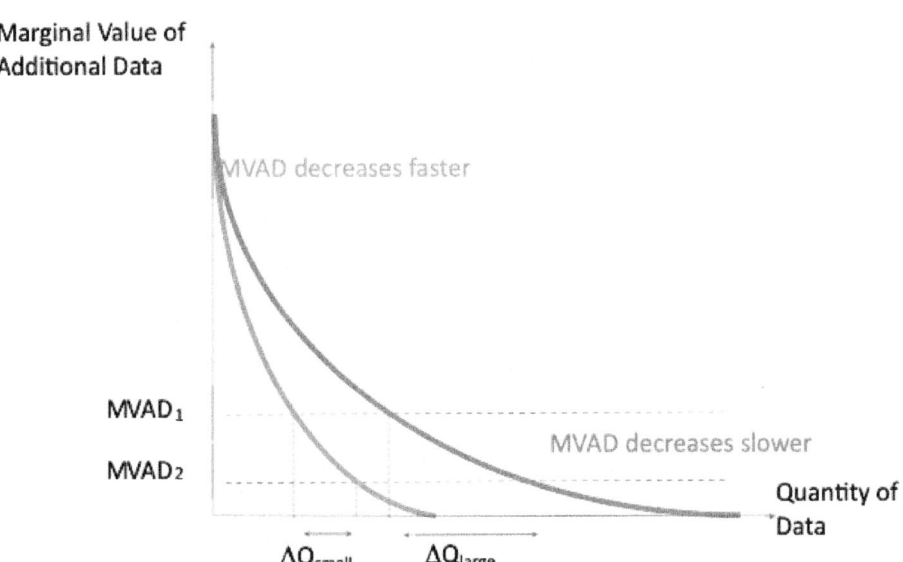

III. ENDOGENOUS CONDITIONS AFFECTING SPEED OF MVAD DECLINE: UNDER-STANDING THE MARKET

A. First Mover Advantages

When MVAD decreases at a slower speed, that is when the downward sloping curve in Figure 1 is flatter, there are advantages to being first in the market. Gathering data at the initial stages confers a significant boost in this case, as larger volumes of data are required in order to make inferences about purchasing or patterns of use for current customers. Thus, a firm that begins the gathering process early on will

---

6 For a brief discussion see Hagiu, Andrei & Julian Wright, 2020, "When Data Creates Competitive Advantage," *Harvard Business Review*, January-February 2020. Accessible at: https://hbr.org/2020/01/when-data-creates-competitive-advantage.

have a significant advantage over late entrants if this data is not shared. Examples of this would be comparing the innate advantage of a first mover search engine, such as Google, compared to the disadvantage faced by Bing in gathering intelligence from internet users — no matter the efforts that Bing invested in catching up, the data advantages from Google's search engine have been deemed insurmountable but this has more to do with the problem of scale (network externalities which we take on below) and less so with a problem of the ability to extract useful information from the data.

In contrast, an example of an industry characterized by a steeper MVAD curve, that is where the speed of decline of the value added of data falls faster. An example is an industry characterized by specialized data gathering such as Alexa and Siri. In this case, both systems will learn about their respective individual consumers very fast, but this information cannot be easily extrapolated to other consumers and a new operating system could more easily enter without a significant disadvantage. Many of the products currently being sold that "learn" from consumers' behaviors face similar limitations about extrapolation to other consumers — think of Nest™, intelligent coffeemakers and refrigerators, among other intelligent consumer products.

B. Exploiting Network Effects

Network effects occur when the value of belonging to a network increases with more participants in the network. We distinguish direct and indirect network effects when there is only one type of user in the network (direct) vs. two or more types of users in the network (indirect). Direct network effects occur when the number of same type of participants in the network increases and this increases the value of the network both for the new user as well as for all existing users in the network. Indirect network effects occur when users of one type within a network benefit from a greater number of users of the other type in the network. Here we are referring to direct network effects.

In the context of data, exploiting network effects allows the rapid scalability of data that can be used to successfully obtain valuable information and learn from consumers. In this way, it becomes easier to:

1) extrapolate insights garnered from actual consumers to future consumers, and

2) generate insights into creating new products and services.

Enhanced learning about products and services, for example, exploits the first possibility. This learning is based on data obtained from current customers, and this information can be used to improve products for existing customers as well as to attract new consumers. In this sense, data and its exploitation convey a competitive advantage.

In industries where network externalities are possible, exploiting the second possibility can lead to lock-in, as consumers may find it in their interest to remain with the same provider who is now offering new products and services that are catered to their particular preferences. Taken to the extreme, the high costs of switching can eventually lead to tipping.

C. Open vs. Closed Systems

Another endogenous element that will have effects on competition is whether the type of architecture on which information is captured is open or closed. With a closed system, an advantage can be garnered when being first as learning occurs only within the proprietary space. In addition, the ability to exploit data, which becomes limited with closed systems, is of greater concern where the MVAD curve is flatter as catch up becomes even more difficult for those firms that follow a first mover. If proprietary data can successfully limit replication, then a first entrant may have an advantage in obtaining and exploiting information to grow until innovation can exploit nonproprietary means of learning and open the possibilities of faster learning and broader data to exploit for those that use the open system — again, as before, the problem of the scale of data is a problem of network effects rather than open or closed systems.

In sum, we want to illustrate through these three examples of endogenous conditions affecting the speed of MVAD, that it is not data alone which introduces barriers or concentrates markets, it happens through important first-mover advantages, through the use of proprietary systems that cannot be easily replicated or approximated, or by exploiting networking externalities successfully — to the point where tipping can happen.

There are a series of additional industry conditions and business opportunities that can lead to competition or regulatory problems that are not inherent in the data, speed of entry, type of systems used or the relationship between network externalities and the use and scale of data to be exploited and that can be successfully used by entrepreneurs who have the foresight to do so. These issues are exogenous to the firms and we discuss them next.

IV. EXOGENOUS CONDITIONS AFFECTING SPEED OF MVAD DECLINE: THE ROLE FOR PUBLIC POLICY

We look at three types of public policy as it relates to data: consumer policy, regulation and antitrust policy, with the latter one divided into *ex post* interventions — unilateral conduct and coordinated behavior — and *ex ante* analysis, namely mergers.

A. Data and Privacy: The Issue of Consumer Protection

By type of good: non-excludable has to do with access, means that anyone can have access; non rivalrous means that simultaneous consumption is possible. In the case of data, and argument can be made that it is non rivalrous and only partially excludable which makes it similar to both a club good and a public good.[7] What is interesting about data is that even when data is public, sometimes the value added is the arrangement of this data in a way that is valuable to users, in this case, excluding others from "free" consumption of this structured data has been deemed valid — think of newspapers for example vs. simple free online news.[8]

Public/Private realm: even private data includes information that is not exclusively personal, it may have actual or potential consequences for others, even consequences for that same individual that can or cannot be foreseen in the present. In the parlance of economics these are externalities, they may be positive or negative externalities,[9] they may be realized or not, thus these are risk externalities which are defined as the risk that a user faces dependent on the risk mitigation decision of adjacent individuals.[10] In the context of data this means that any infringement to my privacy will depend on the actions that others have taken to mitigate diffusion of my information to other parties. Thus, the only insurance against this risk is for me to cease sharing any of my information or to coordinate with my friends and family — assuming we can resolve the collective action problem — so that we all agree to not share our information.[11]

---

7   By Public Good, we mean a goods that is both non-excludable and non-rivalrous. By Club Good, we mean goods that are excludable in property but non-rivalrous in consumption.

8   We do want to add that although the logic from the point of view of economics may be clear, from a legal point of view, the issue of privacy and property rights is not. For some jurisdictions, privacy may be an unalienable human right while others have a laxer standard. Thus, the issue of privacy can become a binding restriction in some cases, while for others it is part of a contract negotiation.

9   Choi, Jeon & Kim, (2019), "Privacy and Personal Data Collection with Information Externalities," Working Paper, January 29, 2019, accessible at https://www.tse-fr.eu/sites/default/files/TSE/documents/doc/wp/2018/wp_tse_887revised.pdf.

10   Sanyo Fianu, Emmanuel (2017), "A Concise Note on Risk Externalities: A Critical Review," Advances in Economics and Business, 5(10): 568-573, 2017, DOI: 10.13189/aeb.2017.051005.

11   For example, see the dissenting statement of FCC commissioner Pamela Harbour in the Google-DoubleClick decision (2007) where she stated her opposition to closing the investigation of the merger, "The transaction will combine not only the two firms' products and services, but also their vast troves of data about consumer behavior on the Internet. Thus, the transaction reflects an interplay between traditional competition and consumer protection issues." See https://www.ftc.gov/sites/default/files/documents/public_statements/statement-matter-google/doubleclick/071220harbour_0.pdf.

B. Data as a Bottleneck: The Issue of Regulation

In addition to the semi-public good nature of data, its production function has characteristics that make it similar to a natural monopoly. Data can have significant economies of scale — more is better — as well as scope — more varied information for each data point is best. This opens the discussion on the suitability of regulating its production and its access.[12]

Concerns about data also involve considerations that some of this information may have a strategic or essential nature and thus access to it becomes vital or, alternatively, slow or burdensome access to data affects transactions significantly so that it behaves like a bottleneck. It may be worth recalling how we define and analyze a bottleneck in this context. A bottleneck is *"a point on a network through which all service products must pass to reach the ultimate buyers. When there is limited capacity at this point, decisions are necessary to prioritize deliveries and determine whether to build additional facilities to relieve the constraint."*[13]

The only similar type of good where bottlenecks are involved excluding utilities (electricity, water, gas, railways, airports, etc.) would be a financial regulator dealing with banking secrets. But contrary to the more general "data," financial information tends to be individual and excludable, and any breaches to privacy in this realm can be calculated in dollars and cents. Furthermore, a decision involving regulation will require to carefully carve out the problem areas vs. those areas where *ex ante* rules are not necessary or where potential costs of regulation outweigh their benefits. Regulators need to consider, however, that their actions will have an effect on company incentives: greater protection will mean that companies with internal policies aimed at protecting user information will have an edge over those that don't. In some cases, this may be recommendable, but not in all cases.

C. Data as an Antitrust Problem

1. Abuse of Dominance and Foreclosure

A less rigid way of evaluating exclusionary behavior on a case-by-case basis is by using *ex post* antitrust analysis. Here, it is not individual data that is the problem but access to databases that have been compiled over time by incumbents and that are refused to entrants who cannot easily replicate them. The problem, from a purely antitrust position is similar to the refusal to license patents. As in patents, a case needs to be made that these are essential patents so that licensing becomes compulsory.

---

12 Yan Carrière-Swallow & Vikram Haksar, (2019), "The Economics and Implications of Data: An Integrated Perspective," International Monetary Fund. Strategy, Policy, and Review Department (Series).

13 http://regulationbodyofknowledge.org/glossary/b/bottleneck-facility/.

Access considers only the use of data from a horizontal competitor's point of view; however, data can be used as a means of leveraging an advantage from one market to another exploiting economies of scope in particular. Recent theories of harm in digital markets have argued that it is possible for incumbents in market A with large volumes of data to use this information to enter other markets (call them B) more effectively than B players, thus affecting nascent competition in these markets. The recent discussion of Amazon reviewing its customer and supplier data to pick which markets to enter comes to mind.[14] On many occasions, this information is obtained from customer data without their knowledge of how or where it will be used, even where the data can be a tool to more easily displace or foreclose competition to the detriment of those consumers who, through ignorance or passive behavior, end up facilitating anticompetitive practices.

2. Data as a Coordinating Mechanism: *Per Se* Analysis

If data is non rivalrous then it can be shared by multiple players without detracting from others. If the data is excludable then this becomes a "club good" and the antitrust issue in question may be one of foreclosure which we've discussed previously. In this case, a database that has use for all market participants may imply that there is no need to duplicate an investment in creating it, for example, when information from customers in a given market is available to all. Even if there are savings to be made from sharing data, care must be taken that it does not become a coordinating mechanism even if it is legal; for example, a credit bureau.

The issue here is how much collaboration is required to construct this public good (database) before the collaboration becomes a facilitating practices where users of the database can allot themselves customers or market segments or can decide on an "optimal price" to set for similar services – all of these, clearly harming competition in the market and possibly constituting a cartel. In the beginning, the analysis may require a rule of reason approach to weigh the benefits and costs of the data base as a coordinating mechanism.

3. Data as a Strategic Asset: Mergers

Just as firms have bought other firms to avail themselves of strategic assets which allow them to place themselves in a stronger competitive position relative to their actual or potential competitors, we now count data as a "special" strategic asset. This asset, the argument goes, is so valuable to render the remaining assets belonging to the business as completely worthless. Thus, a firm with a very valuable database or an algorithm that exploits this database very successfully or that learns from it in a particularly novel way, can be a target for an acquirer who simply wants the informa-

---

14   See Zhu, Feng and Qihong Liu, 2018, "Competing with complementors: An empirical look at Amazon.com," Strategic Management Journal, 2018: 39: 2618-2642.

tion and the technology surrounding it. This "predator-buyer" has no interest in the underlying business and will acquire the "prey-target" to fold the data into its own business. We can even think of this wealth destruction argument as equivalent to standard predatory pricing analysis, where a predator is willing to lose money – destroy wealth – for the sole purpose of displacing its competitors or creating a reputation for toughness that will keep others away.

Hence, "killer acquisitions" as they relate to data, are transactions aimed at purchasing databases of functioning businesses with no concern to maintaining or growing the business. In this case, antitrust agencies are justifiably worried about an inefficient allocation of resources, regardless of whether the new controlling party has fully committed to upholding privacy and legal principles relating to the handling of data. In fact, if we follow a similar analytical logic as that used in a predatory pricing analysis, the standard of proof for killer acquisitions should be similarly stringent: a reasonable expectation that the buyer's only interest in the business is the database, just as in predation there is an expectation that once the company has expended resources and incurred in losses there is a reasonable expectation of recouping these investments.

V.   AN ANALYSIS OF ACTUAL AND POTENTIAL EFFECTS OF DATA USING A MERGER EXAMPLE

We describe next a recent merger case to illustrate our previous examination of data and its role in antitrust analysis, that of Mexico's review of the *Walmart/Cornershop* merger.[15,16]

Traditional "brick and mortar" firms, such as Walmart, have become aware of the importance in using data linked to consumer decisions and preferences. They have progressively developed business models that take this into account and begun to

---

15 *Walmart/Cornershop*. Resolution CNT-161-2018.
https://www.cofece.mx/CFCResoluciones/docs/Concentraciones/V6008/9/4845885.pdf.

16 Although the case raised various antitrust issues relating mostly to unilateral effects centering on horizontal displacement concerns in the brick and mortar business, as well as vertical displacement of potential competitors in both the online marketplace as well as e-commerce businesses, the core issue that we will center on are the concerns raised in the use of data as a strategic asset. Regardless, we list the key competition concerns brought up by COFECE: Horizontal displacement: Walmart, directly or indirectly, could unduly displace its traditional competitors from the Cornershop platform, among others, by forcing the newly purchased Cornershop to stop offering its products and/or privileging Walmart stores over other stores in the market. Vertical displacement: Walmart inhibits innovation in the digital market by refusing to deal with any platform that competes with Cornershop, thus ensuring that Cornershop is a dominant market for fresh produce. Displacement through the use of data: Walmart may have access to strategic data of its competitors that sell in the Cornershop market and use this data to displace them, whether in the world of the brick and mortar market and virtual, where it drives a significant market share.

insert this intelligence into their growth strategies in the field of digital commerce. The accumulation, processing and analysis of consumer data — viewed as a central tool for digital businesses in developing competitive advantages — is now also vital for brick and mortar businesses as well.

Thus, firms have explored different business models for implementing their digital strategies. One business model has relied on approaching their consumers by developing intermediation services that offer products and services catered to specific needs, such as the configuration of consumer baskets based on previous purchases and/or offering home delivery services. To implement this model, they have used two different strategies.

The first strategy uses self-insertion and growth into digital commerce markets as an additional sales outlet. Some companies have opted for the creation of electronic commerce business units within their organizations (organic growth), which not only allows companies to integrate their commercial logistics units with e-commerce logistics and gradually train their work teams as they develop new markets, but also to leverage their experience of better understanding their own traditional consumers.

When organic growth is not the chosen option, companies have opted for a second strategy, that of acquiring companies already operating in electronic commerce environments and who have already acquired knowledge of the logistics and data processing capabilities required in a digital environment. This strategy allows them to rapidly climb the learning curve of data management and electronic commerce and to more quickly adapt themselves to a new business environment to advertise, select, transport and sell similar products and services.

Since the early 2000s, Walmart developed an electronic service unit with integrated fresh food transportation service directly to the homes of its consumers. Nonetheless, in September 2018 having exploited with relative success its business model for a brick and mortar business, it decided to venture into the second strategy and notified Mexico's Federal Economic Competition Commission ("COFECE") of its intention to acquire Cornershop. Cornershop is an online multi-sided platform that offers logistics services for the display, purchase and delivery of products offered by self-service stores, price clubs and other stores through a software application for mobile devices and its website for end users, in other words, a digital marketplace for fresh produce that links consumers, stores and shoppers.

But what does this mean in terms of the structure we laid out at the beginning of this piece?

a)   Is Cornershop a new business medium? A new market?

b)   How does it use and exploit data? How fast does the marginal value of additional data decline? Is the market susceptible to first mover advantages, exploitation of network externalities, and/or successful use of proprietary information in a way that enhances these advantages or strengthens network effects?

c)   Are there other exogenous elements that should be analyzed and that could pose problems? And if so, what are the different policy instruments that could be used to reduce potential problems?

We will take each of these questions in turn.

A. Cornershop is a transformative means to sell retail, it is a new medium not a new market

Cornershop transforms an old medium, the traditional brick and mortar retail business, by using digitization. The same goods and services are being sold but are now advertised, purchased, packaged and delivered in a new way. This forces the old business model to change.

This new type of business model has decentralized the traditional intermediation services, using open market platforms or marketplaces where different suppliers and consumers can concur, and where a greater offering of suppliers and variety of products can give greater value to users on various sides of the platform who can take advantage of *indirect network externalities* that arise from this interaction. In other words, Cornershop grants access to the last mile, obtention of consumer level data, not just producer (competitor) comparison data already available through Nielsen and market intelligence in the traditional business model.

B. Data gathering for all sides of the multisided platform reveals that the MVAD is steeper for consumer and store level data and unimportant for shoppers in terms of the amount of data. First mover advantages are therefore not relevant in terms of data in this market

To analyze whether data acquisition would be a problem, we need to understand the slope of the Marginal Value of Additional Data curve ("MVAD") that characterizes this market, for all sides of the multisided platform business that it represents: consumers, stores and shoppers.

Shopper information we will ignore since we assume it is simply a data base of persons interested in delivering goods and services that have user reviews associated to them which grants them tips and other additional payments commensurate to the review. The effect of data is not relevant here and what truly becomes relevant is the indirect network externality associated with having a critical mass of users on all sides of the platform (consumers and stores) in a way that attracts more and better shoppers to the platform.

To understand the value of consumer data for Cornershop we first need to characterize the products it sells. Even though it is a marketplace, it is a platform that mostly sells food and perishable goods. Amazon may be a marketplace, but the nature of the goods sold in the Cornershop platform are different. Here goods sold are perishable and nondurable, and they tend to involve repeat purchases that are linked to individual consumer tastes. The knowledge that can be gained from crossing consumer information is therefore limited.

For example, the marginal value of additional data in this case would more likely look like the steeper curve rather than the flatter curve that we have depicted before in this paper. Experience in the consumption of the goods may not be a good proxy here for the likelihood of purchasing a good, so that consumer reviews have less value than they do in the case of Amazon's section of durable and nonperishable goods that represent a greater share of household expenditures. Consequently, direct externalities have only a very limited possibilities of being exploited in the case of Cornershop relative to Amazon.

Consequently, as it relates to consumer level data, new entry is more likely to succeed, and first mover advantage concerns should be less important.

Looking at how Cornershop exploits store level data requires understanding the order of choices that it provides consumers. Consumers are first given a choice of store and, once in the store, they are given a choice of goods to purchase. Hence nesting of choices goes from store to goods and not vice versa. This is relevant because the algorithm cannot nudge consumers into making purchases of similar products at different stores, it can instead present discounts of different products within a store once the consumer has selected it.

With this background in mind, store level data cannot easily be extrapolated among the different member stores of Cornershop. Knowing how much milk is sold in Costco or HEB is not necessarily a good predictor of how much milk will be sold by Walmart. More data points do not provide more intelligence so that, similarly to consumer data, the MVAD curve is also steeper rather than flatter for one side of the market, namely the consumer side of the platform. If instead we focus on the other side of the market, the data gathered from suppliers who sell in this marketplace regarding inventory management, purchases and in-store offerings, for example, the MVAD curve may be flatter rather than steeper. This suggests that having market power, particularly for those products with standard handling and stable consumption, may be beneficial.

Similarly. to consumer level data, in the case of store level data, data is not likely to impede new entry, and first mover advantage concerns should be less important.

C. Are there other exogenous elements that should be analyzed and that could pose problems? And if so, what are the different policy instruments that could be used to reduce potential problems?

Privacy of consumer information is always a concern, but in this case, it is unrelated to antitrust since the dataset does not represent a bottleneck. It can be replicated as there are no first mover advantages, multihoming is possible to purchase and sell fresh produce that does not use Cornershop only and there are no exclusive arrangements among any of the demands serviced by the platform: consumers, stores or shoppers. Furthermore, Cornershop's algorithm is based on an open system and there are other competing logistics platforms that can easily modify their algorithms to adapt them for the sale of a larger basket of goods, including fresh produce.

Reviewing data as a potential antitrust problem, there are three potential problems that Cornershop's database could pose: its use as a mechanism to foreclose competition given its dominance (unilateral effects), its use as a facilitating mechanism for stores (coordinated effects), and its use as a strategic asset (the killer acquisition argument). We will take each one of these in turn.

The last argument, the purchase of a company simply to acquire its data set and then to close the business — a killer acquisition — is only reasonable when the accumulated data in the database allows for valuable predictions in the future for any of the economic participating in the multisided business and/or when replicating this database is difficult. Neither of these conditions are met, as we have argued previously.

Regarding the likely abuse of dominance hypothesis based on the use of data to maintain or increase substantial market power, i.e. potential unilateral effects caused by a Walmart-Cornershop merger, we need to identify first whether market power is derived from the data. In this case, the authority's analysis identified unilateral effects as arising from leveraging Walmart's market power in brick and mortar into a new medium. Data, therefore, plays no role in unilateral effects analysis. If a merger were to involve companies with complementary datasets or potential for algorithmic improvements in a way that would grant them a substantial advantage over the other platforms, unilateral analysis should consider looking into this more carefully.

The use of the database as a facilitating mechanism whereby member stores jointly construct the database and/or can communicate or share product purchases or consumer information in a way that allows them to allot themselves consumers or market segments or can decide an "optimal price" for similar products would be a concern. Here behavioral or structural remedies could be expected to reduce potential anticompetitive conducts. Nonetheless, as with any potential collusive behavior, be it tacit or explicit, the authority would need to review participation and incentive compatibility constraints which would require the analysis of potential retaliatory measures by the members of the cartel in order to preclude unilateral deviation from the agreement. In any case, a structural analysis of a potential cartel would need to take into account the nature of the goods involved, and in many cases, most cartels hare based on homogeneous and durable goods while the goods involved in this platform are heterogeneous and perishable.

VI. FINAL THOUGHTS

We began our discussion about the transformative effects that a new medium has both in the area where it is emerging as well as in the industries that it is disrupting. How an incumbent industry — not just a firm — decides to adapt to this new medium, in this case digitalization and more specifically its more intensive and expansive use of data.

We also discussed how digitization has rendered the intermediary unnecessary in many cases, allowing companies to have direct contact with their final consumers, thus opening the possibility for them to mine data directly, catered to their immediate and changing needs. But all of this is only possible when algorithms are built to reap the information contained in a universe of zeros and ones.

As algorithms become more effective at unravelling information from Big Data, reaching equilibrium in a market may be possible with a lower variance, thus enhancing the allocation process in terms both of welfare and speed. So, provided these algorithms are not designed to coordinate interactions among competitors,[17] the central question for any antitrust analysis is not really whether large volumes of data exist associated to a conduct, merger or market, but how it can be exploited and analyzed.

In particular, whether there are endogenous and exogenous conditions in place that affect competition in a market and make it relatively easy or hard for economic agents to behave in anticompetitive ways, or for markets to tip, or to become increasingly less efficient. All of this taking into account that data may have positive market effects in terms of information gathering to more efficiently reach a market equilibrium, but that certain endogenous and exogenous conditions may limit or reverse these positive effects. The difficulty, of course, is to imagine a counterfactual.

---

17   See for example, Harari's thesis regarding algorithm's control of human choices in Yuval Noah Harari, 2018, *21 lessons for the 21st Century*, London: Jonathan Cape.

The Role of Competition in Promoting Digital Economies in Developing Nations

By Tembinkosi Bonakele[1]

Abstract

Despite all the achievements of the industrial economy, it has however also resulted in the skewed allocation of available resources. South Africa is a case in point, as it continues to be characterized by persistent high levels of inequality, poverty, and unemployment. The increasing prominence of the digital economy, therefore, presents an opportunity to reverse these outcomes to achieve an equitable allocation of available resources thus shifting South Africa from inequality to equality, from poverty to shared prosperity, and from unemployment to meaningful participation. These would be the attributes of an inclusive digital economy.

The increasing demand for the digital economy nevertheless presents new challenges in competition enforcement including whether the current competition regime and enforcement tools are geared to deal adequately with competition problems in digital markets. It is imperative that these challenges are addressed and that proper tools are designed to enable the digital economy to fully realize and achieve its meaningful benefits. Therefore, these markets need unified regulation, legislation to enable an environment poised for innovation and dynamic growth. Competition policy and regulation therefore have a major contribution to make in this regard.

I. THE PROMISE OF A DIGITAL ECONOMY

According to UNCTAD's 2019 Digital Economy Report *"…[D]igitalisation has [ ] given rise to fundamental challenges for policymakers in countries at all levels of development. Harnessing its potential for the many, and not just the few, requires creative thinking and policy experimentation. And it calls for greater global cooperation to avoid widening the income gap."*[2] UNCTAD's report also acknowledges that the advent of the digital economy holds great promise for developing nations but recognizes that

---

1 Commissioner of the South African Competition Commission.

2 https://unctad.org/en/PublicationsLibrary/der2019_en.pdf.

developing nations cannot reap these benefits unless they apply creative thinking, experiment with innovative policy, and cooperate with others in reducing the income gap.

One might ask what a digital economy is, given its dynamic and ever-evolving character. Its very definition undergoes constant changes. More than a market, the digital economy cuts across all markets in which goods and services utilize an internet base for production, distribution, trade, and consumption by different agents. While a market is considered to be one stream within an economy – for example a financial market – the digital economy has become an entire economic system running parallel to the industrial economy and threatening to, one day, overtake the industrial economy as the primary base for economic activity. The developments around the COVID-19 pandemic have brought this prospect ever closer.

The purpose of an economy is to organize the allocation of available resources.[3] Unfortunately, for all the achievements of the industrial economy, it has also resulted in the skewed allocation of available resources. South Africa is a case in point, as it exhibits high levels of inequality, poverty, and unemployment. The arrival and rapid rise of the digital economy presents an opportunity to reverse these outcomes to achieve an equitable allocation of available resources thus shifting us from inequality to equality, from poverty to shared prosperity, and from unemployment to meaningful participation. These would be the attributes of an inclusive digital economy.

Even with the limited uptake of digital innovation in some developing countries it has become clear that the digital economy has the potential to succeed where the industrial economy has failed developing nations. When managed correctly and harnessed optimally, digitalization can contribute to addressing specific social or economic development challenges in developing nations. It can facilitate access to basic services such as health (e.g. e-health services), education (e.g. remote teaching) and financial services.[4] High traction of digital technology can be found in the automotive and agricultural sectors in South Africa. Technology enables manufacturers to synchronize production, improve planning and productivity. Increasingly, precision farming innovations are enabling farmers to manage large fields of crops by gathering information in real-time and then responding to the variability in the crops.[5] This ultimately leads to efficiency gains from the technology such as reduced costs, improved quality, and choice for consumers.

---

3 Hall (September 2017) *Purpose of Economics.*

4 UNCTAD, "Investment and the Digital Economy," (2017) at page 156, available at https://unctad.org/en/PublicationChapters/wir2017ch4_en.pdf.

5 OECD, "The digital economy, new business models and key features," (2014) at page 72, available at https://www.oecd-ilibrary.org/docserver/9789264218789-7-en.pdf?expires=1584362876&id=id&accname=guest&checksum=FBF40091B7C1BA0B755934309E681164.

II. CHALLENGES TO REALIZING BENEFITS OF THE DIGITAL ECONOMY

A. External Challenges

While countries acknowledge the potential benefits of large scale digitalization, there are hindrances that prevent the unfettered uptake of digital technologies and thus the roll out of the promised outcomes that digitalization can bring about. While these challenges differ from country to country, they can broadly be summarized as follows:

- Low levels of connectivity and internet penetration. The lower the rate of connectivity in a country the lower the uptake of digital technologies by consumers, business, and potential innovators. Internet penetration figures differ among developing nations with countries like India and Egypt hovering 45 and 50 percent; China and Mauritius between 60 and 65 percent; while Malaysia and Kenya reflect higher numbers of 80 and 90 percent respectively.[6]

- Low level of skills in information technology, programming, artificial intelligence, and other innovations. From the educational curriculum in school to the ability of countries to retain digital skills in the work place, developing nations lag behind the more developed nations in cultivating, attracting, and retaining digital skills in the economy.

- The digital divide. Internet products and services, and thus internet usage, tend to be skewed in favor of middle to upper income consumers. This is partly due to a dearth of technologies specifically targeting lower income consumers.

- Slow regulatory adoption. The regulatory framework in some developing nations takes a considerable amount of time to change and so has not yet caught up to the realities of operating in a digital economy. One South African example is labor laws that have not yet evolved to cover the transient income generating opportunities prevailing in digital markets. Another example is the disruption that Uber and AirBnB have brought to the regulatory framework established for transport and tourism respectively.

---

6 2018 figures taken from an April 2020 report by Genesis Analytics.

- Limited funding for the information technology sector. In some developing nations, funding models are still structured for the industrial economy and thus not promoting investment in the digital economy. These models are burdened with financial regulations and funding models that fail to take advantage of the rapid pace and massive scale of digital transformation.

- Limited market access. In a somewhat circular way, the low levels of connectivity in some developing nations limits the ability of people and businesses to participate meaningfully in the digital economy. The COVID-19 crisis, for instance, has exposed the crippling inability of markets that rely only on physical infrastructure to trade in an increasingly digitalized world.

B. Internal Challenges

The challenges of regulating digital markets equally apply to the application of competition law and economics to digital markets. The competition authorities, like other regulators, have had to grapple with competition issues arising from the increased digitalization of markets.

The major discourse in competition law relating to digital markets currently is whether the current competition regime and its tools are sufficient to deal with competition problems in digital markets. There are two main characteristics of digital markets that challenge the adequacy of current competition laws and tools. First, some digital platforms are two-sided in nature. Second, innovation in digital markets is rapid. The interplay of these factors challenges the adequacy of competition law tools in dealing with digital markets.

Two-sided markets generally create difficulties for competition authorities because, procedurally, the first step in assessing dominance and its abuse is to define the relevant market within which the alleged abuser's conduct has an effect. The SSNIP[7] test is the tool that is commonly used to separate close substitutes from distant substitutes in an effort to determine the boundaries of the relevant market. The SSNIP test is used to establish whether customers of the respondents would switch to readily available products or suppliers located elsewhere in response to a hypothetical small but significant relative increase in the products in the areas being considered. In digital platform markets, some customers face a very low price or sometimes no price at all.

---

7 SSNIP is an acronym for "small but significant non-transitory increase in price."

As such, the SSNIP test would only be applied to the paying-side of the market and leave the impression that, on the other side, there is no market to investigate. Hence, if the SSNIP test is applied to multi-sided markets where some consumers pay a price of zero, it may lead to overly narrow market definitions. And if a market is not correctly defined, this could result in either over enforcement or under enforcement of competition law.

Because of rapid innovation in digital markets and given their two-sided nature, the SSNIP test is challenged even further. This is because if the different sides of the platform are highly dependent on each other and customers prefer to use the platform of the dominant player, markets tend to tip.[8] If innovation is quick, the market can tip to the platform of a new player. As a result, newer and better platforms may replace older and outdated platforms such that competition does not exist between markets, but firms compete for the markets. This does not only cast doubt on the SSNIP test as an effective tool in market definition, but also questions the effectiveness of market shares as an indicator of market power, as a firm with a high market share at one stage may quickly be overtaken by innovative rivals.

Cases involving digital platforms also require competition practitioners to carefully identify what amounts to pro-competitive and anti-competitive effects. In markets where customers prefer to multi-home, network effects become a weak indicator – if at all – of market power. In the *Google Android* case, for instance, the European Commission held that there were high barriers to entry in the market because of the existence of network effects (the more users use a smart mobile operating system, the developers develop apps for the system – which in turn attracts more users). The European Commission was criticized for adopting this approach in the *Google* case. In traditional assessments of market power based on network effects, the underlying assumption is that consumers derive more benefits from being part of the network of a large (or dominant firm) and therefore will tend to be reluctant to use platforms of smaller players. This is the case when consumers do not derive value from multi-homing. However, in social media platforms, consumers tend to multi-home. For example, social network users use multiple social networks such as Facebook, Twitter, Instagram, and WhatsApp complementarily and in that way make network effects less important as a barrier to entry in these markets. Hence, there is an added need for investigators to carefully consider customer behavior when faced with cases in digital platforms.

Given that digital markets are driven by rapid innovation which is normally associated with efficiencies and benefits for consumers, a critical question for competition authorities is whether regulatory intervention is necessary at all in these markets.

---

8 Tipping occurs when all sides of a network eventually converge to using one large network such that competing networks are cannibalized. This occurs when customers of the network do not use other platforms simultaneously with the primary platform (multi-homing).

Regulatory intervention is undertaken to protect competition and consumers, but where innovation is the *modus operandi* for competitiveness, ill-considered intervention by competition authorities can hamper innovation or have unintended exclusionary effects.

However, given the possible competitive risks posed by mergers in digital markets, particularly those involving firms with an entrenched dominant position, Motta & Peitz (2020) propose a presumption of harm in relation to mergers involving an actual or potential competitor. This view is shared by the Stigler report (2019) as well as the Australian Competition and Consumer Commission report (2019) which states that it "*may be worthwhile to consider whether a rebuttable presumption should also apply, in some form, to merger cases in Australia. Absent clear and convincing evidence put by the merger parties, the starting point for the court is that the acquisition will substantially lessen competition.*" We however note that the Furman report (2019) suggests the introduction of a new "balance of harms" test, which would enable the UK Competition and Markets Authority to weigh up – in broad terms – both the probabilities and magnitudes of potential outcomes and as such reject the suggestion of a presumption of harm. On the other hand, the Cremer report (2019), for the European Commission, does not propose any formal change to the merger assessment test, nor does it seek to create any general reversal of legal presumption.[9]

A further challenge for developing nations has been that of jurisdiction, especially in merger control as many of the social platforms are internationally based. For example, the *Facebook/WhatsApp* merger in 2015 was not notifiable in South Africa because WhatsApp did not generate any revenue in the country. While South Africa does have the power to investigate small mergers within six months after implementation, these do not trigger a mandatory notification to the competition authorities.

Finally, another challenge faced by the competition agencies of developing nations in the digital age is the ability to detect and investigate cartels operating in the digital economy. The traditional approaches used to initiate cartel investigations include corporate leniency programs and the dawn raids. These traditional approaches seem to be less suitable for digital markets which are more internet based. In the developed world, competition authorities are more analytical and data based in their approaches to cartel investigations. As indicated above, other international jurisdictions use digital tools to analyze data from public procurement or from the Internet in assessing cartel investigations.

Overall, from a local perspective, establishing jurisdiction; creeping acquisitions; and the adequacy of traditional competition assessment tools; all come up as

---

9   We note however that the Cremer report does introduce a new theory of harm that effectively involves major digital platforms buying up small digital start-ups as a defensive strategy to create and protect their ecosystems (p. 124).

challenges developing countries are likely to face when considering mergers and acquisitions in the digital economy.

III. STEPS TO A MORE INCLUSIVE DIGITAL FUTURE

Despite the regulatory, structural, and systemic challenges that exist in developing nations, and thus slowing down the large-scale uptake of digital transformation, there are opportunities for developing nations to harness the promised benefits of digital transformation for the growth and development of their economies. Some of the opportunities are elaborated on below.

Competition regulators are in a position to lead from the front with regulation and enforcement that deliberately sets out to broaden access to technologies and to markets. An example lies in South Africa's recent market inquiries into the price of data.[10] This inquiry ultimately led to the conclusion of settlement agreements with two of the country's largest mobile network operators in which the mobile network operators agreed to reduce the price of data to lower income segments of the market.

Firms operating in the digital economy, particularly those in positions of power – by virtue of their ownership of big data or must-have technologies – also have a role to play in ensuring competitive markets that remain open to all. Such firms should refrain from engaging in exclusionary tactics such as leveraging their power in one market in order to bind consumers to related markets. Engaging in collusion and concluding exclusive agreements in digital markets are two sets of conduct that could also come under scrutiny by competition agencies.

Industry regulators should regulate in a manner that promotes the inclusion of new technologies and applies rules equally among competitors rather than further entrenching the power of incumbents. One example is in the area of financial technology where old regulations may have the effect of excluding new applications from gaining access to the national payments system, banking platforms, and from securing licensing in a fair regulatory landscape. Rather than protecting incumbents, regulation should protect the payments system for the benefit of consumers. Any risks posed by allowing new technologies into the payments system should be managed by regulation rather than allowing the proliferation of unregulated technologies to permeate the market unchecked. The same consideration applies to regulators of communication technology.

As a whole, regulators should adopt a coordinated approach to the regulation of their digital markets. The impact of technological innovations cuts across all levels of society, hence the need for a broad perspective that provides an overarching

---

10   Data Services Market Inquiry Final Report, Dec 2019. Available at http://www.compcom. co.za/wp-content/uploads/2019/12/DSMI-Non-Confidential-Report-002.pdf.

focus for the entire economy. The pillars of cross-cutting regulation must ultimately promote greater investment in the digital economy.

If developing nations are to harness the promised benefits of a digital economy, they must regulate intentionally. These markets need unified direction, enabling legislation and a business environment poised for innovation and dynamic growth. As explained, competition policy and regulation have a major contribution to make in this regard. Of course, competition regulation alone is insufficient to achieve these outcomes; therefore, regulators and corporate stakeholders also need to play their part – as set out above – in contributing to more equitable outcomes from the digital revolution.

The Digital Economy and Competition Law in Japan

By Hideo Nakajima[1]

Abstract

In this article, I would like to discuss an issue concerning the digital economy and competition law in Japan, mainly focusing on online platform businesses from the enforcers' perspective, since I worked at the Japan Fair Trade Commission ("JFTC") as Secretary General prior to joining my present law firm in September, 2017. Section 1 gives a general overview of developments concerning the regulatory framework for online platform businesses in Japan. Section 2 delineates the possible future directions competition policy would need to take in enforcing competition law in online platform businesses, after pointing out why law enforcement faces difficulties in that area. Any views mentioned below should be regarded as entirely my own.

I.   RECENT DISCUSSIONS ABOUT THE REGULATORY FRAMEWORK FOR ONLINE PLATFORMS

Most jurisdictions, including Japan, are fully aware of the importance of digital online platforms which provide the very basis for the modern way of people's economic and social life. Consumers and business users benefit greatly from online platform services. By taking advantage of online platforms businesses are able to reach more customers and reduce costs, and consumers can enjoy more convenience and tailored online experiences. Such online platforms are results of past innovation and can be sources of future innovation.

There have been, however, several concerns raised regarding the recent rapid expansion of online platform businesses, and the digital economy in general. One concern is that the interests of users of these online platforms, whether businesses or consumers, may be or may have been jeopardized by gigantic platform businesses, or big tech companies. The other is that new entry to the platform business markets may be or may have been hampered by big tech companies. Those concerns are closely related to consumer privacy, transparency and fair-trade practices, and competition policy.

---

1   Special Advisor, White & Case LLP.

Regulators around the world have been actively taking measures to address those concerns. For example, last year the EU enacted a regulation intended to increase transparency and fairness in transactions conducted over digital platforms with EU consumers. In the U.S., under apparent political pressure, the Department of Justice, Federal Trade Commission and state attorneys general have reportedly launched investigations against many of the trade practices of major digital platforms.

Such regulations and investigations into online platform businesses may have negative side-effects on the sound and sustainable development of business activities for innovation, depending on their content and means of enforcement. Therefore, every country has been exploring regulatory frameworks in the digital economy that strike the correct balance between enhancing innovation and ensuring fair trade practices to protect the interests of online platform users. In the area of competition policy, it is of the utmost importance to ensure a free and fair competitive environment without chilling sound and sustainable incentives to innovate.

In Japan, in order to avoid new regulations on business diminishing incentives for innovation to the extent practically possible, the government prefers not to resort to comprehensive, inflexible and intrusive *ex ante* regulation, which may result in stifling business innovation or discouraging new entrants. Instead, the government places higher importance on competition law enforcement which is *ex post* and flexible on a case-by-case basis, as well as self-regulation and comply-or-explain type implementation rules, which are less intrusive.

The Japan Ministry of Economy, Trade and Industry ("METI"), the Japan Fair Trade Commission ("JFTC") and the Ministry of Internal Affairs and Communication ("MIC") have been tasked with collectively formulating a policy framework to regulate certain aspects of digital platform businesses since the latter half of 2018. To that end, a number of study groups were formed jointly by those agencies to analyze and recommend policy choices that Japan may take as the basis for the formulation of new regulations.

After the reports were issued by those expert groups earlier last year, the Japanese Government determined the future course of specific actions for improving the trade practices of digital platform businesses in Japan by a cabinet decision last June, essentially in accordance with the recommendations of those reports. The major thrust of the government actions delineated mainly by its cabinet decision, and actually taken by its relevant branches by the end of last year, is the following:

A. Establishing a New Specialized Unit Composed of Experts Having Diversified and High-Level Expertise at the Cabinet Office

In order to ensure a competitive environment in the digital platform sector, it is necessary to discuss and take actions from varieties of perspectives, such as an appropriate control by sector-specific regulations, implementing a scheme to promote data transfers and openness, an appropriate protection of personal information, as well as enforcement of the AMA.

The Conference for Digital Market Competition was established at the cabinet office last September for the purpose of overseeing the developments of trade practices and competitive environment in the digital market for supporting and coordinating law enforcement and policy formulations of the relevant government branches. The secretariat of the unit is composed of officials seconded from JFTC, METI, MIC, and other relevant branches of the government.

Its main missions include: (i) carrying out competition assessments on the digital market; (ii) conducting fact-finding surveys and making recommendations on the development of further rules governing platform business as well as on issues regarding the AMA and the Personal Information Protection Act; (iii) making recommendations for methods to promote the further development of small and venture businesses; and (iv) making recommendations concerning rules regarding competition assessments in the digital market under international frameworks, such as the G7.

B. Digital Platform Transparency Act: To Ensure Fairness and Transparency in Online Platform Transactions

Though digital platforms enhance remarkably the possibility of market access by small and venture businesses, there reportedly has been problematic conduct in transactions with users, including the unilateral imposition of contractual terms and conditions, imposition of excessive cost burdens, and excessive restrictions on access to data. In order to address those problems by making trade practices transparent through various measures, including self-regulation to the extent possible so as not to hamper innovation, the Conference for Digital Market Competition prepared a bill for "Improving Transparency and Fairness of the Specified Digital Platforms," particularly taking into account the EU's regulation on promoting fairness and transparency for business users of online intermediation services. The bill was submitted to the Diet last February.

The bill requires disclosure of terms and conditions concerning online platform services provided by large-scale online stores and app stores concerning their changes, termination of a user accounts, access to data, and ranking in search results. It also requires the Specified Digital Platforms report annually the status of their disclosure.

C. Enforcement of the Antimonopoly Act ("AMA") to Ensure Fair and Free Competition on Online Platform Business

In case the JFTC finds any specific conduct that raises competitive concerns, it is to apply the AMA to such conduct in a prompt and strict manner.

For the last couple of years, the JFTC has been dealing with several cases regarding online platform businesses, both domestic and foreign. For example, on June 1, 2017, the JFTC publicly announced the closing of its investigation into Amazon Japan. In this case, the price parity clauses and selection parity clauses (MFN clauses) included in those contracts made by Amazon Japan allegedly violated unfair trade practice rules under the AMA. The JFTC closed its investigation without taking any legal measures, since Amazon Japan voluntarily proposed specific remedial measures to deal effectively with competitive concerns raised by the Commission, which included restrictions on sellers' business activities, distortion of competition among platforms, and discouragement of innovation by platforms, or new entry. As typified by this case, the JFTC's recent investigation activities concerning single firm conduct regarding e-commerce seem to have been aiming more at restoring competitive environments in a prompt and effective manner, if appropriate, instead of taking longer amounts of time to complete investigations or issuing legal orders.

In this context, it should be noted that an EU-type commitment procedure was introduced in Japan at the end of 2018. The introduction of a commitment procedure provides the JFTC with clear legal authority to resolve alleged violations with the consent of the authority and the parties subject to the enforcement action, and this procedure is expected to enable the JFTC to take up more cases of single-firm conduct, including exploitative ones, due to abuses of superior bargaining position. as discussed below.

In fact, the JFTC applied its commitment procedure to a Japanese online platform operator concerning an alleged AMA violation as recently as last October.[2]

Looking ahead, it is worth noting that if a digital platform operator which has a superior bargaining position over consumers collects and uses personal information unduly against their interests, it may be subject to the regulation on abuse of a superior bargaining position (the "ASBP rules") under the AMA. The JFTC issued new enforcement guidelines to clarify its enforcement policy in this regard last December.[3]

The ASBP rules seem unique as compared to the antitrust regulations in other jurisdictions since they do not require market dominance but only a superior bargaining position over the counterparties of transactions.

Until now the JFTC have been applying the ASBP rules only to the B2B transactions, although there is no legal restriction under the AMA. It has now publicly announced through its new guidelines that it will apply them to the B2C transactions, in particular when the conduct of online platform operators is found to violate privacy law (the Personal Information Protection Act in Japan), or, more generally, to misuse

---

2 https://www.jftc.go.jp/en/pressreleases/yearly-2019/October/191025.html.

3 https://www.jftc.go.jp/en/pressreleases/yearly-2019/December/191217_DP.html.

personal information when they collect, hold and use it against the explicit consent of the relevant individuals.

Therefore, large technology companies would more likely be subject to ASBP enforcement in Japan, in their transactions both with businesses and consumers, since large platform businesses will often be found to be in a superior position to its customers. Therefore, they would need to pay special attention to compliance with privacy law as well as Digital Platform Transparency Act, a new legislation mentioned above.

In addition, last December, the JFTC amended the Business Combination Guidelines to clarify how it will assess the value of data, technology and innovation as well as multi-sided markets in its merger review decisions. Further, in order to address the issue of merger cases concerning acquisitions which do not meet the notification thresholds under the AMA, the JFTC recommends that the relevant parties make prior consultation with the commission for those acquisition plans that would meet several conditions set out in amendments to its business combination procedures policies. Those include the acquisitions with a value exceeding 40 billion yen, and a certain level of nexus between the parties and the Japanese economy.[4]

In parallel to the enforcement of the AMA, the JFTC has launched large-scale, comprehensive and thorough fact-finding surveys on various digital-related markets to familiarize itself with actual trade practices, thereby enabling it to apply the AMA in a prompt and effective manner. Last October, the JFTC issued a report regarding its fact-finding survey on digital platforms, which focused on B2B transactions on online retail platforms and app stores. Its report identified and assessed from competition policy viewpoints those trade practices which may disadvantage trading partners, exclude competitors, or restrict trading partners' business activities. The JFTC has now engaged, under the direction of the Conference for Digital Market Competition, in conducting another fact-finding survey in other areas of the digital sector such as online advertisement markets to develop and organize competitive assessments on trade practices there.

D. Amending the Personal Information Protection Act to Strengthen the Rights of the Individual

The Personal Information Protection Agency recently prepared a bill to amend the current Personal Information Protection Act for the purposes of strengthening the rights of individuals concerning disclosure, deletion, and suspension of the use of personal data. The bill was submitted to the Diet on March 10, 2020.

---

4 https://www.jftc.go.jp/en/pressreleases/yearly-2019/December/191217.html.

These amendments are in response to growing public concerns over the handling of personal information by big tech companies, while striking the appropriate balance between the protection and use of personal information and ensuring an equal footing between domestic and foreign companies. The bill is supposed to be submitted to the Diet early this year.

II. POSSIBLE FUTURE DIRECTIONS OF COMPETITION LAW ENFORCEMENT IN THE DIGITAL ECONOMY

A. Sources of the Challenge Competition Policy is Facing in the Digital Economy

In the present global economy, in which ICT has been developing rapidly and significantly, thereby transforming businesses and society fundamentally, the establishment of predictable and effective competition policy and enforcement in the digital economy are among the most imminent but difficult challenges every competition agency in the world is now facing.

This challenge seems particularly difficult to address due to the following several reasons:

1) First of all, the very nature of the digital economy, in particular, online platform businesses, raises difficult tasks for competition policy. Those markets or business models in the digital economy fully utilizing ICT tend to develop with significant speed and scale because of direct and indirect network effects, a relatively low level of entry barriers, and significant first-mover advantages, which tend to lead to monopoly or oligopoly.

2) Accordingly, competition policy to ensure free and fair competition there needs to be flexible and versatile enough to be applicable to conduct or trade practices in such rapidly developing markets. Those desirable attributes of competition policy in the digital economy may not be always compatible with transparency and predictability, which are other essential requirements of competition policy.

3) As for most single firm conduct, conventional competition policy usually argues that whether the conduct under investigation violates competition law or not should be determined on a case-by case basis, through effect-based considerations or economic analysis, not a form-based approach. As such, it would most likely take a certain period of

time for enforcers to investigate and reach a conclusion in an individual case. However, the very nature of the digital economy, as mentioned above, also requires that competition concerns, if any, be removed effectively at an early stage. It may be too late or ineffective for antitrust enforcers to try to restore competition on the relevant markets through measures that are taken only after a long period of investigation.

4) Third, competition in digital economy may not be conventional "competition on the market," but often "competition for the market."

Competition agencies as well as competition academics have developed quite extensively the framework and content of competition policy, including the theories of harm or specific criteria for antitrust infringements, applicable to "competition on the market." However, such concepts may not be applicable to "competition for the market," at least as they are. For example, the concepts of market dominance and market share may not be so instrumental in considering competition for the market.

In fact, it does not appear to be easy for competition policy for "competition for the market" to develop without compromising sound business incentives to innovate, particularly for disruptive innovations which are conducive to remarkable enhancements of consumer welfare and economic growth.

Big data and AI in the digital economy have raised issues such as protection of personal data (privacy) and cybersecurity, which may not to be adequately addressed by competition policy alone. Even though those regulations were introduced from the viewpoints of data protection and other policy considerations they may affect competitive conditions on the relevant market. Such new regulations or policies may affect competition on the relevant markets either in a positive or negative manner. While some of them could be properly integrated into, or work in the same direction as competition policy, others may hamper effective competition and thereby stifle innovation.

Accordingly, the development of such regulations and policies needs to be closely monitored and discussed from the viewpoint of competition policy in order to strike the right balance between competition and other policies. Also, competition agencies need to take fully into account relevant policy developments in other fields when they enforce competition policy or law. In this regard, since there is an argument that businesses could face double jeopardy if competition agencies stray too far into other policy areas, a clear line needs to be drawn between the remits of different kinds of regulators to avoid such situation.

Businesses in the digital economy are very often carried out across borders. Accordingly, competition policy addressing issues regarding those business models in the digital economy preferably requires competition policy to be universal or global.

Of course, it would be quite natural that the outcome of enforcement by antitrust agencies against the same kinds conduct may vary among jurisdictions, even when they have the same competition policy, depending, partly, on specific factors relating to the individual markets subject to the agencies' investigations.

However, if competition policy or competition law enforcement applied to the same conduct varies from one jurisdiction to another, it would likely hamper business development and innovation. A common competition policy needs to be developed among jurisdictions. Harmonization of competition policy in this area would be desirable.

Though abuse of market dominance is prohibited by competition laws all over the world, there quite often seem to have been differences in the fundamental approaches and philosophies of antitrust enforcers in this regard. In particular, there is a significant difference between the two major leading competition authorities in the world, the U.S. DOJ and the EU Commission.[5] Such differences have been widely and increasingly perceived through antitrust enforcement in the digital economy.

These days the situation has apparently been changing, particularly on the U.S. side, but the existence of such a difference shows the practical difficulties of convergence in the digital economy.

B. Future Directions for Competition Policy in Enforcing Competition Law on Online Platforms

Considering the points noted above, I believe that competition policy, in particular competition law enforcement, should aim at pursuing, among other things, the following courses of action for addressing issues raised by the digital economy.

1. Continuous and Timely Issuance of Fact-finding Survey Reports

In addition to enforcement guidelines, continuous and timely issuance of fact-finding survey reports to identify conduct that may raise competitive concerns is desirable to enhance predictability and transparency, and to avoid ambiguity in competition law enforcement.

Fact-finding surveys targeting some areas or markets of the digital economy,

---

5 Broadly speaking, the EU tends to emphasize the special responsibility of dominant companies to maintain competition on whatever markets they are going to engage in, while the U.S. tends to argue for monopolists to be, no less than any other competitors, encouraged to compete aggressively, stressing the importance of monopoly which induces risk taking, thereby producing innovation and economic growth.

whether they are called market studies or sector inquiries, can provide competition agencies with precious opportunities to present their views on novel forms of conduct, practices or business models in the digital economy which raise antitrust concerns. In fact, through those surveys, competition, agencies could enjoy much broader over-sight than through the enforcement of individual cases, whose number is necessarily limited due to resource constraints.

Further, such studies are, like enforcement guidelines, expected to encourage the companies concerned to review and modify their conduct, practices or business models voluntarily to deal effectively and promptly with the antitrust concerns held by the agencies, though, of course, if any voluntary measures are not taken by the companies concerned, the agencies need to proceed to regular antitrust investigations.

2. Flexible Law Enforcement, Considering Cooperation Provided by the Companies Concerned

A flexible approach to law enforcement, including flexible imposition of sanctions against alleged or real violations of competition law should be applied, if appropriate, to avoid chilling effects on incentives to innovate.

In the digital economy, it may be desirable and in fact necessary under some situations for competition agencies to give higher priority to prompt and effective restoration of the competitive environment to the extent possible, in particular in those cases where the relevant parties voluntarily take appropriate actions to allay competitive concerns.

Prompt and effective restoration of the competitive environment should be of utmost importance for the sound and sustainable development of the rapidly chang-ing digital economy. Should appropriate remedial measures be taken voluntarily by the parties under investigation, the agencies could close their investigation without issuing legal orders, or they may not impose administrative fines on the parties. Such decisions will should only be taken if appropriate, taking into account the degree of the deterrent effect that fines may have against future infringements.

Also, commitment procedures could be fully utilized to enable prompt and effective removal of competitive concerns raised by businesses' unilateral conduct or practices.

In this context, I would like to emphasize the importance of close collabora-tion and smooth communication by competition agencies with businesses subject to enforcement, as well as through fact-finding surveys. Such collaboration should be conducive to ensuring or restoring competition in the digital economy in a prompt and effective manner without causing chilling effects and undermining innovation.

3. Enhanced Inter-agency Cooperation for Converging Law Enforcement

I believe that a significant breakthrough in developing appropriate competition policy for the digital economy can be made by further enhancement of bilateral or multilateral inter-agency cooperation to converge or harmonize, as much as possible, law enforcement, or competition policy in general, among various jurisdictions. The recent convergence or harmonization of procedures and substantial criteria for merger review among jurisdictions all over the world is an excellent precedent. As we have seen, various endeavors to respond to such a challenge in the digital sector have already started bilaterally and multilaterally, but they need to be urgently enhanced. For example, I believe that the OECD is in a suitable position to take a strong and effective initiative in addressing this difficult and imminent challenge by leading and organizing the discussion among the antitrust community towards its recommendation on competition policy in the digital economy, as it did regarding artificial intelligence in May, 2019.

III. CONCLUSION

In Japan, the regulatory framework for digital online platforms has recently been developed through the government's strong initiatives. This includes an active and extensive enforcement of the Antimonopoly Act, the introduction of Digital Platform Transparency Act, amendments to the Personal Information Protection Act, and the establishment of the Conference for Digital Market Competition at the cabinet office. A fact-finding survey continues on various areas of the digital platform business, such as online advertisement markets. It is expected that the free and fair competitive environment for online platform businesses will be enhanced under this regulatory framework in Japan in 2020.

That said, ensuring the effective enforcement of competition law on online platforms is a great challenge for every competition agency around the world. It requires, among other things, (1) not only transparent and predictable, but also versatile and flexible enforcement; (2) not only effect-based approaches through economic analysis, but also prompt and effective enforcement; (3) appropriate enforcement not only as regards competition on the market but also competition for the market; and (4) global convergence or harmonization of law enforcement. The entire antitrust community, consisting of academics, practitioners and enforcers, needs to step up its efforts to meet those requirements, in full cooperation with ICT experts and the business community.

Setting Sail on a Sea of Doubt Again?: Antitrust Review of Data-Driven Non-Horizontal Mergers

By Andy C. M. Chen[1]

Abstract

The arrival of the digital economy has spurred a new wave of enforcement interest in data-driven non-horizontal mergers by global competition agencies. At the same time, new theories concerning the likely competitive harms from such mergers are reshaping what used to be a relatively clear and predictable enforcement landscape in antitrust law. We explore this issue in this paper. Beginning with a brief summary of the definition and basic features of "big data," we consider the types of anticompetitive harms and procompetitive benefits produced by data-driven non-horizontal mergers. Enforcement experience from the United States, the European Union, and Taiwan are then described and analyzed to illustrate how these theories were applied in relevant cases. As will be shown, although new theories specific to competition related to big data have been proposed, most of the competitive concerns raised by these theories can still be contained and reviewed under existing analytical frameworks for vertical and conglomerate mergers involving the acquisition of big data. However, the challenges to non-horizontal merger reviews from big data are duly recognized and we suggest several of the policy responses to these challenges at the end of this paper.

I.   INTRODUCTION

In *United States v. Addyston Pipe & Steel Co.* by the U.S. Supreme Court,[2] Justice Taft famously stated that a full-blown rule-of-reason analysis of collusive agreements would be forcing the court to "set sail on the sea of doubt."[3] He argued for understanding the "proper limits of the relaxation of the rules for determining the unreasonableness of restraints of trade."[4] In comparison with cartel investigation, antitrust review of non-horizontal mergers followed a relatively clear course in the past. Conven-

---

1   Dean and Professor of Law, Department of Financial and Economic Law, School of Law, Chung Yuan Christian University, Taiwan.

2   85 F. 271 (6th Cir. 1898), aff'd 175 U.S. 211 (1899).

3   85 F. at 284.

4   85 F. at 283.

tional antitrust thinking tended to view vertical and conglomerate mergers as innocuous to market competition and generally to be efficiency-enhancing. In cases where the likelihood for the post-merger competitive harms to occur was high, these could be addressed by conditioning the approval of the mergers on the imposition of behavioral or structural remedies on the merged entities. This optimistic and simplified view toward market impacts from non-horizontal mergers has received recent challenge,[5] specifically in mergers involving the acquisition of big data. Mergers involving data acquisition have rekindled the debate on how to design and implement an analytical framework for pre-merger review by competition authorities to properly assess competitive effects from abusive uses of big data after mergers occur. The word "rekindle" in this instance indicates that this is not a new competition issue. Antitrust has a long history of dealing with data, or more broadly, information, being strategically employed to facilitate collusion or to boycott rivals.[6] What makes it a more appealing concern today might be attributable to the rapid development and application of web technologies and the popularization of online business models. The collectible amount of data has increased unprecedentedly, while the time needed to organize and disseminate it has substantially declined. Consequently, it has been argued that the incentive for merged entities to abuse acquired data for anticompetitive gains has also heightened.[7] More controversially, the regulatory framework is being extended to include issues typically not covered by antitrust law, such as privacy protection under this new development. This in turn requires the competition authorities to assess factors that are difficult to verify objectively, adding to the complexity and unpredictability of merger review. Are we back in the unchartered water that Justice Taft advised us to avoid more than a century ago?

II. THE DEFINITION AND FEATURES OF "BIG DATA"

The explosion of data and its challenges to data storage and processing have long been recognized by researchers in information science.[8] In 1997, two scholars from NASA, Michael Cox & David Ellesworth, presented a paper on the storage

---

5   For example, four renowned antitrust scholars have recently proposed that the enforcement agencies should "[c]onsider and investigate the full range of potential anticompetitive harms." Jonathan B. Baker, Nacy L. Rose, Steven C. Salop & Fiona Scott Morton, *Five Principles for Vertical Merger Enforcement Policy*, 33 ANTITRUST 12, 13 (2019).

6   See e.g. *Associated Press v. United States*, 326 U.S. 1 (1945).

7   See generally, MAURICE E. STUCKE & ALLEN P. GRUNES, BIG DATA AND COMPETITION POLICY, Chapter 6 & 15 (2016).

8   Peter J. Denning, *Saving All the Bits*, 78 AMERICAN SCIENTIST, 402 (1990) ("The rate and volume of information flow overwhelm our networks, storage devices and retrieval systems, as well as the human capacity for comprehension.") See also Gil Press, *A Very Short History of Big Data*, FORBES, (May 9, 2013) (describing the emergence and evolution of the concept of Big Data), available at https://www.forbes.com/sites/gilpress/2013/05/09/a-very-short-history-of-big-data/#473d15c665a1.

problem for computers caused by the huge dataset generated by visualization technology. They called it "the problem of big data."[9] Subsequent advancements in data storage technology helped to popularize the application of big data to disclose the unknown correlation and hidden patterns among events that in turn facilitate market forecasts. The vastly enhanced value of this technology was depicted in a 2012 commentary in the New York Times, entitled "The Age of Big Data," in which it listed the likely commercial or non-commercial (i.e. government policy, health care, politics, sports, social activities) future applications of big data.[10] Given its importance, however, a lack of consensus still exists among academics and practitioners on the definition of big data. For the purpose of antitrust analysis, "bigness" is no longer the only or even the most decisive feature of big data. Qualitative elements such as the ability to better collect, process, manage, analyze, and apply data could provide a firm with competitive advantages over its competitors, even though it may not be able to secure as much data as its competitors can.[11] Currently, the most frequently cited definition of big data is the "4Vs" definition initially proposed by Doug Laney in 2001 and later followed by the OECD Competition Committee.[12] Under this definition, big data typically demonstrates the features of large volume, high velocity, and variety. Stucke & Grunes add "value" to the list as the additional feature of big data.[13]

A. Volume

The improvement of data storage technologies has dramatically lowered the costs of data collection, processing, and analysis. As the trend toward networking is

---

9   Michael Cox & David Ellesworth, *Application-Controlled Demand Paging for Out-of-Core Visualization* PROCEEDINGS OF THE 8TH CONFERENCE ON VISUALIZATION '97, IEEE COMPUTER SOCIETY PRESS 235 (1997). ("Visualization provides an interesting challenge for computer systems: data sets are generally quite large, taxing the capacities of main memory, local disk, and even remote disk. We call this the problem of big data.").

10   Steve Lohr, *The Age of Big Data*, THE NEW YORK TIMES (February 11, 2012), available at http://www.nytimes.com/2012/02/12/sunday-review/big-datas-impact-in-the-world.htm.

11   For example, the number of users of Myspace were greater than those of Facebook when Facebook initially entered the market of online platform for social media but was eventually outcompeted by Facebook. Similarly, better technologies for data collection and analytics might explain why Google replaced Yahoo to be the key provider of the service for online search. Xavier Boutin & Georg Clemens, *Defining "Big Data" in Antitrust,* 1 COMPETITION POLICY INTERNATIONAL: ANTITRUST CHRONICLE 26 (August 2017).

12   Doug Laney, *3D Data Management: Controlling Data Volume, Velocity, and Variety*, posted on February 6, 2001, available at https://blogs.gartner.com/doug-laney/files/2012/01/ad949-3D-Data-Management-Controlling-Data-Volume-Velocity-and-Variety.pdf;   OECD Competition Committee Roundtables (Background note by the Secretariat), *Big Data: Bring Competition Policy to the Digital Era* 5 (29-30 November 2016), available at http:///one.oecd.org/document/DAF/COMP(2016)14/en/pdf.

13   STUCKE & GRUNES, *supra* note 7, at 15.

becoming increasingly prominent and the devices for wireless data transmission are becoming more portable and customized, it was predicted that the global volume of data transmission will grow exponentially.[14]

B. Velocity

Once big data becomes an important input for service provision, the ability to manage huge datasets in a swift, orderly, and timely manner will be vital for participating firms to compete effectively in the relevant markets. Again, the progress in transmission technologies makes real-time data management and analysis possible and enhances the impacts of their analytical results. Ranging from the prediction of unemployment rates to matching real estate transactions, big data has been used to significantly improve the quality of business decisions and governmental policy making.[15]

C. Variety

Increasing collectible data volume and velocity for data transmission in turn renders the types of data utilized by participants in big data industries highly diversified.[16] Data gathered from written messages, e-mails, websites, tweets, and satellite photos allow data holders to obtain information concerning the locations (IP or real addresses), birthdays, genders, family members, dietary preferences, shopping habits, and frequency and time spent surfing the Internet. This sort of "data fusion," as was dubbed by the OECD, generates new types of data that enable product or service providers to better understand and develop markets.[17]

D. Value

The added value to relevant industries from big data is attributable to the following two factors. First, better analytical tools have been created to more precisely interpret data and to assist data holders to better influence and control data targets, be they natural phenomena, social systems, or individuals.[18] In addition, the "volume," "velocity," and "variety" dimensions of big data also contribute to

---

14 OECD, *supra* note 12.

15 OECD, *id.* at 7.

16 Big data today consists of the following five major sources: (1) large scale enterprise system; (2) online social graphs; (3) mobile devices; (4) internet-of-things; (5) open data/public data. Bart Baesen, Ravi Bapna, James R. Marsden, Jan Vanthienen & J. Leon Zhao, *Transformational Issues of Big Data and Analytics in Networked Business*, 40 MIS QUARTERLY 807, 808 (2016).

17 OECD, *supra* note 12, at 6.

18 STUCKE & GRUNES, *supra* note 7, at 22.

enhancing the value of big data for industries. Several new and creative business models, such as online-to-offline commerce, networks of smart vehicles, and pro-active customer care, would not be possible had big data not been involved in the operation process.[19]

III. ASSESSMENT OF COMPETITIVE EFFECTS OF NON-HORIZONTAL MERGERS INVOLVING BIG DATA

Under antitrust classification, non-horizontal mergers include vertical and conglomerate mergers. Vertical mergers refer to combinations or acquisitions be-tween firms at different levels of production or distributional chains. These also include mergers between IPR licensing firms and their licensees. Conglomerate mergers refer to mergers that are neither horizontal nor vertical. Conventional thinking in antitrust law treats non-horizontal mergers more leniently than hori-zontal mergers because both vertical and non-horizontal mergers do not, at least in the short run, increase the post-merger horizontal market power of the merging parties; their potential adverse effects to market competition are typically the prod-ucts of post-merger business arrangements, not the mergers themselves. In addition, non-horizontal mergers typically produce substantial procompetitive effects, such as mitigating successive-monopoly problems, creating synergies efficiency, or avoid-ing free-riding behavior that has the potential to undermine consumers' welfare.[20] However, this favorable enforcement attitude toward non-horizontal mergers seems to be changing in recent years.[21]

A. The Theories of Competitive Harm and the Reviewing Frameworks

As non-horizontal mergers do not directly alter the existing distribution of market share among horizontal competitors in the relevant markets, competition au-thorities have typically been concerned about the potential anticompetitive effects created by post-merger contractual arrangements between merged parties. Accord-ingly, the review process tends to focus more on the behavioral rather than structural dimension of the mergers.

1. Vertical Mergers

Most jurisdictions have based their reviews on the "foreclosure" theory to assess the competitive harms created by vertical mergers and have applied the "ability-

---

19　Baesen et al., *supra* note 16, at 811-12.

20　Einer Elhauge & Damien Geradin, Global Antitrust Law and Economics 1146 (3rd ed. 2018).

21　See generally, Steven C. Salop, *Invigorating Vertical Merger Enforcement*, 127 Yale L. J. 1962 (2018).

incentive-effect" reviewing framework to evaluate the probability of the market being foreclosed by the merger and its potential procompetitive effects.[22] Under the foreclosure theory, vertical mergers could lead to *input* foreclosure. The merged entity may refuse to supply a critical input to its downstream competitors or implement discriminatory trading terms for such transactions after mergers in order to raise its rivals' costs of participating in downstream competition.[23] Vertical mergers could also facilitate a merging firm to practice *customer* foreclosure. Namely, the downstream unit of the merged entity commits after the merger to purchasing all of its input requirements exclusively from its upstream unit or to reducing its purchases from the merged entity's upstream rivals.[24]

Whether the foreclosure strategy would be implemented and effective depends on whether the merging firm has the incentive and ability to exclude upstream and downstream competition via vertical integration.[25] Both the *incentive* and *ability* elements are required to declare a vertical merger problematic. The ability to foreclose should not be interpreted to mean that the merging firm will definitely have the incentive to implement the foreclosure strategies and vice versa.[26] Ability to exclude rivals through vertical mergers is closely related to the market power that the merged entity has after the merger. As the EU Guidelines on Non-horizontal Mergers had described:[27] "For input foreclosure to be a concern, the vertically integrated firm resulting from the merger must have a significant degree of market power in the upstream market. It is only in these circumstances that the [integrated] firm can be expected to have a significant influence on the conditions of competition in the upstream market and thus, possibly, on prices and supply conditions in the downstream market." Similarly, the integrated firm needs to have market power at the downstream market to successfully implement the foreclosure strategy. Market power is primarily assessed by the market share commanded by the merged entity in a properly defined relevant market. In addition to market share, market power could also be inferred in some jurisdictions, including Taiwan, from the uniqueness or importance of an input (e.g. the essentiality of a patent) that is controlled by the merged entity and that is indispensable for downstream production.

---

22 International Competition Network, *Vertical Mergers Comparison Study* 2 (May 2019), available at https://www.internationalcompetitionnetwork.org/wp-content/uploads/2019/05/MWG-Vertical-Mergers-Comparison-Study.pdf.

23 Salop, *supra* note 21, at 1975.

24 Salop, *id.*

25 OECD Competition Committee Policy Roundtables (Background Note), *Economic Evidence in Merger Analysis* 27-29 (2011).

26 *Id.* at 28.

27 Commission Notice, *Guidelines on the assessment of non-horizontal mergers under the Council Regulation on the control of concentrations between undertakings,"* paragraph 35 (2008).

The incentive to foreclose is in essence a cost-benefit analysis to the merging firm. In the case of input foreclosure, for example, the merging firm faces a tradeoff between profit lost in the upstream market due to reduced input sales and profit gains from short or near-term sales expansion at the downstream market.[28] Only when the profits outweigh the costs will the merged entity have the incentive to implement a foreclosure scheme.

Finally, the "effect" test requires the competition authority to review whether the vertical merger may substantially lessen market competition in the sense of reduced market share or trade volume at either the upstream or downstream market, given its foreclosure potential. This test aims to ensure that competition law would not be directed toward protecting "competitors" rather than "competition." However, the procompetitive effects of a vertical merger should also be considered and counterweighted against its market foreclosure effects. As will be introduced later in this paper, numerous well-recognized efficiencies exist that vertical mergers might create to decrease the costs from divergence in promotional incentives within the distribution chain. These benefits have led commentators to suggest that competition authorities should adopt a more permissible reviewing standard for vertical mergers than that used for horizontal mergers.[29]

2. Conglomerate Mergers

A conglomerate merger raises two types of competitive concerns: (1) it may eliminate potential horizontal competition; and (2) it could enable the merged entity to engage in vertical exclusionary conduct.[30] By "potential" competition, this could be further divided into *perceived* and *actual* potential competition.[31] The former refers to the elimination of the pre-merger "threat" or "pressure" not to price high, which is imposed by the presence of the firms at the edge of the market. Once the threat is weakened or eliminated, the incumbent firm would have the incentive to set a new and higher price. Similarly, the harms to actual potential competition refer to the *lost opportunity* for the existing firm to improve its market performance that results from the entry of an additional competitor via a more procompetitive manner, such as new entry or entry through a "toehold" acquisition of a present small competitor.[32]

---

28 *Id.* at paragraph 40.

29 See James A. Keyte & Kenneth B. Schwartz, *Getting Vertical Deals Through the Agencies: "Let's Make a Deal,"* 29 ANTITRUST 10, 11–12 (2015); Michael H. Riordan & Steven C. Salop, *Evaluating Vertical Mergers: A Post-Chicago Approach*, 63 ANTITRUST L. J. 513, 519 (1995); David T. Scheffman & Richard S. Higgins, *Vertical Mergers: Theory and Policy*, 12 GEO. MASON L. REV. 967, 976 (2004); Paul Yde, *Non-Horizontal Merger Challenges: A Solution in Search of a Problem*, 22 ANTITRUST 74, 81 (2007).

30 ELHAUGE & GERADIN, *supra* note 20, at 1181-82.

31 See U.S DOJ HORIZONTAL MERGER GUIDELINES, paragraphs 4.11 & 4.12 (1984).

32 *Id.* at paragraph 4.112.

Alternatively, foreclosure via a *reciprocity* arrangement and *portfolio* effect are two of the most frequently discussed types of exclusionary conduct in the literature on conglomerate mergers. In conglomerate mergers involving a buyer of product *A* and the seller of product *B*, reciprocity theory describes a scenario under which the merged entity bundles the obligation to purchase product *B* as a condition for its purchase of product *A* from a third party. Modern U.S. antitrust courts, however, have generally refused to follow this line of reasoning in order to block a conglomerate merger,[33] while the EU has appeared to be more receptive to this anticompetitive theory.[34] A portfolio effect from a conglomerate merger is a rather broad and somewhat vague term. According to the OECD, this could be defined as "the pro- and anticompetitive effects that may arise in mergers combining branded products in which the parties enjoy market power, but not necessarily dominance, and which are sold in neighboring or related markets."[35] The main anticompetitive concerns for conglomerate mergers with portfolio effects lie in their potential to maintain or expand the merged entity's market power by facilitating various post-merger exclusionary conducts rather than directly changing the market structure.[36] In *Guinness/Grand Metropolitan*,[37] for example, the European Commission argued that the merger of the two largest spirit suppliers in the European Union would allow them to combine the two parties' ranges or portfolios of products and brands. The market position of the holder of the portfolios in relation to its customers was stronger because:

---

33   The reciprocity theory was indeed applied by the U.S. Supreme Court in 1965 in *FTC v. Consolidated Foods*. 380 U.S. 592 (1965) In this case, the respondent attempted to induce reciprocal buying of products by the respondent's suppliers after the merger. The FTC held that the opportunity for reciprocal buying in this oligopolistic industry would significantly lessen market competition. The Court of Appeal disagreed and reversed the decision. The Supreme Court then reversed the decision by the Court of Appeal, holding that the findings by the FTC regarding the anticompetitive effect from reciprocal buying was supported by substantial evidence. Nevertheless, the rather reserved attitude toward the reciprocity theory was echoed more recently in the comments from former Deputy Assistant Attorney General William Kolasky on the case of *GE/Honeywell*: "After fifteen years of painful experience with these now long-abandoned theories, the U.S. antitrust agencies concluded that antitrust should rarely interfere with any conglomerate merger.... U.S. agencies simply could not identify any conditions under which a conglomerate merger would be likely to give the merged firm the ability and incentive to raise prices and restrict output." William Kolasky, *Conglomerate Mergers And Range Effects: It's A Long Way From Chicago To Brussels* (address before the George Mason University Symposium Washington, DC, November 9, 2001), available at https://www.justice.gov/atr/speech/conglomerate-mergers-and-range-effects-its-long-way-chicago-brussels.

34   The most famous case was the *GE/Honeywell* merger. *General Electric v. Commission*, T-210/01 [2005] E.C.R. II-5575.

35   OECD Policy Roundtables, *Portfolio Effects in Conglomerate Mergers* 22-23 (Background Note) (2001).

36   *Id.* at 23.

37   Commission Decision 98/602/EC, OJ 1998 L. 288/24.

"[H]e is able to provide a range of products and will account for a greater proportion of their business, he will have greater flexibility to structure his prices, promotion, and discounts, he will have greater potential for tying, and he will be able to realize economies of scale and scope in his sale and marketing activities. Finally, the implicit (or explicit) threat of a refusal to supply is more potent."[38]

Similar to vertical mergers, to block a conglomerate merger based on either a reciprocity or a portfolio theory requires the competition authority to show that the merged entity has the ability and incentive to implement the exclusionary strategies.[39]

3. Procompetitive Effects of Non-Horizontal Mergers

Various procompetitive effects have been proposed to justify vertical and conglomerate mergers. In addition to mitigating the inefficiency produced from two-level pricing decisions, the benefits from vertical mergers are mostly associated with their contribution to controlling the incentive disparity inherent in vertical distribution. Although profit maximization may be the unifying goal pursued by both the upstream supplier and downstream distributor, they may have diverging views on the way in which that goal should be realized. The upstream supplier may wish to increase its profits by increasing the *sale amounts* of its products at the downstream market, and therefore, increase the derived demands of its products from the distributors at the wholesale market. In contrast, the distributor may simply try to accomplish its profit-maximizing goal by reducing the costs for each unit of product sold, including, for example, the promotional costs that may enhance the popularity of the distributed product, and thus expand its overall sale. By merging the downstream distributor, suppliers could internalize this type of "externality" generated by the distributor's self-interested considerations.

Specifically, vertical mergers can bring forth the following benefits:[40]

---

38 *Id*. paragraph 39.

39 See e.g. *Commission v. Tetra Laval BV*, paragraph 74, Case C-12/03 P. [2005] E.C.R I-987 (to establish that conglomerate merger is an essential step in leveraging market power, the court must examine "both of the incentives to adopt such conduct and the factors liable to reduce, or even eliminate, those incentives, including the possibility that the conduct is unlawful."); *GE/Honey*, *supra* note 34, paragraph 327 ("[I]t was for the Commission to establish not only that the merged entity had the ability to transfer [its reciprocity in the engine market] … to the markets for avionics and non-avionics products but also…that it was likely that the merged entity would engage in such conduct.").

40 OECD Policy Roundtables, *Vertical Mergers in the Technology, Media and Telecom Sector* (Background Note) 27-28 (June 7, 2019).

(1) control of the successive monopoly problem, referring to the mark-up effect on the final price of the distributed product due to two-level profit-maximizing pricing decisions individually and independently made by the supplier and the distributor.

(2) avoidance of free-riding behavior to control the cost-saving distributor from taking advantage of the promotional efforts provided by other distributors to increase its own sales without sharing its costs.

(3) elimination of the hold-up problem emerging from the idiosyncratic investments made specifically for the operation of the distribution network. These investments are frequently without salvage value if the distribution relationship is terminated and would subject the party making the investment to the risk of being forced to accept unfair or disfavored trading terms by the party to which the investments were made.[41]

(4) elimination of input substitution as a result of not using the more expensive input supplied by an upstream monopolist and switching to less expensive but low-quality input by the downstream competing firms. For example, a telecom company may integrate an upstream company in order to access optical fiber cable at a cheaper cost and to avoid substituting it with cheaper copper cable.[42]

(5) facilitation of price discrimination[43] by allowing the vertically integrated firm access to information concerning various demand preferences to design different price schemes for preference divergence. A vertical merger could also enable the integrated firm to monitor and avoid arbitrage among favored and disfavored buyers, which could disrupt price discrimination.

(6) promotion of inter-brand competition was demonstrated by the Microsoft/Nokia merger. After acquiring Nokia's device department,

---

41   See Benjamin Klein, Robert G. Crawford & Armen A. Alchian, *Vertical Integration, Appropriable Rents, and the Competitive Contracting Process*, 21 J. L. & ECON. 297 (1978).

42   OECD, *supra* note 40, at 28.

43   Although the term "price discrimination" carries a negative tone in law, it could be welfare-enhancing for both the consumers and the market. OECD, *id.*

Microsoft would be able to enter the mobile telecommunications market and offer a new operating system for smartphones so that it could compete with the existing Android and iOS systems.

For conglomerate mergers, the most frequently mentioned efficiency is consumption synergy, through which the merged entity could offer consumers the opportunity to do one-stop shopping and reduce transaction costs. Conglomerate mergers can also create the incentive and demand to form new firms and can facilitate the transfers of unproductive assets to more efficient users. In addition, the threat of being taken over by firms outside the industry could further broaden and strengthen the pressure on a manager to improve management. Finally, conglomerate mergers enhance the efficiency from economies of scope and may assist domestic firms to effectively compete in world markets.[44]

4. Incorporating Big Data into the Framework

In non-horizontal mergers driven by the consideration to acquire big data, certain data-specific anticompetitive harms have been raised and debated by antitrust commentators. These debates have centered on the need and scope for competition authorities to consider these harms when conducting merger reviews.[45]

First, when big data is an important or essential input for market competition, acquisition and control of datasets may assist the merged entity to fortify the network effect created from using big data. The "volume" dimension of big data might significantly raise the costs for competitors to obtain the sufficient amount of data required in order to compete successfully with the merged entity. In addition, the merger could further enhance the "variety" of the big data controlled by the merged entity, making it costlier for competitors to produce or collect its own datasets with the same or higher degree of variety in order to overcome the data-centered entry barrier created by the merged entity.

Second, vertical and conglomerate mergers provide the merged entity with the opportunity to interact directly with its competitors at the upstream, downstream, or neighboring markets. The probability of the merged entity being able to access sensitive information concerning its competitors or to share its own with its rivals could also be increased. This collusion-facilitating concern might be more legitimate in data-driven than traditional mergers because the "velocity" feature of big data reduces the negotiation cost for organizing cartels and the monitoring cost for detecting cheating by cartel members.

---

44   See Joseph F. Brodley, *Limiting Conglomerate Mergers: The Need for Legislation*, 40 Ohio St. L. J. 867, 875 (1979).

45   See e.g. Darren S. Tucker & Hill B. Wellford, *Big Mistakes Regarding Big Data*, Antitrust Source (December 2014); Stucke & Grunes, *supra* note 12, Chapter 6.

Third, big data and data analytics generate new types of information that could assist the merged entity in predicting where future business is and who a future competitor could be. This enables the merged entity in data-driven mergers to acquire preemptively the companies that are likely to become its competitors and to eliminate competition as early as possible.[46]

Finally, recent investigations have also revealed the possibility of founding the theory of competitive harm for conglomerate mergers on the "interoperability" issue, particularly for mergers that occurred in the software industry. Under this theory, the merged entity could intentionally degrade the interoperability of its acquired data or software with the products or services provided by its downstream rivals. If interoperability is vital for a rival to engage in downstream competition, then this can be an effective foreclosure strategy.

In contrast, there might also be procompetitive effects that are specific to data-driven non-horizontal mergers.[47] For example, new data acquired through a merger may create the effect of a "user feedback loop" to enable the merged entity to innovate and to improve the quality of its services offered to users of digital platforms. Furthermore, the increased availability of big data post-merger could also allow a merged entity to better monetize its online platform through targeted advertising.[48] In a two-sided market, better targeted advertising and the increased profits from advertisements could be used to subsidize the free service provided by the merged entity at the other side of the market for search or social networking. Contrary to prediction by the foreclosure theory, several studies have shown that platform integration of applications developed by third parties, such as Facebook's integration of Instagram, may help to promote competing third-party app developers.[49]

Facilitating the design of different pricing schemes for consumers with diversified preferences may be the primary trigger for data-driven mergers. With the data acquired becoming more "voluminous" and "various," this enhances the merged entity's ability to provide price combinations more precisely tailored to individual needs.

---

46 See Lear, *Ex-post Assessment of Merger Control Decisions in Digital Markets-Final Report* 7 (prepared for the Competition and Market Authority, May 9, 2019), available at https://assets.publishing.service.gov.uk/government/uploads/system/uploads/attachment_data/file/803576/CMA_past_digital_mergers_GOV.UK_version.pdf.

47 See Ben Holles de Peyer, *EU Merger Control and Big Data*, 13 JOURNAL OF COMPETITION LAW AND ECONOMICS 767, 776-78 (2018).

48 *Id.* at 777.

49 Zhuoxin Li & Ashish Agarwal, *Platform Integration and Demand Spillovers in Complementary Markets: Evidence from Facebook's Integration of Instagram*, 63 MANAGEMENT SCIENCE 3438, 3449 (2017) ("[T]he resulting demand increase for Instagram creates a positive spillover effects on the demand for big third-party applications causing an overall increase in the demand for big third-party apps.").

As the OECD has described, a telecom company could acquire a media company in order to access personal data to provide better telecom services to consumers.[50] Similarly, in mergers involving financial institutions and Fintech companies, detailed data concerning income and credit history acquired through a merger and coupled with sophisticated methods of data analytics would allow the merged entity to provide affordable financial products whose prices would vary with the wealth of the buyers. This would facilitate the realization of "inclusive finance," an important goal championed by international organizations and pursued by countries to increase the accessibility of financial services for disadvantaged groups in society and to maintain economic stability.[51]

IV. CASE ILLUSTRATIONS

A. United States

After the 1977 landmark decision of *GTE v. Sylvania* by the Supreme Court,[52] U.S. antitrust jurisprudence for vertical cases has henceforth been quite lenient to antitrust defendants. In the context of data-driven mergers, no deal has been blocked simply because of the competitive concerns that arise from owning or controlling additional data.

In *Amazon/Whole Foods*, Amazon planned to acquire all of the stock of Whole Foods Market, the largest retailer of high end, organic groceries in the United States. As Amazon already sold groceries online and made home deliveries, the proposed merger could be characterized as a horizontal merger. The vertical and data dimensions of this merger were that Amazon might want to "transform online shopping for groceries by combining its data/software resources and logistics with Whole Foods' networks of food suppliers, its superb brands, and its network of retail outlets in major urban centers, using these assets as a launching pad so that it can take over online orders for groceries."[53] After investigation, the U.S. Federal Trade Commission

---

50 OECD, *supra* note 40, at 28.

51 OECD, *Financial Inclusion and Consumer Empowerment in Southeast Asia* 9 (2018) ("The benefits of digitalization include lower consumer costs as well as more convenient, faster and secure transactions. Further, there are opportunities for innovative product design to reach disadvantaged groups (such as women and the poor) and, in doing so, integrate these vulnerable groups into the formal financial system.")

52 433 U.S. 36 (1977).

53 William Markham, *Amazon's Merger with Whole Foods Market* (June 27, 2017), available at https://www.markhamlawfirm.com/amazons-merger-whole-foods-market-william-markham-2017/.

("FTC") decided to clear the merger.[54] Although the reasons for not challenging the merger are unavailable, we could infer from the statement by a former Commissioner who investigated this case that efficiency (particularly dynamic efficiency) that could be realized from the merger played an important role in the FTC's decision: "When you embrace competitive markets, you also embrace change and the need for firms to constantly improve or risk being left behind. These are all things that the antitrust laws exist to foster, not prohibit."[55]

In *Google/ITA*,[56] Google announced its plan to acquire ITA software in 2011. ITA software was a travel software company that owned the airfare pricing and shopping system QPX. QPX provided online travel agencies such as Kayak or Expedia with information about, *inter alia*, airline pricing, schedules, and seat availability, and was therefore a crucial input for online travel agencies. Google sought to upgrade its search services by launching a travel website after the merger. After review, the U.S. Department of Justice ("DOJ") concluded that the merged entity would have the ability and incentive to either deny or degrade access to the QPX system to competing travel websites. In particular, the DOJ was concerned that if Google refused to renew existing QPX licensing contracts or signed new contracts on less favorable terms with competing travel websites, it could fully or partially foreclose downstream competition. Google, on the other hand, argued that the transaction would provide it with a platform on which to develop new and innovative flight search services for consumers. The DOJ conditionally cleared the merger by imposing on Google the following behavioral remedies:

- The duty to extend existing licensing agreements and grant new licenses for QPX to flight search companies on similar or fair, reasonable, and non-discriminatory terms;

- The duty to continue improving QPX, not reduce R&D expenses, and make any upgrades available to competitors;

- The duty to establish an internal firewall to protect confidential data; and

---

54 Statement of Federal Trade Commission's Acting Director of the Bureau of Competition on the Agency's Review of Amazon.com, Inc.'s Acquisition of Whole Foods Market Inc., (Aug. 23, 2017), available at https://www.ftc.gov/news-events/press-releases/2017/08/statement-federal-trade-commissions-acting-director-bureau.

55 Maureen K. Ohlhausen, *Reflections on Recent Competition Enforcement at the FTC*, available at https://www.ftc.gov/system/files/documents/public_statements/1408329/09072018_posting_version_mko_fordham.pdf.

56 See *United States v. Google Inc.*, available at https://www.justice.gov/atr/case/us-v-google-inc-and-ita-software-inc.

- The duty not to tie ITA software to other Google products.

In clearing the *Microsoft/Yahoo!* merger in 2010,[57] the DOJ maintained that the transaction would allow Microsoft to have access to a larger set of queries, which should "accelerate the automated learning of Microsoft's search and paid search algorithm and enhance Microsoft's ability to serve more relevant search results and paid search listings, particularly with respect to rare or 'tail' queries." The transaction would also provide Microsoft with a much larger pool of data than it currently has or is likely to obtain without this transaction, and would enable Microsoft to conduct more effective testing and rapid innovation. With respect to the potential anticompetitive concerns from the merger, the DOJ argued that they could be neutralized by the competitive constraints from Google, and therefore "the competitive focus of both Microsoft and Yahoo! is predominately on Google and not on each other."

Regardless of this enforcement trend, the debates continue on how to establish an analytical framework that could reflect the genuine and dynamic market impacts from non-horizontal mergers. In practice, the DOJ's recent investigation on the merger between Google and Fitbit demonstrated the relevance of the debates to data-driven mergers and the DOJ's willingness to extend the debates to issues conventionally not covered by antitrust law, such as privacy protection. The DOJ is concerned with the Fitbit user data that Google will have access to after the merger because much of this data collected by tracking devices concerns the health of consumers and is extremely sensitive. In addition, the investigation was spurred by Fitbit users' own concern about their information being sold to Google without their consent. Furthermore, there exists the concern that after the acquisition, Google could extend its dominance to the market of smart wearable devices.[58]

---

57 Statement of the Department of Justice Antitrust Division on Its Decision to Close Its Investigation of the Internet Search and Paid Search Advertising Agreement Between Microsoft Corporation and Yahoo! Inc., available at https://www.justice.gov/opa/pr/statement-department-justice-antitrust-division-its-decision-close-its-investigation-internet.

58 See Gabriela Barkho, *DOJ Probes Google's Fitbit Acquisition Over Consumer Health Data Concerns,* Observer (December 11, 2019), available at https://observer.com/2019/12/google-fitbit-acquisition-doj-probe-health-data/.; Both the EU and Australia had also initiated investigations on this merger. See Press Release, *Mergers: Commission Opens In-depth Investigation into the Proposed Acquisition of Fitbit by Google* (4 August 2020), available at https://ec.europa.eu/commission/presscorner/detail/en/ip_20_1446; Australian Competition & Consumer Commission, *Statement of Issues: Google LLC – proposed acquisition of Fitbit Inc* (18 June 2020), available at https://www.accc.gov.au/system/files/public-registers/documents/Google%20Fitbit%20-%20Statement%20of%20Issues%20-%2018%20June%202020.pdf.

B. European Union

In *Apple/Shazam*,[59] Apple intended to acquire Shazam, a developer and distributor of music recognition apps for smartphones, tablets, and personal computers. The EU Commission reviewed several theories of harm in this case, but the likely foreclosure effects on competing providers of automatic content recognition ("ACR") remained the major competitive concerns. The Commission first reviewed the possibility that Apple might provide different levels of integration of ACR functionalities between Apple Music apps and competing digital music streaming apps to exclude competing rivals. However, this scenario was considered implausible by the Commission because there were already several alternative ACR providers in the market and the merger might have had the positive effect of encouraging digital music distributors to partner with providers of ACR technology.[60]

The Commission then reviewed the second possibility that Apple might leverage its market power in other markets, in particular the hardware market, into the ACR market. The Commission focused on three strategies likely to be adopted by Apple: (1) Apple might pre-install the Shazam app on Apple's PCs, smart mobile devices, and other platforms; (2) deeper integration of Shazam's app on Apple's products and services; and (3) reduction of interoperability between Apple's products and services (and, specifically, Apple device microphones) and third party ACR apps and software solutions.[61] However, the Commission found this potential anticompetitive effect to be non-merger-specific as there is already a partnership and integration in place between Apple's Siri and Shazam's ACR technology.[62]

In *Microsoft/LinkedIn*,[63] the Commission evaluated the assertion that Microsoft would practice an input foreclosure strategy to deny access by competing providers of customer relationship management ("CRM") software to LinkedIn user data.[64] Some have worried that LinkedIn would become a key input for innovation, but such a concern was eventually rejected by the Commission.[65] The Commission argued that the merged entity would not have the *ability* to foreclose competing providers of CRM software solutions by restricting or denying access to LinkedIn full data for the

---

59   Case N. COMP/M.8788–*Apple/Shazam*, Commission decision of 6/9/2018, available at http://ec.europa.eu/competition/mergers/cases/decisions/m8788_1279_3.pdf.

60   *Id.* at paragraphs 310 and 344.

61   *Id.* at paragraph 336.

62   *Id.* at paragraph 342.

63   Case M.8124, Commission Decision of December 6, 2016, available at http://ec.europa.eu/competition/mergers/cases/decisions/m8124_1349_5.pdf.

64   *Id.* at paragraph 246.

65   *Id.* at paragraphs 250, 256.

following two reasons. First, LinkedIn has not currently licensed any data to any third party and the only data valuable for CRM purposes that it made available to third parties were those displayed to users irrespective of whether the data was integrated with CRM software solutions. The merger would not affect competition because LinkedIn did not "appear to have [a] significant degree of market power … in any potential relevant upstream market."[66] Second, the Commission considered that LinkedIn data could not be qualified as, and was not likely to become in the next two to three years, an important input with respect to the provision of CRM software solutions.[67] Even assuming that LinkedIn data was an important input, numerous sources of data were still available for CRM service providers and LinkedIn data would not be "essential" for CRM market competition.[68]

With respect to the *incentive* to foreclose competition, the Commission concluded that it was unclear at least whether such an incentive might be present after a merger.[69] In particular, after investigating relevant documents and testimonies by business stakeholders,[70] the Commission maintained that "it appears that any strategy restricting access to LinkedIn full data to competing CRM software solutions risks translating into significant losses which may not be compensated by the gains from expanding market shares in the CRM software solutions market."[71]

The Commission reviewed the risk of post-merger bundling arrangements by the merged entity in two recent conglomerate mergers.

In *IMS Health/Cegedim Business*,[72] IMS and Cegedim Business entered into an agreement in 2014 whereby the former would acquire sole control over the latter. Both IMS and Cegedim Business were active in the information and technology sector and provided companies in the pharmaceutical, biotech, life sciences, and healthcare sectors with solutions to measure and improve their performance.[73] IMS provided sales tracking data to pharmaceutical companies to assist them in organizing their sales forces and marketing efforts and "has been acknowledged as the *de facto* standard for the pharmaceutical industry."[74] Cegedim Business was not an active player in

---

66 *Id*. at paragraph 254.

67 *Id*. at paragraph 256.

68 *Id*. at paragraphs 262, 276.

69 *Id*. at paragraph 272.

70 *Id*. paragraphs 267 to 271.

71 *Id*. at paragraph 269.

72 Case COMP / M 7337, Commission Decision of December 19, 2014, available at http://ec.europa.eu/competition/mergers/cases/decisions/m7337_20141219_20212_4101276_EN.pdf.

73 *Id*. at paragraph 4.

74 *Id*. at paragraphs 20, 21.

the market of sales tracking data and its provided services were not included in this transaction.[75] The two products that would be added to IMS's product portfolio were CRM software, where IMS had only a limited presence, and healthcare professional databases, which IMS did not offer at the time of the merger. The Commission was concerned that those products could be bundled with or tied to IMS's strongest product, sales tracking data.[76] Nevertheless, the Commission concluded after investigation that the merger would not give rise to the concerned anticompetitive effect because there would still be a sufficient number of alternative providers post-merger.[77] Moreover, there were a significant number of market participants who did not purchase the products and services concerned as part of the same contract.[78] As a result, it was feasible for customers to counteract any foreclosure strategies used by the merged entity. For example, a supplier of CRM software for the pharmaceutical industry could partner with a data solutions company to provide similar integrated offerings as IMS provided.[79]

In *Google/Sanofi*,[80] Sanofi, through its wholly-owned subsidiary, Aventis, and Google, through its wholly-owned subsidiary, Verily Life Sciences, created a new joint venture, Onduo. Sanofi was a global pharmaceutical group engaged in the research, development, manufacture, and marketing of healthcare products; Verily Life Sciences was established by Google to group together its life science-related projects.[81] The purpose of the conglomerate merger was to offer services for the management and treatment of diabetes, including collection, processing, and analysis of data, as well as commercialization of certain products, such as specialized continuous glucose monitoring devices, insulin pumps, and insulin that can be used alongside these services.[82]

The Commission analyzed the following two issues concerning conglomerate effects. First, the possibility that the merged entity bundled products with a service providing data analysis. Second, that the merged entity limited the interoperability with competing offerings to foreclose rivals.[83] Regarding the *ability* to foreclose rivals, the Commission noted that the merged entity would not have a market position to be leveraged to exclude third-party device manufacturers, insulin providers, or providers

---

75 *Id*. at paragraphs 23.

76 *Id*. at paragraph 265.

77 *Id*. at paragraph 267.

78 *Id*. at paragraph 268.

79 *Id*. at paragraph 269, 270.

80 Case M.7813 – *Sanofi/Google/DMI JV*, Commission Decision of February 23, 2016, available at http://ec.europa.eu/competition/mergers/cases/decisions/m7813_479_2.pdf.

81 *Id*. at paragraphs 3, 4.

82 *Id*. at paragraph 5.

83 *Id*. at paragraph 78.

of digital services for the management and treatment of diabetes from these individual markets.[84] In addition, as the choice of treatment devices or products was primarily determined by healthcare professionals on the basis of a patient's specific needs, the number of patients that would use the devices alongside the data analysis services was unknown. Therefore, the merged entity would also lack the incentive to practice bundling strategy "given that by preventing third parties' insulins and devices to work with [third-party products and services], the joint venture would drive patients away, *making such a strategy unprofitable* for the joint venture."[85] Insofar as the "interoperability" issue was concerned, the Commission rested in part on the commitment made by the merging parties to maintain the "portability" of data and "interoperability" of the e-platform after the merger to refute these concerns.[86] Interestingly, the Commission also mentioned that the then soon-to-be effective General Data Protection Regulation would further safeguard data portability.[87]

C. Taiwan

Between 2011 and 2018, the Taiwan Fair Trade Commission ("TFTC") received and reviewed thirty-three vertical mergers,[88] several of which also involved conglomerate issues. Most of these cases were mergers that took place in the technology, media, telecommunications, financial and insurance services, integrated circuit, and IT hardware sectors.[89] The TFTC also follows the ability-incentive-effect framework to review non-horizontal mergers, and with respect to anticompetitive effects, the TFTC may consider whether a merger under review might increase rivals' costs, create entry barriers, facilitate or stabilize concerted actions, or assist merging parties to circumvent price regulations.[90] On the procompetitive side, the TFTC considered the efficiency of saving transaction costs, improving asset specific investments, avoiding free-riding behavior, and the successive-monopoly problem that would result from the mergers.[91] However, very few of these cases had the acquisition of big data as their core reviewing issue.

---

84 *Id.* at paragraph 80.

85 *Id.* (emphasis added).

86 *Id.* at paragraphs 68, 82.

87 *Id.* at paragraph 69.

88 TFTC Submission to the OECD Competition Committee Meeting, *Vertical Mergers in the Technology, Media and Telecom Sector-Note by Chinese Taipei* paragraph 22(3) (June 7, 2019), available at https://one.oecd.org/document/DAF/COMP/WD(2019)22/en/pdf#_ga=2.45123940.1549380068.1559867970-707968676.1528544464.

89 *Id.*

90 *Id.* at paragraph 7.

91 *Id.* at paragraph 8.

The *Easycard Co./DDPowers Co.*[92] joint venture may be one of the few cases during the 2011–2018 period that involved more direct discussion of data and competition by the TFTC. In this case, the merging parties along with seven other companies in various markets, including telecom, chain convenience stores, micropayment tools, 3C product distribution, and venture capital, intended to establish a joint venture to operate a bonus points business through DDPowers. According to findings by the TFTC, bonus points represented only a small fraction of the market for payment systems and could be substituted by several competing payment methods. As this was a conglomerate merger, the TFTC also found that the merger would not be able to create significant entry barriers to the respective markets involved in this merger in the foreseeable future. Alternatively, the merger would enhance competitive efficiency and overall economic benefits by expanding the scope of the business of the merging companies through joint investment, as well as by sharing their research and development and production costs and realizing economies of scope. However, the TFTC also noticed the two-sided feature of the relevant markets involved in this joint venture, with Chunghwa Telecom, the leading telecom company in Taiwan at one side of the market, and Easycard Corporation, who was the largest issuer of electronic stored value cards, at the other. Both parties controlled vast amounts of user data and information before the joint venture. The "network effect" likely to be generated from such a joint venture (and the sharing of data) could have created the long-term possibility that DDPowers would gain a monopoly in the bonus points market. To prevent post-merger anticompetitive practices by the merged entity, the TFTC conditioned its clearance of the merger on several behavioral remedies on DDPowers, including the duty of continuing supply, dealing on equal terms, prohibition of denial without proper causes to an application to join the joint venture, and the establishment of firewall mechanisms to prohibit participating companies from obtaining the personal information and transaction records of DDPowers' members.

On July 30, 2019, the Financial Supervisory Commission of Taiwan approved three applications to operate online banking activities, including the application filed by Line Financial Taiwan Ltd., a Fintech subsidiary controlled by Naver Corporation, a Korean company whose messaging app LINE and service held nearly a 90 percent penetration rate in Taiwan ("LINE Group"). In addition to Line Financial, who held 49.9 percent of the shares of the established online banking business ("LINE Bank"), it also consisted of companies from banking and telecom industries holding in aggregate the remaining 50.1 percent shares of the joint venture.[93] In its review that cleared the joint venture in December 2019, the TFTC provided perhaps the most detailed competitive assessments to date of a data-driven non-horizontal merger.

---

92   TFTC Decision of April 2, 2014 (the 1169th Commissioners' Meeting), available at http://www.apeccp.org.tw/htdocs/doc/Taipei/Case/dec2014/1186-1169case01.html.

93   Mathew Strong, *Taiwan Approves Three Online Banks*, Taiwan News (July 30, 2019), available at https://www.taiwannews.com.tw/en/news/3755178.

First, the TFTC concluded that it was unlikely that the merger would eliminate potential competition among participating Fintech, telecom, and banking companies because the banking industry is highly regulated and the government was not planning to liberalize it. Due to legal constraints, it was still unlikely that non-financial firms would be able to enter the banking market without collaborating with existing financial companies. Namely, no potential competition existed among those firms before the joint venture.

Second, with regard to the "portfolio effect" from this joint venture, the concern was raised that the LINE Group might pre-install the LINE Bank app within its highly popular LINE app to entice LINE users to use LINE Bank while using other services from the "LINE ecosystem," such as online shopping, entertainment, traveling, or payments. However, the TFTC found this market-foreclosure concern implausible for the following reasons:

(1) even if LINE Group implemented this bundling strategy, each service in the LINE ecosystem faced intense competition from other online commerce providers. For LINE users, each service in the ecosystem had a wide array of substitutes. They would not be forced to use LINE Bank simply because they used LINE.

(2) under the regulatory principle of "know your customer," LINE Bank was prohibited from establishing bank accounts for LINE users before obtaining their consent. The users would still have the choice to use or not to use LINE Bank.

(3) even though the penetration rate for LINE was nearly 90 percent, there were other alternative messaging apps in the market (e.g. Facebook Messenger and WeChat). Moreover, mobile device users tend to practice "multi-homing" strategies, installing and using various apps on the same device for the same communication purposes. LINE app was not a bottleneck for other competitors of online banking to reach LINE users. In addition, they could also cooperate with other messaging app developers to offer their own online banking systems.

(4) messaging apps are only one among a variety of ways to promote the service of online banking. Competitors of LINE Bank can still team up with other non-messaging app developers or develop their own apps for their own services.

Similar reasoning was applied by the TFTC to refute the concerns of bundling LINE Bank with the services offered by telecom venture partners. In particular, the TFTC argued that any attempted bundling strategy would be counteracted by the other two online banks with similar competing strategies.

Finally, the TFTC recognized the ability for LINE Group to collect vast amounts of data through the LINE ecosystem. In response to the emergence of online banking in Taiwan, LINE Group also revealed its intention to launch LINE Score to collect and analyze data concerning the preferences of LINE users and the relevance of online social media. The resulting scores from data analytics would be used to assist LINE Bank in designing products that most fit the needs of potential customers and would be integrated into its credit-rating system. The TFTC then approached the issue of data and competition in this case from the following two perspectives.

The TFTC maintained that the collection and utilization of data typically is non-rivalrous, namely, that it could be collected and used by various users simultaneously without diminishing its value. Furthermore, the application value from data analytics may be transient; firms may not be able to gain competitive advantages simply through long-term aggregation of historical data. Data itself is not a ticket to market dominance; the skill and technique used to analyze data is what matters. Therefore, concentration of data ownership is not necessarily equivalent to the acquisition of additional market power. The TFTC pointed out further that the data or data set controlled by LINE Group were not unique or essential in terms of market competition. The two competing online banks, through their e-commerce and telecom shareholders, could easily acquire a large amount of their own users' data to assist them in implementing competing strategies with LINE Bank. Competing online banks could also partner with independent social media networks, search engine providers, or online shopping websites for the same data-gathering purposes.

The TFTC also held the view that the issue of protecting the privacy of data suppliers should be reviewed under competition law by treating privacy protection as a type of non-price or quality competition among data collectors. This is particularly true for industries demonstrating the feature of two-sided markets. LINE Group offered free messaging services to users and was compensated with revenue from selling advertising services to advertisers. As there is no price indicator at the free side of the market, the policy and scope of privacy protection implemented by LINE Group was important information that most users would consider before joining the network. Given this, the TFTC was of the opinion that there was no evidence showing the existence of privacy-based competition among LINE Group and its telecom and banking venture partners *before* the merger. Therefore, the joint venture would not lessen market competition. Even though the LINE Score service might raise concerns of privacy invasion, this was a persistent concern regardless of the establishment of a joint venture and was thus not a merger-specific competitive harm that should influence the reviewing result.

V. A NEW LIGHTHOUSE FOR CRUISING THE SEA OF DOUBT? REASSESSING THE CHALLENGES TO EXISTING ANALYTICAL FRAMEWORKS

In its Background Note for the 2001 roundtables on portfolio effects in conglomerate mergers, the OECD Competition Committee began with a statement suggesting that "in general terms, the paper finds that conglomerate mergers involving portfolio effects do not present new competition concerns. Rather they present traditional issues in new guises and combinations. To a considerable degree, the analysis applied in vertical mergers that are suspected of having exclusionary effects is found to be applicable to conglomerate mergers involving portfolio effects."[94] We agree. From the previous case illustration, it is evident that current analytical frameworks under which both the coordinated and exclusionary effects of vertical and conglomerate mergers are evaluated by the ability-incentive-effect standard should be capable of addressing most of the competitive concerns from the acquisition and abuse of big data. To be sure, big data brings new challenges to the regulation of non-horizontal mergers and should be duly recognized. We propose some of our initial thoughts and policy responses to these challenges in this section.

A. The Characterization Challenge

Big data, data analytics, and the digital technologies upon which they are operated have created an immense number of new business opportunities for the market. This is due primarily to the progress of online technologies that have allowed firms interested in experimenting with new business models to shift and change more easily and quickly. Traditional business categories and boundaries shift in an unpredictable pattern as well.[95] The immediate challenge to merger reviews is that the characterization of a merger as horizontal, vertical, or conglomerate will become increasingly complicated and laborious. The safe harbor for exempting mergers from review founded primarily on market-share criteria will also be questioned because the characterization challenge renders the definition of a relevant market more demanding and unverifiable. Competition authorities will need to offer sophisticated economic reasoning in order to defend an enforcement policy that applies divergent degrees of reviewing efforts to mergers of different and statically drawn formats. In addition, the characterization challenge might serve as a reason to question the operability of the theory that depicts data acquisition as a means of preempting future competitors.[96] To apply the theory accurately, competition agencies will need to observe how close the data of the merging parties would be in the same competing space had the merger not occurred.[97]

---

94   OECD Policy Roundtables, *supra* note 35.

95   See Bart Basesens et al., *supra* note 16, at 812-13.

96   See note 45 and its accompanying text.

97   Lear, *supra* note 46, at 135.

B. The Challenge of the Definition of Relevant Markets

As the collection and transaction of big data today are conducted predominantly in a digital environment, the two-sided market theory currently dominating the discussion of market definition for digital platforms will certainly continue to interest antitrust commentators on data-driven mergers. Although economic literature on this topic is growing rapidly and certain operational criteria have been developed,[98] delineating relevant market for two-sided market is still an arduous task for most competition agencies. To meet this challenge, competition authorities need to keep abreast of the recent theoretical developments in this area and learn from the enforcement experience of other jurisdictions regarding how theories on two-sided markets could be incorporated into practical guidance for merger reviews. The other challenge in practice is how to construct a method that would assist competition authorities in observing and judging the *substitutability* among different types of data under the SSNIP defining rule. Supposedly, the variety and voluminous features of big data will make the scope and scale of comparable data very difficult to determine. The evolving nature of data adds an additional layer of complexity to this problem. As was described in *Microsoft/ LinkedIn*, depending on how they are used, other types of data may be more relevant than LinkedIn, and "[i]t is difficult to predict how this will evolve in the future."[99]

C. Big Data and Market Power Analysis

The 4V features of big data have been highlighted by antitrust commentators to establish the "uniqueness" of big data and the enhanced market power that is gained from controlling them. Some have gone further to portray big data as an "essential facility" for market competition.[100] In contrast, those who hold a dynamic view on data competition support the argument that data are "ubiquitous,"[101] not

---

98   See Lapo Filistrucchi, Damien Geradin, Eric Van Damme & Pauline Affeldt, *Market Definition in Two-Sided Markets: Theory and Practice*, 10 JOURNAL OF COMPETITION, LAW & ECONOMICS 296 (2014); OECD Competition Committee Roundtables (Background Note), *Big Data: Bring Competition Policy to the Digital Era* (29-30 November 2016), available at https://one.oecd.org/document/DAF/COMP(2016)14/en/pdf.

99   Paragraph 261.

100   See e.g. INGE GRAEF, EU COMPETITION LAW, DATA PROTECTION AND ONLINE PLATFORMS: DATA AS ESSENTIAL FACILITY (2016).

101   Executive Office of the President, *Big Data: Seizing Opportunities, Preserving Values* (2014) ("We live in a world of near-ubiquitous data collection."), available at https://obamawhitehouse.archives.gov/sites/default/files/docs/big_data_privacy_report_may_1_2014.pdf; James Manyika et al., *McKinsey Global Institute, Big Data: The Next Frontier for Innovation, Competition, and Productivity* 2 (June 2011) ("Digital data is everywhere-in every sector, in every economy, in every organization and user of digital technology."), available at https://bigdatawg.nist.gov/pdf/MGI_big_data_full_report.pdf.

costly to collect,[102] and unlikely to be used as an entry barrier. For example, in *Apple/Shazam*, the EU Commission found that "the majority of respondents to the market investigation took the view that there are plenty of sources for music chart data in the music industry" and that "several respondents have indicated that they collect and do have access to music tag data. Therefore, the same type of data could be available from others."[103] Similarly, in *IMS/Cegedim Business*, the Commission noted that "pharmaceutical companies source their products and services from different providers at different points in time.... IMS and Cegedim Business sell their data and service offerings at different points in time and to different individuals within pharmaceutical companies. Indeed, the duration of the contracts for the different products and services varies."[104]

Understandably, it is tempting for competition authorities to infer the existence of market power from the mere control of big data when defining relevant markets for data-driven mergers is difficult. However, it is vital for the competition authorities to notice that the *quality* rather than the *quantity* of data acquired could be more useful in assisting the controlling firm to gain a competitive edge over its competitors. As *Apple/Shazam*, *IMS/Cegedim*, and *LINE Bank* have demonstrated, a large amount of "raw" or basic data are widely available from various sources. Competitively valuable data are frequently structured and analyzed data; they require substantial investments made by the controlling firms in the technologies necessary for conducting these value-added activities. A reviewing policy that equates the acquisition of data directly with the increase of market power risks deterring efficient innovation.[105]

VI. ASSESSING COMPETING THEORIES OF HARM FOR DATA-DRIVEN NON-HORIZONTAL MERGERS

The competing theories of harm for non-horizontal mergers are multifaceted and frequently advocated with equal persuasiveness. Whether the procompetitive or anticompetitive theories prevail should be assessed by market realities, not by mere theoretical possibility. This is particularly critical to merger review because the review-

---

102 Tucker & Wellford, *supra* note 45, at 2.

103 Paragraphs 179, 319.

104 Paragraph 268.

105 This is particularly the case when competition authorities condition their clearance decisions on the duty of the merged entity to share big data with its competitors after a merger has taken place. The remedy of sharing data reduces the market value for the shared data, rendering it more difficult for tech startups to make profitable exits through vertical mergers. This may in turn reduce their incentives to invest in creating data. D. Daniel Sokol, *Vertical Mergers and Entrepreneurial Exit*, 70 FL. L. REV. 1357, 1377 (2018).

ing results are typically based on *prediction* of a merger's future competitive effects.[106] To competition agencies, this proposal is equally implicative when they attempt to block a merger based on its *strategic* motivation. Substantiating the existence of strategic purposes requires the verification of not only the assumed market conditions incentivizing the merging parties to adopt the strategy, but also the causation between these conditions and the implementation of the merger. This entails further that the enforcement agencies might be required to probe into the merging parties' subjective deliberation process. Empirically testing the reasonableness of the assumptions and robustness of the predicting outcome is indispensable for sound merger reviews.

The need to empirically evaluate competing theories also counsels against adopting highly intrusive behavioral remedies when clearing non-horizontal merger cases. Take open access to big data as an example. This sort of remedy typically requires the competition authority to assess the quality of data in order to determine the content and scope of the dataset subject to mandatory access. The chances of making improper assessments are higher when the competing evidence on market impacts has close or equivalent probative values.

The challenge from assessing competing theories also implies that evidentiary rule, in particular the standard for burden of proof, might be the legal mechanism most relevant to the reviewing result. This point has been emphatically highlighted in the *AT&T/Time Warner* decisions by the District Court and the D.C. Circuit. For example, the District Court contended that "[t]he case at hand therefore turns on whether, notwithstanding the proposed merger's conceded procompetitive effects, the Government has met its burden of proof of establishing, through 'case-specific evidence,' that the merger of AT&T and Time Warner, at this time and in this remarkably dynamic industry, is likely to substantially lessen competition in the manner it predicts."[107] The D.C. Circuit sustained that "[w]hile the existence of this effect from the merger may be intuitive, its size and significance is not, and U.S. law makes mergers unlawful only if they have a "*reasonable probability*" of substantially lessening competition."[108] Similarly, in *Commission v. Tetra Laval* ("Laval II"), the European Court of Justice required the evidence submitted by the Commission to be able to "establish convincingly the merits of a decision on a merger."[109] By "convincingly," this meant "factually

---

106   As the D.C. Circuit confirmed in its recent decision on the *AT&T/Time Warner* merger, "the Clayton Act applies to vertical mergers to halt "incipient . . . trade restraints" and, therefore, requires "a much more stringent test than does the rule-of-reason analysis under section 1 of the Sherman Act." *United States v. AT&T, Inc.*, 916 F.3d 1029, 1032 (D.C. Cir. 2019) (quotes omitted.)

107   310 F. Supp. 3d 161, 194 (D.D.C. 2018).

108   916 F.3d at 1031.

109   ECJ Case C-12/03 P, [2005] ECR I-978, paragraph 41. See also ANDRIANI KALINTIRI, EVIDENCE STANDARDS IN EU COMPETITION ENFORCEMENT: THE EU APPROACH, Chapter 3 (2019) (a recent and succinct discussion of the evidentiary rules for EU competition law.).

accurate, reliable, and consistent."[110] Due to its predictive nature, merger reviews must "envisage various chains of cause and effect with a view to ascertaining which of them are the most likely."[111] More importantly, the Court stressed that when evaluating the "incentive" to foreclose competition, the Commission needed to consider the factors that were "liable to reduce, or even eliminate, those incentives."[112]

The implication from the reasoning in those decisions is that a clear guideline stipulating the operational factors for the application of the evidentiary rule in merger review, in particular the allocation of the duty to present evidence and to persuade, would enhance the predictability of merger reviews.

VII. THE ISSUE OF PRIVACY PROTECTION IN MERGER REVIEWS

In commenting on the role that competition law could play to protect privacy issues in digital markets, U.S. Assistant Attorney General Makan Delrahim maintained that "[a]lthough privacy fits primarily within the realm of consumer protection law, it would be a grave mistake to believe that privacy concerns can never play a role in antitrust analysis."[113] In theory, the demand to protect users' data on digital platforms will encourage firms to provide more secure platforms than their competitors do and trigger a sort of non-price (quality) competition among platform operators. Assessing non-price competition is no stranger to merger analysis in antitrust law.[114] Nevertheless, this enforcement approach has its limit and should be implemented with care. Daniel Sokol has pointed out that there was no empirical evidence that supported the merit of using competition law to regulate privacy. In particular, this could deter the emergence of the positive effects gained from using big data.[115] James Cooper argued that regulating privacy under competition law requires the competition authority to deal with the "subjectivity" issue inherent in privacy protection (i.e. the widely distributed preference for the need and degree of privacy protection). This could further induce the regulated parties to engage in rent-seeking activities and activate the contro-

---

110 *Id.* at paragraph 39.

111 *Id.* at paragraph 43.

112 *Id.* at paragraph 74.

113 Remarks at Harvard Law School & Competition Policy International Conference on "Challenges to at Harvard Law School & Competition Policy International Conference on "Challenges to Antitrust in a Changing Economy" (November 8, 2019), available at https://www.justice.gov/opa/speech/assistant-attorney-general-makan-delrahim-delivers-remarks-harvard-law-school-competition.

114 See OECD, *Data-driven Innovation for Growth and Well-being: Interim Synthesis Report,* (October 2014)" available at https://www.oecd.org/sti/inno/data-driven-innovation-interim-synthesis.pdf.

115 D. Daniel Sokol & Roisin E. Comerford, *Does Antitrust Have a Role to Play in Regulating Big Data?* (January 27, 2016), available at https://ssrn.com/abstract=2723693.

versy over the attack on free speech.[116] Actually, most of the concerns around privacy protection associated with big data mergers rest not so much on the failure of market competition to encourage the provision of protection as on the failure of the market to provide a *preordained minimum amount* of protection. In response to this sort of concern, merger reviewers would need to formulate a pre-determined minimum degree of privacy protection that cannot be compromised throughout the process of market competition. However, this view runs against one of the underlying principles for competition law: competition authorities should refrain from pre-determining the *outcome* of competition. This deprives market participants of the opportunities to experiment with reaching an optimal degree of privacy protection that mirrors the changes of market conditions and individual preferences for privacy protection over time. It also neglects the fact that the duty to protect privacy should be dynamically allocated between data users and suppliers in accordance with the costs and benefits from the allocations. In the spirit of the Coase Theorem,[117] sometimes the most effective way to avoid privacy invasion may not be to endow upon data suppliers the right to be let alone after they have voluntarily disseminated the data to the platform, but to impose upon them the duty not to reveal for abuse from the beginning the data they consider to be highly sensitive and vulnerable.

VIII. CONCLUSION

With the advent of the digital economy, we have witnessed a parallel and increasing interest in enforcing competition law to data-driven non-horizontal mergers. The introduction of new theories concerning the competitive harm from such mergers is also reshaping what used to be a relatively clear and predictable enforcement structure. We begin in this paper with a brief summary of the definition and the 4V features of "big data," followed by the introduction of the pro and anticompetitive theories concerning data-driven non-horizontal mergers. We then illustrate the theories by using the enforcement experience from the United States, the European Union, and Taiwan. Our initial findings suggested that the existing reviewing framework should be able to address most of the competitive concerns arising from data-driven non-horizontal mergers. Instead of seeking to create a new framework specifically tailored to the challenges of data acquisition, we might as well focus on integrating the responses to these challenges into the existing framework to improve its regulatory quality. In doing so, we highlight and propose our initial thoughts on some of the most commonly raised challenges at the end of this paper. First, increasing difficulty in characterizing data-driven mergers and defining their relevant mar-

---

116   James C. Cooper, *Privacy and Antitrust: Underpants Gnomes, the First Amendment, the Subjectivity,* 20 GEORGE MASON LAW REVIEW 1129 (2013).

117   See Ronald H. Coase, *The Problem of Social Cost,* 3 JOURNAL OF LAW AND ECONOMICS 1 (1960) (suggesting legal rights be allocated in a manner that could have the concerned social problems addressed with minimal costs).

kets could be mitigated primarily by the development of empirical studies on digital platforms and markets and the progress of economic thinking in two-sided markets. Second, although the control of big data denotes competitive advantage, competition authorities should not be tempted to equate more data with higher degrees of market dominance. Quality rather than quantity of data acquired is more decisive in terms of measuring market power.

Third, the validity of competing theories of harm for merger reviews should be assessed by market realities. The need to empirically test these theories also counsels against imposing highly intrusive behavioral remedies, such as mandatory access to big data when clearing mergers. This will require the competition authority to delineate the scope and types of accessible data, which is error-prone given the vast amount of data that needs to be considered. As the competing theories of harm are frequently of equal probative value, this further implies that the evidentiary rule applied by the enforcement agency will be key in the final decisions of merger reviews. A clear guideline containing the reviewing factors when applying the evidentiary rule would enhance the predictability of merger reviews. Finally, although the supply of privacy protection might be viewed as a non-price (quality) competition and therefore reviewable under the analytical framework for non-horizontal mergers, we argued that competition authorities may not be the most competent agencies to deal with this issue. This will place competition agencies in a thorny situation where they are required to understand the relevance and degree of privacy protection over data belonging to various individuals. Furthermore, this will also deprive market participants from experimenting with reaching an optimal degree of privacy protection that mirrors the changes of market conditions and individual preferences over time.

Editors' Bios

David S. Evans' academic work has focused on industrial organization, including antitrust economics, with a particular expertise in multisided platforms, digital economy, information technology, and payment systems. He has authored eight books, including two award winners, and more than one hundred articles in these areas. He has developed and taught courses related to antitrust economics, primarily for graduate students, judges and officials, and practitioners, and have authored handbook chapters on various antitrust subjects.

David's expert work has focused on competition policy and regulation. He has served as a testifying or consulting expert on many significant antitrust matters in the United States, European Union, and China. He has also made submissions to, and appearances before, competition and regulatory authorities with respect to mergers and investigations in those and other jurisdictions. David has worked on litigation matters for defendants and plaintiffs, on mergers for merging parties and intervenors, and for and in opposition to competition authorities.

Allan Fels AO graduated in economics (first class honors) and law from the University of Western Australia in 1965. He has a PhD in Economics from Duke University and was a research fellow in the Department of Applied Economics at the University of Cambridge from 1986-1972, where he wrote The British Prices and Incomes Board (Cambridge University Press, 1972).

On his return to Australia Professor Fels joined the Economics Department of Monash University as a Senior Lecturer, before becoming Professor of Administration and Director of the Graduate School of Management from 1984 until 1991.

The career of Professor Fels in Australia falls into two parts. He was generally regarded as the nation's leading regulator, serving as inaugural Chair of the Australian Competition and Consumer Commission (and its predecessor bodies) from 1989 until 2003. The Australian Competition and Consumer Commission is the country's regulator of competition law and consumer law; it also regulates public utilities in the telecommunications and energy industries (in a similar manner to industry-specific bodies such as Ofcom in the UK and FCC in the US). He has had numerous other regulatory roles (for example, in insurance, agriculture, telecommunications, and aviation).

Professor Fels remains a leading figure globally in competition policy. He co-chaired the OECD Trade and Competition Committee from 1996 to 2003 and continues regularly to be a keynote speaker at major global competition events including the world's two peak events, the International Competition Network Annual Conference and the OECD Global Competition Forum.

He was a participant in the 15-year process of drafting the Chinese Antimonopoly Law 2008 and currently advises the Chinese government on the law's implementation. Academically, he is co-director of the Competition Research Centre at the Chinese Academy of Science, a prestigious position, and an international adviser to the Chinese Academy of Social Science.

The second part of Professor Fels' career has been academic. He was appointed Foundation Dean of the Australia and New Zealand School of Government and served in that position from 2003 until 2012. The predominant activity of the School has been the provision of management development programs to senior public servants in the two countries. There is also a substantial research program and other professional and outreach activities.

Catherine Tucker is the Sloan Distinguished Professor of Management and a Professor of Marketing at MIT Sloan. She is also Chair of the MIT Sloan PhD Program.

Her research interests lie in how technology allows firms to use digital data and machine learning to improve performance, and in the challenges this poses for regulation. Tucker has particular expertise in online advertising, digital health, social media, and electronic privacy. Her research studies the interface between marketing, the economics of technology, and law.

She has received an NSF CAREER Award for her work on digital privacy, the Erin Anderson Award for an Emerging Female Marketing Scholar and Mentor, the Garfield

Economic Impact Award for her work on electronic medical records, the Paul E. Green Award for contributions to the practice of Marketing Research, the William F. O'Dell Award for most significant, long-term contribution to Marketing, and the INFORMS Society for Marketing Science Long Term Impact Award for long-run impact on marketing.

She is a cofounder of the MIT Cryptoeconomics Lab which studies the applications of blockchain and also a co-organizer of the Economics of Artificial Intelligence initiative sponsored by the Alfred P. Sloan Foundation. She has been a Visiting Fellow at All Souls College, Oxford. She has testified to Congress regarding her work on digital privacy and algorithms, and presented her research to the OECD and the ECJ.

Catherine Tucker is coeditor at Quantitative Marketing and Economics, associate editor at Management Science, Marketing Science, and the Journal of Marketing Research and a research associate at the National Bureau of Economic Research. She teaches MIT Sloan's course on Pricing and the EMBA course "Marketing Management for the Senior Executive." She has received the Jamieson Prize for Excellence in Teaching as well as being voted "Teacher of the Year" at MIT Sloan.

She holds a PhD in economics from Stanford University and a BA from the University of Oxford.

Authors' Bios

Jonathan B. Baker is Research Professor of Law at American University Washington College of Law. He specializes in the areas of antitrust and economic regulation. Professor Baker served as the Chief Economist of the Federal Communications Commission from 2009 to 2011, and as the Director of the Bureau of Economics at the Federal Trade Commission from 1995 to 1998.

Previously, he worked as a Senior Economist at the President's Council of Economic Advisers, Special Assistant to the Deputy Assistant Attorney General for Economics in the Antitrust Division of the Department of Justice, an Assistant Professor at Dartmouth's Amos Tuck School of Business Administration, an Attorney Advisor to the Acting Chairman of the Federal Trade Commission, and an antitrust lawyer in private practice. Professor Baker is the author of *The Antitrust Paradigm*, the co-author of an antitrust casebook, a past Editorial Chair of *Antitrust Law Journal*, and a past member of the Council of the American Bar Association's Section of Antitrust Law.

He has published widely in the fields of antitrust law, policy, and economics. Professor Baker has received the Jerry S. Cohen Award for Antitrust Scholarship, American University's Faculty Award for Outstanding Scholarship, Research, and Other Professional Accomplishments, and the Federal Trade Commission's Award for Distinguished Service. He has a JD from Harvard and a PhD in economics from Stanford University.

Tembinkosi Bonakele has been the Commissioner of the South African Competition Commission since 2013. Mr. Bonakele joined the Commission in 2004 and occupied various positions in the Commission's core divisions. He was appointed Deputy Commissioner in 2008, and prior to that worked as head of mergers, head of compliance, and senior legal counsel respectively. Mr. Bonakele's accomplishments at the Commission include establishing the Cartels division. He has worked on all of the Commission's major cases and overseen its policy evolution for over ten years. He has been involved in negotiating most of the Commission's ground-breaking settlements and helped develop the Commission's Corporate Leniency Policy, among others.

Mr. Bonakele is an admitted attorney and previously practiced with Cheadle Thompson and Haysom in Johannesburg largely in the areas of labor law, regulation, and health and safety. He has also spent a year working in corporate finance and antitrust groups at Clifford Chance, New York office. He is an adjunct visiting professor of law at Wits Law School, an Associate of the European Summer School and Conference in Competition and Regulation of Athens University of Economics and Business, a Fellow of the University of Johannesburg's Centre for Competition, Regulation and Economic Development and a Board Member of the University of Stellenbosch's Centre for Competition Law and Economics. He has published widely in academic journals and writes for newspapers and business magazines on competition matters. He has recently co-edited a book titled, Competition Law for the New Era.

He holds a BJuris and an LLB from the University of Fort Hare and an MBA from Gordon Institute of Business Science, University of Pretoria. He took law and social science courses at the University of Amsterdam as an exchange student. Mr. Bonakele currently serves as the Chairperson of the African Competition Forum, is a member of the BRICS competition forum and a member of the International Competition Network Steering Group. Mr. Bonakele is also a member of the JSE's Take-Over Regulation Panel and is the Chairperson of Buffalo City Development Agency. Mr. Bonakele is an activist who has been a leader in the youth and student movement and is a former President of the Student Representative Council of the University of Fort Hare. He is a recipient of the Black Management Forum's Black Excellency Award and is a regular speaker at international competition policy conferences.

Antonio Capobianco is a Senior Competition Expert with the OECD Competition Division and is currently the Acting Head of the Division. In this position, he is responsible for the proceedings of the OECD Competition Committee and for all the other competition work streams of the Division. Over the years at the OECD, Mr. Capobianco was responsible for a series of projects and work streams, including the work on fighting bid rigging, on transparency and procedural fairness, on SOEs and competitive neutrality, as well as the work on international enforcement co-operation. He authored numerous Secretariat Background Notes on a variety of competition law enforcement and policy topics.

Prior to joining the OECD in 2007, Mr. Capobianco was a Counsel in the Competition Department of WilmerHale LLP in Brussels. He also spent three years with the Italian Competition Authority. Mr. Capobianco authored several antitrust articles for major international competition law journals and he co-authored books on Italian and European competition law and economics. He regularly speaks at international conferences on antitrust and regulatory issues. Mr. Capobianco is a graduate of the L.U.I.S.S. - Guido Carli in Rome and holds LLM degrees from New York University Law School and from the Institute of European Studies at the Université Libre de Bruxelles.

Gabriele Carovano PhD candidate at King's College London, Dickson Poon School of Law. Mr. Carovano is an Italian qualified lawyer who holds a PhD from Sapienza University in Public, Comparative, and International Law, a degree (Cum Laude) from L.U.I.S.S. Guido Carli in Administrative and Public Law and a specialized Master of Law (LLM) in Competition law (Distinction) from King's College London. He worked as Junior Competition Expert at the Competition Division, OECD (Organisation for Economic Co-operation and Development), published several articles in professional and academic journals, and often participates as speaker in national and international competition law conferences.

Andy C. M. Chen Professor Chen is currently the Dean of the School of Law and Professor in its Department of Financial and Economic Law at Chung Yuan Christian University in Taiwan. He served as Commissioner of the Taiwan Fair Trade Commission ("TFTC") from 2007 to 2010. His familiarity with international competition laws and policies has made him a regular speaker on related topics to government agencies, private companies, and leading academic institutions and professional organizations. He also regularly provides expert opinions in lawsuits and actively participates in public hearings, conferences, and workshops hosted by the TFTC, regulatory agencies as well as private business. Professor Chen earned his law degrees from National Taiwan University (LLB), Soochow University (LLM), Duke University (LLM) and Northwestern University (Doctor of Juridical Science). He has published extensively on antitrust and regulatory issues in Chinese and English, mainly from the perspective of economic analysis. His most recent publications include:

- *Justifications and Limitations for Adopting Divergent Competition Policy and Law in Emerging Economies*, Denver Journal of International Law and Policy (Volume 43, Summer 2015);

- *Patent Assertion Entities in Merger Review in Taiwan: Issues of Characterization and Remedies* (book chapter in Patent Assertion Entities and Competition Policy, Cambridge University Press, January 2017);

- *Due Process and Transparency Requirements for Investigating Competition Cases in Taiwan* (book chapter in Antitrust Procedural Fairness, Oxford University Press, January 2019);

- *Political, Economic and Legal Driving Forces Shaping the Developmental Contours of Competition Law: the Experience of Taiwan* (book chapter in Research Handbook on Asian Competition Law, Edward Elgar Publishing, 2020).

Lesley Chiou is a Professor of Economics at Occidental College in Los Angeles. Her fields are industrial organization and applied econometrics. Her research interests include consumer search and firm competition on the Internet. Her recent work includes examining advertising, vertical integration, and antitrust issues in internet search markets. Lesley's prior research also investigated the effects of trademarks and content provision by aggregators on consumer search.

Lesley's work is featured in the *Journal of Econometrics, Marketing Science*, and the *Journal of Economics and Management Strategy*. She received the Paul Geroski Prize for best paper in the *International Journal of Industrial Organization*. Her work was also supported by grants from the National Bureau of Economic Research and the NET Institute.

She holds a PhD in economics from MIT, and a BA from the University of California, Berkeley.

Alexander Elbittar Professor in Economics at the Center for Economic Research and Teaching ("CIDE"), Mexico City. His research has focused on Economic Competition, Industrial Organization, Auctions, Theory of Individual Decision and Experimental and Behavioral Economics. He has published his work in several peer-reviewed academic journals. He is the current Director of the Interdisciplinary Program for Regulation and Economic Competition ("PIRCE") of the CIDE and General Coordinator of the Diplomas in Economic Competition and Regulation of the CIDE.

He has collaborated with the Federal Commission for Economic Competition, the Energy Regulatory Commission, the National Commission for Regulatory Improvement, the Federal Institute of Telecommunications, the Ministry of Economy, the Center for Public Finance Studies of the Chamber of Deputies, the National Laboratory of Public Policies, the Federal Judicial Council and the Specialized Courts in Economic Regulation and Competition, for which he was appointed as Expert in Economics before the Bodies of the Judicial Power of the Federation of Mexico. He is currently a member of the Mexico's Antitrust Regulator ("COFECE") advisory group on the digital economy and member of the National System of Researchers Level II of CONACYT.

He obtained his PhD in Economics from the University of Pittsburgh, PA, USA.

David S. Evan's academic work has focused on industrial organization, including antitrust economics, with a particular expertise in multisided platforms, digital economy, information technology, and payment systems. He has authored eight books, including two award winners, and more than one hundred articles in these areas. He has developed and taught courses related to antitrust economics, primarily for graduate students, judges and officials, and practitioners, and have authored handbook chapters on various antitrust subjects.

David's expert work has focused on competition policy and regulation. He has served as a testifying or consulting expert on many significant antitrust matters in the United States, European Union, and China. He has also made submissions to, and appearances before, competition and regulatory authorities with respect to mergers and investigations in those and other jurisdictions. David has worked on litigation matters for defendants and plaintiffs, on mergers for merging parties and intervenors, and for and in opposition to competition authorities.

Allan Fels AO graduated in economics (first class honors) and law from the University of Western Australia in 1965. He has a PhD in Economics from Duke University and was a research fellow in the Department of Applied Economics at the University of Cambridge from 1986-1972, where he wrote The British Prices and Incomes Board (Cambridge University Press, 1972).

On his return to Australia Professor Fels joined the Economics Department of Monash University as a Senior Lecturer, before becoming Professor of Administration and Director of the Graduate School of Management from 1984 until 1991.

The career of Professor Fels in Australia falls into two parts. He was generally regarded as the nation's leading regulator, serving as inaugural Chair of the Australian Competition and Consumer Commission (and its predecessor bodies) from 1989 until 2003. The Australian Competition and Consumer Commission is the country's regulator of competition law and consumer law; it also regulates public utilities in the telecommunications and energy industries (in a similar manner to industry-specific bodies such as Ofcom in the UK and FCC in the US). He has had numerous other regulatory roles (for example, in insurance, agriculture, telecommunications, and aviation).

Professor Fels remains a leading figure globally in competition policy. He co-chaired the OECD Trade and Competition Committee from 1996 to 2003 and continues regularly to be a keynote speaker at major global competition events including the world's two peak events, the International Competition Network Annual Conference and the OECD Global Competition Forum.

He was a participant in the 15-year process of drafting the Chinese Antimonopoly Law 2008 and currently advises the Chinese government on the law's implementation. Academically, he is co-director of the Competition Research Centre at the Chinese Academy of Science, a prestigious position, and an international adviser to the Chinese Academy of Social Science.

The second part of Professor Fels' career has been academic. He was appointed Foundation Dean of the Australia and New Zealand School of Government and served in that position from 2003 until 2012. The predominant activity of the School has been the provision of management development programs to senior public servants in the two countries. There is also a substantial research program and other professional and outreach activities.

Pedro Hinojo is Senior Advisor in the Market Studies Unit in the Spanish National Commission on Markets and Competition ("CNMC"), since December 2015. Specialized in digital economy and general advocacy matters. Previously (from May 2014), he worked in the Unit of State Aid and Regulatory Reports of the CNMC. Before joining the CNMC, he held several positions in the Ministry of Economy and Competitiveness and in the Ministry of Industry and Trade, dealing with economic policy and analysis issues. Pedro Hinojo holds a degree in Economics from the University of Salamanca (Spain) and a Master in Economic Analysis from the University of Alcalá (Spain) and is pursuing PhD studies at the same university.

Stephen King is a Commissioner at Australia's Productivity Commission and an adjunct Professor at Monash University. Prior to joining the Productivity Commission in July 2016, Stephen was a Member of the Western Australian Economic Regulation Authority, a Member of Australia's National Competition Council and Professor of Economics at Monash University. Stephen was also a Member of the Australian Competition and Consumer Commission from 2004 to 2009, where he chaired the mergers review committee.

Stephen has researched and published widely in competition economics, regulation and industrial organization. He has advised numerous government agencies and private businesses and has provided expert testimony to the courts on regulation and competition economics.

Stephen received the University Medal from ANU for his undergraduate studies in Economics. He also has a Masters in Economics from Monash University and a PhD from Harvard University. He is a Fellow of the Academy of Social Sciences in Australia and a Lay Member of the High Court of New Zealand.

Robert Klotz is a partner in the Antitrust & Competition Practice Group of Sheppard Mullin Richter & Hampton LLP. He is admitted to the Hamburg Bar and the Brussels Bar (E-List). Based in Brussels for 25 years, Robert first served, for almost a decade, as an official of the European Commission in DG Competition, where he gained first-hand experience in EU competition law and enforcement practice, with a particular focus on regulated network industries such as telecommunications and energy. In this role, he was directly involved in some of the leading cases in this area. Since 2007 he established himself as a private practitioner in the same fields of law. He represents numerous clients before the European Commission and national authorities, notably in Germany, in cartel and abuse of dominance investigations, merger notifications as well as State aid investigations. In addition, he teaches EU competition law at the Universities of Berlin, Bonn, and Saarbrücken and is a frequent speaker/panel chair at international conferences. He is co-editor of a standard EU competition law treatise in German ("NOMOS"), and managing editor of the European Competition and Regulatory Law Review ("CoRe").

Alexandre Cordeiro Macedo is the General Superintendent of CADE and a former Commissioner. He holds a Master's degree in Constitutional Law from the Instituto Brasiliense de Direito Público and is a PhD Student in Economic Law at the Universidade Federal de Minas Gerais. His educational background includes graduate certificates in law and economics. He is a visiting scholar and International Fellow of the Global Antitrust Institute and Antonin Scalia Law School – George Mason University. Since 2006, he has been an Auditor at the Brazilian General Comptroller's Office, where he also worked as an adviser and chief of staff. Between 2012 and 2013, he was the Executive Secretary of the Ministry of Cities. Currently, he is a professor of Economic Law and Economic Analyses Law of the Escola de Direito de Brasília/IDP and a visiting professor at the UNICAMP, UFRGS, Universidade do Vale do Rio dos Sinos, and at the Faculdade de Direito de Vitória. He has spoken at various international events and universities such as Harvard Law School, Northwestern University, Competition Policy International, American Bar Association, International Bar Association, International Competition Network, Global Competition Review.

Elisa Mariscal has worked in competition matters for more than 20 years. She is Managing Director with Global Economics Group, a firm specializing in independent and rigorous economic analysis in legal, regulatory, and policy matters throughout the world. She is an Economics and Law Adjunct Professor at CIDE (*Centro de Investigación y Docencia Económicas*), and an associated fellow of its Interdisciplinary Program in Competition and Regulation ("PIRCE"). She was a founding member of Mexico's Federal Telecommunications Regulator ("IFT") Advisory Council between 2015 and 2019 and is currently a member of Mexico's Antitrust Regulator ("COFECE") advisory group on the digital economy.

Dr. Mariscal has participated as an Expert Witness on behalf of private actors in economics and antitrust matters, as well as being a named expert witness for the specialized tribunals in economic competition, telecommunications, and broadcasting. She has also been deposed as a damages expert in a telecommunications matter involving international arbitration in Washington DC. She is listed as a Who's Who Legal: Consulting Expert, Economics since 2018.

Elisa Mariscal is currently President of Competition Policy International ("CPI") and prior to this was its Editor-in-Chief. CPI is an online knowledge resource and continuing education fora for the global antitrust and competition policy community. Created and managed by leaders in the competition policy community, through a variety of media, it publishes a bi-monthly magazine, and a daily newsletter that covers antitrust and competition policy issues around the world.

Prior to her work in the private sector, Dr. Mariscal headed the General Directorate for Unilateral Conduct Investigations at the Federal Competition Commission ("CFC") of Mexico. In this role, she led one of the largest unilateral conduct investigations for the CFC into exclusive dealings and fidelity rebates programs. During her seven-year tenure at the CFC, she held positions as advisor to the Chairman, Deputy General Director of Economic Studies, and Deputy General Director of International Affairs. Before this, she was an economic consultant at Cornerstone Research and LECG, where she worked in antitrust, regulation, and intellectual property issues in the U.S., Canada, and Latin America.

Dr. Mariscal has authored various papers including several studies on behalf of the CFC for the OECD's Competition Committee and the Regional Center for Competition in Latin America. Research analysis in support of market investigations for COFECE, and various academic papers on competition and telecommunications matters.

Elisa Mariscal received her bachelor's degree with honors from ITAM (*Instituto Tecnológico Autónomo de México*), and a PhD and MA in Economics from the University of California, Los Angeles.

John Moore has been working as an economist for the *Autorité de la concurrence* (French Competition Authority) since 2017. He holds a PhD from the Sorbonne Business School and has previously worked as an economist for the French railway regulatory body (*"Autorité de Régulation des Transports"*).

Hideo Nakajima is a Special Advisor in White & Case's Global Antitrust Practice. Mr. Nakajima is based in Tokyo.

Prior to joining the Firm, Mr. Nakajima served for more than three years as Secretary General of the Japan Fair Trade Commission ("JFTC"), since January 2014.

In that position, Mr. Nakajima encouraged cooperation among competition authorities, contributed to the convergence of competition law enforcement, and policy and consultation and compliance programs for corporations and trade associations.

Mr. Nakajima previously served as Director General of the Bureau of Economic Affairs, where he engaged in JFTC competition advocacy activities, was responsible for competition policy in the government, compliance program for businesses, and reviewing merger proposals. Prior to that, he worked as a Director General of the Investigation Bureau, where he was in charge of the enforcement of the Antimonopoly Act.

Mr. Nakajima joined the Ministry of Finance in 1978 after graduating from Tokyo University. There, he worked in various bureaus including the International Financial Bureau and the Financial Bureau. He was twice stationed in Manila, Philippines, from 1986 to 1989 and again from 2002 to 2005, serving as Special Advisor to the President and Director General of Budget, Personnel & Management. He is regularly consulted by Japanese media on competition issues.

Etienne Pfister has been chief economist at the Autorité de la concurrence (French Competition Authority) since 2013. He holds a PhD from the Sorbonne Business School and has previously worked as a university assistant professor and then as an economist and as a deputy rapporteur general for the Autorité de la concurrence.

Henri Piffaut is a Vice President of the French Competition Authority. He is a former Adviser to the Deputy Director General for mergers at DG Competition of the European Commission. He has spent most of his career in the competition policy field. During the academic year 2016/17 he served as a fellow at Harvard University where he pursued research on the interaction of competition policy and platform industries. He has been a head of unit for merger control and for conduct cases. Both at DG Competition and in the private sector, he dealt with pay-for-delay cases in the pharmaceutical industry, conduct and merger cases in the energy, payment systems, IT, and telecom industries, State intervention in the transport industry and merger cases in a variety of industries. He holds degrees in science and engineering, political science, and economics.

Pierre Régibeau is the Chief Competition Economist at DG Competition. Dr. Régibeau received a BSc in Economics from the University of Liège (Belgium) and a PhD in Economics from the University of California at Berkeley. After graduation, he embarked on an academic career at institutions such as the Massachusetts

Institute of Technology, Kellogg School of management (Northwestern University), the Institute for Economic Analysis (Barcelona) and the University of Essex, where he currently is Honorary Visiting Professor. He has published academic and policy papers in leading reviews. His areas of specialty include industrial organization, with a special emphasis on technology-intensive industry and intellectual property rights and International Trade. He was on the Board of Editors of the Journal of Industrial Economics for more than ten years. He has also been teaching about the interface between IPRs and Competition Policy for the last 14 years in the well-established CRESSE summer school attended by lawyers and personnel from competition and regulatory authorities. Dr. Régibeau has also been a member of the EAGCP (Economic Advising Group on Competition Policy) at the European Commission.

Lara Tobías Peña is Head of the Market Studies Unit in the Spanish National Commission on Markets and Competition ("CNMC"), since October 2018. Lara Tobías Peña joined the Unit in August 2015, specializing in urban services and air transport. Before joining the CNMC, she worked at the Strategic Analysis and International Financial System Unit, Ministry of Economy and Competitiveness. She holds a degree in Economics and a degree in Law from the University Carlos III of Madrid.

Catherine Tucker is the Sloan Distinguished Professor of Management and a Professor of Marketing at MIT Sloan. She is also Chair of the MIT Sloan PhD Program.

Her research interests lie in how technology allows firms to use digital data and machine learning to improve performance, and in the challenges this poses for regulation. Tucker has particular expertise in online advertising, digital health, social media, and electronic privacy. Her research studies the interface between marketing, the economics of technology, and law.

She has received an NSF CAREER Award for her work on digital privacy, the Erin Anderson Award for an Emerging Female Marketing Scholar and Mentor, the Garfield Economic Impact Award for her work on electronic medical records, the Paul E. Green Award for contributions to the practice of Marketing Research, the William F. O'Dell Award for most significant, long-term contribution to Marketing, and the INFORMS Society for Marketing Science Long Term Impact Award for long-run impact on marketing.

She is a cofounder of the MIT Cryptoeconomics Lab which studies the applications of blockchain and also a co-organizer of the Economics of Artificial Intelligence initiative sponsored by the Alfred P. Sloan Foundation. She has been a Visiting

Fellow at All Souls College, Oxford. She has testified to Congress regarding her work on digital privacy and algorithms, and presented her research to the OECD and the ECJ.

Catherine Tucker is coeditor at Quantitative Marketing and Economics, associate editor at Management Science, Marketing Science, and the Journal of Marketing Research and a research associate at the National Bureau of Economic Research. She teaches MIT Sloan's course on Pricing and the EMBA course "Marketing Management for the Senior Executive." She has received the Jamieson Prize for Excellence in Teaching as well as being voted "Teacher of the Year" at MIT Sloan.

She holds a PhD in economics from Stanford University and a BA from the University of Oxford.

Cristina Vallejo is Advisor at the Market Studies Unit in the Spanish National Commission on Markets and Competition ("CNMC"), specialized in digital markets. She holds a degree in Business Administration and a degree in Law from the University of Zaragoza, and an MA in International Trade.

Printed in Great Britain
by Amazon